READING LEO STRAUSS

READING LEO STRAUSS

Politics, Philosophy, Judaism

STEVEN B. SMITH

THE UNIVERSITY OF CHICAGO PRESS
CHICAGO AND LONDON

STEVEN B. SMITH was born in Chicago and received his Ph.D. from the University of Chicago. He is the Alfred Cowles Professor of Political Science at Yale University, where he has taught since 1984, and the Master of Branford College. He has published articles and books on a wide range of topics, including *Spinoza, Liberalism, and the Question of Jewish Identity,* which won the Ralph Waldo Emerson Prize, and most recently *Spinoza's Book of Life.*

The University of Chicago Press, Chicago 60637
The University of Chicago Press, Ltd., London
© 2006 by The University of Chicago
All rights reserved. Published 2006
Printed in the United States of America

15 14 13 12 11 10 09 08 07 06   4 5
ISBN: 0-226-76402-8 (cloth)

Chapter 1 was previously published as "Leo Strauss: Between Jerusalem and Athens" in *Review of Politics* 53 (1991): 75–99.
Chapter 2 was originally published as "Gershom Scholem and Leo Strauss: Notes Toward a German-Jewish Dialogue" in *Modern Judaism* 13 (1993): 209–29, reprinted by permission of Oxford University Press.
Chapter 3 was previously published as "Strauss's Spinoza" in *Cardozo Law Review* 25 (2003): 741–58.
Chapter 4 was previously published as "Leo Strauss's Platonic Liberalism" in *Political Theory* 6 (2000): 787–809, reprinted courtesy of Sage Publications.
Chapter 5 was previously published as "Destruktion or Recovery?: Leo Strauss's Critique of Heidegger" in *Review of Metaphysics* 51 (1997): 345–77.

Library of Congress Cataloging-in-Publication Data

Smith, Steven B., 1951–
　　Reading Leo Strauss : politics, philosophy, judaism / Steven B. Smith.
　　　p.　cm
　　Includes bibliographical references and index.
　　ISBN 0-226-76402-8 (cloth : alk. paper)
　　1. Political science—Philosophy.　2. Philosophy—20th century.　3. Philosophy, Jewish.　4. Strauss, Leo.　I. Title.

JA71.S65 2006
320.01—dc22   2005030549

TO MY STUDENTS,
PAST, PRESENT, AND FUTURE

Men are constantly attracted and deluded by two opposite charms: the charm of competence which is engendered by mathematics and everything akin to mathematics, and the charm of humble awe, which is engendered by meditation on the human soul and its experiences. Philosophy is characterized by the gentle, if firm, refusal to succumb to either charm. It is the highest form of the mating of courage and moderation. In spite of its highness or nobility, it could appear as Sisyphean or ugly, when one contrasts its achievement with its goal. Yet it is necessarily accompanied, sustained and elevated by eros. It is graced by nature's grace. — *Leo Strauss, "What Is Political Philosophy?"*

CONTENTS

I would like to say a word about my motivation for writing this book. The essays contained in this volume have been written over a number of years for diverse occasions. It was not until recently that I conceived the idea of bringing them together in a single volume.

The work of Leo Strauss has long been controversial. A German-Jewish émigré who found a home in America, Strauss has always been something of an exotic plant. He is to some degree an acquired taste. But then not everyone has a taste for philosophy. It is not surprising, therefore, that his work has been subject to frequent and often willful misrepresentation. For reasons discussed below, this has reached a crescendo in recent times due largely to the association of Strauss with the political movement known as neo-conservatism. Suddenly the name of Strauss has been everywhere: in the newspapers, in magazines, on the Internet. Virtually everyone with any power of articulation was weighing in on Strauss. It was in part to register my own discontent with the mountain of nonsense written on this subject that I first conceived of this book.

My own acquaintance with the work of Strauss goes back to my undergraduate days when I first picked up, quite by accident, copies of *Natural Right and History* and *Thoughts on Machiavelli*. At that time I read these works—or tried to read them—as fairly straightforward histories of political thought with little awareness of their larger philosophical context or purport. I recall being warned by a teacher to "be careful," which of course only whetted my appetite to learn more. Since then I have read and reread Strauss always with a deepening appreciation for his subtlety as a writer and his insights as a reader. It is because I do not regard Strauss as a conservative (neo- or otherwise) but rather as a friend of liberal democracy–one of the best friends democracy has ever had—that I felt compelled to enter the current debate. To paraphrase Tocqueville, it is only "foreigners or experience" that will be able to bring home certain hard truths to democracy.

The Leo Strauss who appears in these pages will avoid, I hope, the sometimes comical, occasionally grotesque caricatures created by both his detractors and even some of his friends. I never knew Strauss, although I was privileged to study with students of his as well as with some of the students of his students. An oral tradition has grown up around Strauss, as is bound to happen around all great teachers. My own understanding of Strauss's teaching is based not on lore or on any private communications handed down from teacher to student, but on simply reading and reflecting upon his works over a fairly long period. Readers seeking gossipy stories or salacious anecdotes will simply have to look elsewhere. If I can adapt what Strauss said about his own study of Maimonides, the work that appears here is the result of "about twenty-five years of frequently interrupted but never abandoned study."

Several of these chapters have been presented at conferences or as invited lectures at different universities. Versions of "How Jewish Was Leo Strauss?" were presented at the University of Chicago and the Georgetown Program for Jewish Civilization; "Strauss's Spinoza" was written originally for a conference on "Spinoza's Law" sponsored by the Benjamin Cardozo School of Law and presented later at Waseda University in Tokyo and the University of Notre Dame; "Destruktion or Recovery" was given at a conference on the Legacy of Leo Strauss sponsored by the Olin Center at the University of Chicago and also at the Legal Theory Workshop at the University of Toronto; "Tyranny Ancient and Modern" was given at a seminar at Dartmouth College; and an earlier version of "WWLSD; or, What Would Leo Strauss Do?" was given as the Yuan-Dong Sheu Memorial Lecture at the National Taiwan University. I would like to thank my hosts and interlocutors for their hospitality in inviting me to speak on Strauss.

Some of the essays collected here were originally published as follows: "How Jewish Was Leo Strauss?" was published originally under the title "Leo Strauss: Between Athens and Jerusalem" in the *Review of Politics* 53 (1991): 75–99; "Gershom Scholem and Leo Strauss: Notes toward a German-Jewish Dialogue" appeared in *Modern Judaism* 13 (1993): 209–29; "Strauss's Spinoza" was published in *Cardozo Law Review* 25 (December 2003): 741–58; "Leo Strauss's Platonic Liberalism" was printed in *Political Theory* 28 (2000): 787–809; and "Destruktion or Recovery?: Leo Strauss's Critique of Heidegger" appeared in *Review of Metaphysics* 51 (1997): 345–77.

My reading of Strauss's work has been enhanced over the years by innumerable conversations with teachers, colleagues, friends, and students. Among those who share some burden of responsibility for this book are my former colleague, John McCormick, the first person to suggest that I put together a book on Strauss (although we strongly disagree on how Strauss should be read); Nathan Tarcov, who has been generous with his time and with his usual scrupulous comments; and Mark Lilla, who has encouraged *l'audace, toujours de l'audace*. I would especially like to thank Michelle Tolman Clarke and Justin Zaremby for reading the manuscript as a whole and for their many helpful comments and suggestions.

Why Strauss, Why Now?

Strauss was a towering presence . . . who neither sought nor had any discernible influence on what passes for the politics of the group. — *Joseph Cropsey, "Leo Strauss at the University of Chicago"*

The essays contained in this volume are all intended as a contribution to the understanding of the philosophy of Leo Strauss. They do not purport to provide a comprehensive overview of Strauss's life and work, much less an evaluation of the influence of his teaching and the creation of a school of political thought bearing his name. They do attempt to examine what I consider the central and most enduring theme of Strauss's legacy, namely, what he called the "theologico-political problem," which he also referred to metaphorically by the names Jerusalem and Athens.

Who was Leo Strauss? Strauss was a German-Jewish émigré, the product of the pre–World War I *Gymnasium* who studied at several universities, finally taking his doctorate at Hamburg in 1921. He was a research assistant at an institute for Jewish research in Berlin before leaving Germany in 1932 to settle first in England and later in the United States, where he taught principally at the New School for Social Research in New York and later the University of Chicago. It was during his period in Chicago that Strauss had his greatest influence. He was, by most accounts, a compelling teacher, and like all good teachers everywhere he attracted students, many of whom came to regard themselves as part of a distinctive school. By the time of his death in 1973 Strauss had written (depending on how one counts them) more than a dozen books and around one hundred articles and reviews.

Strauss's works were highly controversial during his own lifetime. When he joined the faculty at the University of Chicago, he was the author of two books published in Germany that were long out of print, a slim monograph on the political philosophy of Hobbes, and an even briefer commentary on a minor dialogue by Xenophon. The future trajectory of his life's work would by no means have been obvious. In the autumn of 1949 he gave a series of lectures under the auspices of the Walgreen Foundation, titled *Natural Right and History*, that was to set his work on a new and distinctive path.[1] It was, literally, his way of introducing himself to the world of American social science from the seat of a major university. The book of the same title was published four years later in 1953. What exactly did Strauss set out to do?

Strauss offered a deliberately provocative account of what might be called the "modernity problem" that had been widely debated in prewar European circles, but which was still relatively unknown to Americans of that era. Prior to Strauss, the most important current of twentieth-century American political thought was John Dewey's "progressivism." Against the view that the advance of science, especially the modern social sciences, was bringing about the progressive triumph of freedom and democracy, Strauss rang an alarm bell. Strauss argued by contrast that the dynamics of modern philosophy and value-free social science, were moving not toward freedom and well-being, but to a condition he diagnosed as nihilism. In Strauss's counternarrative of decline, the foundations of constitutional government as understood by the American framers were gradually being sapped and eroded by the emergence of German-style historicism according to which all standards of justice and right are relative to their time and place. All of this was presented as the outcome of a densely detailed history of political thought in which all the trappings of German scholarship were on full display. His analysis was bold, audacious, and learned. The ensuing controversy pitted those advocates of American progressivism against Strauss, who regarded modernity as a mixed blessing that required certain premodern classical and biblical supports to rescue it from its own self-destructive tendencies.[2]

People on the outside often think of Straussianism as some kind of sinister cult replete with secret rites of initiation and bits of insider information—much like a Yale secret society. Straussians are often believed only to associate with other Straussians and only to read books written by one another. Some actually believe that Straussianism requires the subordination of one's critical intellect to the authority of a charismatic cult leader.[3] Others regard it as a political movement, often allied with "neoconservatism," with a range of prescribed positions and ties to conservative think tanks and policy centers. The liberal historian Arthur Schlesinger Jr.

deplores the influence of what he calls Strauss's "German windbaggery" and compares it to the deleterious influence of Hegel on earlier generations. "Strauss," Schlesinger complains, "taught his disciples a belief in absolutes, contempt for relativism, and joy in abstract propositions. He approved of Plato's 'noble lies,' disliked much of modern life, and believed that a Straussian elite in government would in time overcome feelings of persecution."[4] None of these beliefs could be further from my own understanding.

There is no doubt that the influence of Strauss—or at least his purported influence—is greater now than at any time since his death more than thirty years ago. Of course, Strauss is widely regarded today as a founding father, perhaps the Godfather, of neo-conservatism with direct or indirect ties to the Bush administration. The last few years have witnessed a virtual hostile takeover of Strauss by the political Right. "The Bush administration is rife with Straussians," James Atlas has written in the *New York Times*.[5] Never mind that the Bush administration, like all administrations, is rife with people of all sorts. The association of Strauss with neo-conservatism has been repeated so many times that it leaves the mistaken impression that there is a line of influence leading directly from Strauss's readings of Plato and Maimonides to the most recent directives of the Defense Department. Nothing could be more inimical to Strauss's teaching.

Early readers of *Natural Right and History* like Walter Lippmann saw in the book a support for the belief that the growing debility of modern democracy was due to its loss of faith in the natural law tradition.[6] Straussians have always advocated a strong national government against the crabbed conservatism of "states rights" fundamentalists or the reactionary defenders of a purely federal reading of the Constitution. A textbook on American political thought compiled by two students of Strauss was dedicated to the memory of Franklin Delano Roosevelt and Felix Frankfurter and "to the noble employment of the power they once wielded."[7] The editors of the collection commend FDR for expanding the powers of government beyond securing the bare rights of life, liberty, and the pursuit of happiness to the "higher and grander" conception of the modern welfare state. What distinguished the Straussian approach to politics was its focus on the "philosophic dimension" of statecraft, often at the expense of mass behavior or interest-group politics that attracted the attention of mainstream of political science. Straussians typically studied not only the deeds, but the words of singular political leaders and statesmen, but without any particular ideological pique or animus. Straussians might be either liberal or conservative, although there was a bias toward those who sought to anchor their policies in a reading of the principles of the American founding. Even recently a distinguished student of Strauss served as a prominent member of the first Clinton administration, advising on matters of domestic policy.[8]

The fact is that Strauss bequeathed not a single legacy, but a number of competing legacies. It is a gross distortion to retrofit Strauss's teachings to conform to the agenda of neo-conservatism. His writings on a wide range of subjects continue to spark lively debate among students in a host of fields. New scholarly editions of his work including previously unpublished essays and lectures as well as a voluminous correspondence have all recently appeared, and more are slated for the future. The influence of his ideas on politics and policy-making are continually discussed, debated, and frequently condemned in leading opinion magazines, journals, and newspapers. To the question "why Strauss, why now?" I would say, "if not now, when?"

What Is a Straussian?

Once when I was in graduate school, at a party where there was probably way too much to drink, a friend of mine—now by coincidence a prominent attorney in New Haven—was asked if he was a Straussian. "If you mean by that do I regard everything that Leo Strauss ever wrote as true," he replied, "then, yes, I am a Straussian." We all laughed because my friend's answer so perfectly captured and parodied the common view of Straussianism. The question, am I a Straussian, is something I have been asked on more than one occasion over the years. Sometimes the question seems prompted by nothing more than the idle desire to know what Straussianism means. At other times it has the vague character of an "are you now or have you ever been . . ." kind of accusation. In any case the question has caused me to think about what it is to be a Straussian.

The first point I would make about Straussianism is that it is not all of a single piece. There is rather a set of common problems or questions that characterize Strauss's work: for example, the difference between ancients and moderns, the quarrel between philosophy and poetry, and of course the tension between reason and revelation. None of these problems can be said to have a priority over the others nor do they cohere in anything as crude as a system. Whatever may be alleged, there is hardly a single thread that runs throughout these different interests. Strauss did not bequeath a system, doctrine, or an "ism," despite what may be attributed to him. Rather, he presented a distinctive way of asking questions or posing problems that may have been loosely related but that scarcely derived from a single Archimedean point of view. It is questions that motivate all of Strauss's writings—questions like "Is reason or revelation the ultimate guide to life?" "Has the quarrel between the ancients and the moderns been decided in favor of modernity?" and "Are the philosophers or the poets better educators of civic life?" The point of Strauss's questions is less to provide answers than to make us aware of certain alternatives. In the age-old debate, he was probably more a fox than a hedgehog.

There are many different kinds of Straussians with many and varied interests and perspectives. Some Straussians have devoted themselves entirely to ancient philosophy, while others work on postmodernism; some are deeply religious, while others are proudly secular; some think about politics and policy-making, while others delve into the deepest problems of Being. This diversity reflects, to some degree, the variety of Strauss's own interests. Strauss's writings range from studies of the ancient political philosophy of Thucydides, Plato, Xenophon, and Aristotle, to the Judeo-Arabic writers of the Middle Ages, to such early modern political thinkers as Machiavelli, Hobbes, Spinoza, and Locke, to late nineteenth- and early twentieth-century figures like Nietzsche, Weber, and Heidegger, to issues regarding the philosophy of history, hermeneutics, and the nature of the social sciences. In each of these areas Strauss made notable and lasting contributions that are still widely discussed today.

Few people—one might have to go back to Hegel—have written with as much authority on so wide a range of philosophical, literary, and historical topics. Precisely because Strauss's work covers such a broad landscape, there is not one way of being a Straussian. In fact there are considerable differences among his heirs over precisely what is most valuable in his legacy. Strauss regarded himself as taking the first tentative steps toward the reawakening of substantive interest in the permanent or fundamental problems of political philosophy at a time when it was widely argued that political philosophy was dead.[9] More than this, he expanded the repertoire of political philosophy to include a large number of previously neglected thinkers and topics. The major textbooks of his era made no reference to any of the medieval Judeo-Arabic writers or even to the works of the American founders. Strauss's work treated the American founding as an important philosophical moment in the development of modernity and even encouraged a reconsideration of the ideas of philosophically minded statesmen like Jefferson, Lincoln, and Wilson. His work also inspired a serious engagement with the work of African-American political thinkers from Fredrick Douglass to W.E.B. DuBois to Martin Luther King, Jr. at a time

when their writings received little formal recognition in the academy.[10]
None of this, however, gets us any closer to an understanding of what a
Straussian is.

Careful Readers and Careful Writers

Straussianism is characterized above all by what its practitioners often call
the art of "careful reading." When asked what he taught, it is said, Strauss
often replied "old books." Strauss paid special attention to reading mainly
primary sources, typically in their original languages. This does not sound
terribly controversial today except that at the time the idea of actually reading the great works of political theory had fallen out of favor. It was widely
believed in many circles that the development of the modern behavioral
sciences had put political philosophy on the path to ultimate extinction. It
was believed by many that the meaning of writers like Plato, Hobbes, or
Rousseau had been more or less established and all that was necessary was
to situate them in their place along the historical time line so that the
proper burial rites could be given. Political philosophy had become a kind
of undertaker's art with little relevance or importance for the living issues
of either politics or philosophy.

Strauss helped to change this perception. In the language of the old
Westerns, he came to realize that "there's gold in them thar hills." In contrast to the prevailing historicism that regarded the great works of the tradition as a product of their times, Strauss treated these texts not as
museum pieces to be labeled and catalogued, but as living and vital contemporaries from which there was still much to learn. The history of political thought was not an end in itself, but a necessary propadeutic to the
recommencement of serious political philosophy. Strauss taught that the
interpretations that had been ascribed to the great writers of the past were
far from settled or obvious, that to understand them it was necessary to
bracket our contemporary preconceptions about the path of progress or history, and to consider their writings afresh as part of an ongoing conversation in which we, the readers, were invited to take part. It is possible for us
to participate in such a conversation precisely because the great thinkers
disagree with one another. Is Being one or many? Does it exhibit permanence or change? It thus becomes necessary for us to try to understand and
to judge between rival teachings, to determine which among them is closer
to the truth. The reader is thus invited to participate in a conversation in
which the outcome is far from predetermined, but which remains, in
Strauss's term, an open question.

Strauss was, above all, a reader. He taught his students how to read and how careful writers, like himself, wished to be read. Strauss expanded the scope of our reading to include forgotten figures and others who had been overlooked by the canon of political philosophy. Not only did he breathe new life into familiar figures and texts, he introduced new and unfamiliar writers like Alfarabi, Judah Halevi, Maimonides, and Spinoza to the attention of political philosophers. He pioneered the study of politics and literature by focusing on the literary character of texts and highlighting the "old quarrel" between philosophy and poetry in his reading of thinkers like Plato and Nietzsche. He inquired into the rhetoric in which philosophical arguments are cast long before it became fashionable to talk about "speech acts" and the performative function of language. He paid special attention to ironies, jokes, and puns even in the most serious works and devoted one of his last books to a study of the comedies of Aristophanes.[11] Strauss's most important legacy was teaching his readers how to read. No one can be a Straussian who does not fundamentally love to read.

It is, of course, slightly disingenuous to suggest that Strauss taught the simple art of reading. No reading, we have been taught to believe, is ever innocent, and Strauss was scarcely a naive reader. He was in fact one of the great "masters of suspicion." Strauss's manner of reading unfolded from a single premise that he happened upon slowly and that he developed in a variety of contexts over many years—namely, that great writers often hide or conceal their most profound thoughts from all but the most careful and persistent readers. This seems a simple enough, even a commonsense premise. Do any of us ever say (or intend to say) all that we mean? Do we not speak in different ways to different people depending on the context of the conversation and the extent of our desire to communicate? Strauss's discovery—actually, he called it a "rediscovery"—of esoteric writing can be attributed to a number of causes, from the simple desire to avoid persecution for unpopular or heterodox opinions, to a sense of "social responsibility" to uphold the dominant values of one's society, to the wish to tantalize potential readers with the promise of buried treasure.

Strauss's recovery of the esoteric tradition has been deeply controversial, to say the least. In the first place, there is the question of how we know when an author is writing in a way to deliberately conceal or obscure his teaching. There is, for example, genuine disagreement over whether Descartes's incorporation of God into his system was a strategic ploy or a genuine expression of his religious convictions. One could ask similar questions of a host of thinkers. Did Maimonides write to confirm or undermine a belief in the primacy of revelation? Did Machiavelli write to advise or usurp the prince? Did Locke's theory of natural rights, the virtual corner-stone of the American Declaration of Independence, secretly contain a crypto-atheist and materialist tendency? The answers to these questions are obviously not self-evident. It is clear from what Descartes says about himself that he was writing with the example of Galileo's fate before the Inquisition strongly impressed on his mind, and we know from recent biographies of Locke that he wrote under constant surveillance—so much so that the Master of his Oxford college once referred to him as "the master of taciturnity."[12]

Critics of Strauss's practice of "reading between the lines" have latched onto two potential pitfalls or abuses of the method. There is a genuine problem of how to distinguish careful writers who may disguise their teachings from those who are simply muddled. When is a contradiction simply a contradiction and when is it a clue to a paradox? How do we know whether an author is trying to reveal something through a system of elaborately "contrived deceptions" or is simply confused? Strauss himself expressed caution when applying this method. "Reading between the lines," he wrote, "is strictly prohibited in all cases where it would be less exact than not doing so."[13] Strauss is clearly being deliberately coy here, but his point is a serious one. There is no a priori way of answering this question, any more than there is an a priori way of knowing when a wink is a wink and not a blink. In other words, look and see for yourself. The proof is in the eating.

There are other critics who believe that Strauss's manner of reading leads to the perverse conclusion that whenever a writer says X, we should assume that he really means not-X. Thus a learned classicist—who should know better—has written of Strauss's reading of Plato's Republic that he makes the text mean exactly "the opposite of what it says."[14] This is, of course, absurd. The idea that an esoteric communication could be decoded simply by inverting the literal meaning of a text stands in direct violation of the very principles of esotericism. It would be to turn interpretation into a kind of cryptography. What Strauss did show is that the Republic is a book written for several different types of audiences represented by the different characters in the dialogue and that this helps to explain the very different rhetorical stratagems employed throughout the work.[15] Strauss stressed that every text will inhabit a different set of historical circumstances that delimit what can and cannot be said and that every author will express a very different temperament and sensibility regarding his audience. In contrast to any kind of flat-footed literalism, he sought to avoid the reductionism inherent in the view that every book can be read in exactly the same way.

Perhaps the most revealing (although less often commented upon) aspect of Strauss's manner of reading is his claim that "the real opinion of an author is not necessarily identical with that which he expresses in the largest number of passages."[16] In other words, careful reading must be attuned to the singular, the unexpected, and the anomalous. The true intention of an author may be revealed more clearly in what is left half-said or only subtly alluded to than in what is constantly and relentlessly reaffirmed. The result of this manner of reading is to create what a recent French reader of Strauss has referred to as "two regimes of proof."[17] The one follows the scientific method that regards the true as what is subject to repetition and verification, while the other, Strauss's hermeneutic method, sees the truth in what is singular and nonrepeatable. Truth is to a certain degree "identical with rarity."[18]

Strauss's recovery of esoteric writing could not but leave the impression that his own writings were presented in some kind of code to which only the initiate held the key. Of course, if there ever was such a secret teaching, those who know it aren't saying and those who are saying don't know. Strauss did write cautiously and reticently, especially with regard to the American regime, but certainly not to conceal some sinister intent. He did not write for the sake of undermining democracy, restoring ancient hierarchies, or advocating policies of imperial expansion—all accusations that have been leveled against him—but for the purpose of protecting the regime from the corrosive blasts of skepticism that philosophy necessarily effects on any body of received opinion. He did not sanction the selective use of lies in public life, as has been asserted, and he certainly nowhere claimed that his own works, much less those of others, were written to convey the opposite of what they said. Strauss wrote as he read, that is, with an awareness that there are multiple kinds of readers with different interests and different needs and that like any good teacher it is necessary to address them in different ways.

There is considerable controversy over the sources of Strauss's recovery of the esoteric tradition. Was its source in Plato's artful use of the Socratic dialogue to convey various meanings to different readers without actually speaking in his own name? Was it in Maimonides's allegorical reading of certain scriptural passages and imagery? Or was it in Nietzsche's claim that all that is profound loves masks? Strauss himself loved masks and even admitted in a letter to his fellow émigré Karl Löwith that "Nietzsche so charmed me between my 22nd and 30th years that I literally believed everything I understood of him."[19] Strauss was not a Nietzschean. As he says, Nietzsche's spell on him was broken after he reached the age of thirty.

But he did carry with him something of Nietzsche's love of unmasking others and his desire to hide behind masks of his own making. No one can claim to have read Strauss seriously without attaining an appreciation for the immense sense of playfulness, of hide and seek, that attends his manner of reading and writing.[20]

The Theologico-Political Problem

The great theme of Strauss's life work—what he himself referred to as "*the theme of my investigations*"—is the theologico-political problem, a term he drew from his early studies of Spinoza.[21] At the center of the theologico-political problem is a choice or conflict between two comprehensive and apparently irreconcilable alternatives: revelation and reason, or as he refers to them metaphorically, Jerusalem and Athens.[22] The difference between Jerusalem and Athens is not simply a philosophical or theological problem; it is at heart a political one. It is a matter of authority and who holds ultimate authority. Does final authority rest with the claims of revelation and all that it implies or with one's autonomous human reason as the most fundamental guide to life?

Yet while Strauss sometimes presents Jerusalem and Athens as two incompatible alternatives between which one must choose, he elsewhere presents them as two limbs of the tree of knowledge that have mutually nourished and sustained one another. It is the dialectical tension between these two that has provided the "core" or "nerve" of the Western political tradition.[23] Indeed, Strauss shows that the theologico-political problem is more than just a function of civilizations touched by the great monotheistic religions of Judaism, Christianity, and Islam. It extends as far back as Socrates, the first political philosopher, who was sentenced to death by the city of Athens for corrupting the young and disbelieving the gods of the city. From the outset, the claims of philosophy have been at odds with the ancestral laws of the city and its interpreters. The conflict between Jerusalem and Athens was already something that took place, figuratively speaking, within the heart of historical Athens. It is a problem conceivably coeval with humanity itself.

The conflict between Jerusalem and Athens is, however, more than an extended metaphor for the conflicting claims of revelation and reason. Jerusalem meant for Strauss the spiritual and historical homeland of Judaism and the Jewish people. Strauss was a German Jew who grew up during the final years of Wilhelmine Germany and who came to adulthood during the Weimar Republic, before leaving Germany for good at the onset of the Hitler period. His earliest writings dealt almost exclusively with Jewish themes and Zionist theory. He described himself as having been "converted" to political Zionism at the age of seventeen, and he was later able to write that the establishment of the state of Israel procured "a blessing for all Jews everywhere" whether they realized it or not.[24] The Zionism advocated by Strauss was not of the messianic or redemptivist kind. He strongly opposed the view that the establishment of the Jewish state could provide a solution to the Jewish Question. He once enigmatically referred to the Jewish people and their fate as "the living witness for the absence of redemption."[25] The establishment of the Jewish state was rather a political necessity forced on the Jews not only for the sake of their collective survival, but for the sake of Jewish self-respect.

The question for any student of Strauss's work is where he stood on the theologico-political problem. Was he a citizen of Jerusalem or Athens? As the studies in this work indicate, there is no simple answer to this question. Strauss taught sacred texts as though they were philosophical works and philosophical works as if they were sacred texts. His careful readings have often been called "Talmudic," generally by people who know little of Talmud, and sometimes "kabalistic" by those who know even less of Kabala. What is true is that he often saw things that more conventional readers ignored. In an essay on Thucydides he emphasized the role of piety and "the gods," concluding with the question *quid sit deus* (what does God mean?).[26] In an article on Genesis he could treat the opening chapters of the Bible as if they were a companion to Plato's *Timaeus*.[27]

Strauss taught his readers to listen carefully and to take seriously the claims of Jerusalem, especially at a time when the modern social sciences were treating religion as if it were some atavistic holdover from a dark antedeluvian past. The Enlightenment's "Napoleonic" attack upon revelation, best expressed in Spinoza's *Theologico-Political Treatise*, was beaten back by successive waves of counter-Enlightenment theology and the call for a return to orthodoxy. The rationalist's attempt to overthrow faith is self-refuting, as it rests on a faith in reason that reason itself cannot justify. Nietzsche's announcement of the "death of God" must be considered at best premature. But neither did Strauss's critique of the Enlightenment lead to an endorsement of Jerusalem. "The victory of orthodoxy through the destruction of rational philosophy was not an unmitigated blessing," he wrote.[28] The challenge was not to declare a winner in the struggle, but to remain open to the claims of each and the challenge of each.

The Politics of Philosophy

What were Strauss's politics? This seems to be the question at the heart of the recent debate over Straussianism. To be sure, an extraordinary range of positions have been attributed to him or have been said to be inspired by his writings, from a politics of "national greatness" to expanding an American empire. He has been declared an enemy of democracy and a partisan of the radical Right. But where did Strauss even remotely imply this? His opposition to communism, his rehabilitation of the tradition of natural right, and his skepticism of the general direction of democracy has as much in common with liberalism as with conservatism. On the basis of my own reading, Strauss had no politics in the sense in which that term is generally meant. His works do not endorse any political program or party, whether of the Left or of the Right, Democratic or Republican. He was a philosopher.

If there is a distinctive politics in Strauss's writings, it concerns almost exclusively what could be called the politics of philosophy. Political philosophy meant for him not merely the philosophical treatment of politics, but the political treatment of philosophy. Strauss once declared his writings to be a contribution to the study of the "sociology of philosophy," by which he meant the study of philosophers as a class.[29] What distinguishes all philosophers as a class from all non-philosophers is an intransigent desire to know, to know things from their roots or by their first principles. It is precisely because philosophy is radical that politics must be moderate. Accordingly, Strauss saw a permanent and virtually intractable conflict between the needs of society and the requirements of philosophy. Philosophy understood as the search for knowledge is based on the desire to replace opinion about all things with knowledge of all things. This desire to replace opinion with knowledge would always put philosophy at odds with the inherited customs, beliefs, and dogmas that shape and sustain social life. The politics of philosophy consists of the philosopher's twin needs to show a respect—a decent respect—for the opinions and beliefs that sustain the collective life of society and at the same time to address and recruit new members into the ranks of the potential philosophers.

The question that naturally arises is the relation between the philosopher and the city or the political regime, or (to put the matter a slightly different way) the relation between theory and practice. Strauss often presents these as two virtually incompatible ways of life, that of the philosopher and that of the citizen-statesman or what he sometimes, following Aristotle, calls the gentleman. Is philosophy ministerial to the statesman's life or is politics of value only because it provides the context for the pursuit of philosophy? Which holds the higher rank? Strauss's writings exhibit the same degree of discretion and tact in discussing this problem as in addressing the related theme of Jerusalem and Athens.

It is this problem of the relation of philosophy to the regime that has divided the Straussian legacy between rival East Coast and West Coast camps. Of course this distinction refers not merely to geography, but to a state of mind. At issue is the meaning of the word "political" in the expression "political philosophy." East Coasters are said to believe that "political" refers only to philosophy's mode of expression, the deference philosophy pays to what it is compelled to obey and what it perforce pretends to esteem. West Coasters, by contrast, regard political philosophy as offering substantive moral guidance to political life on issues like religion, patriotism, and the status of America among the nations of the world. Does philosophy ultimately stand above or apart from the world of politics? or are politics and patriotism goods that philosophy, too, must respect? The result, as the founder of the West Coast school has put it, has been a "crisis of the Strauss divided."[30]

The essays collected in this volume all take a stand on the East Coast— the far East Coast—world of Straussian geography. Strauss was, on my reading, a philosopher for whom philosophy meant reflection upon the fundamental or permanent problems of political life. Strauss believed all alleged solutions to such problems, the theologico-political problem for example, to be inherently contestable. He was, as he once described himself, a skeptic in the original Socratic sense of the term.[31] It was, as Strauss saw it, the peculiar heroism of philosophy to live with that sense of uncertainty and to resist the attractions of absolutist positions in both politics and philosophy. Strauss taught the necessity of detachment, of a certain ironic distance from the world of politics and the partisanships that it engenders. Those who put politics before philosophy or who regard philosophy as an instrument of political action threaten to demean philosophy, to reduce it to the status of an ideology, no different from Marxism.

Strauss was fundamentally a skeptic for whom the ends of politics and philosophy were inherently irreconcilable. Strauss taught, if he taught anything, that "there is a fundamental disproportion between philosophy and the city," that is, the ends of philosophy and the ends of politics are irreducible to one another.[32] He was far more impressed with the irreconcilability of basic values than with their harmony. The closest he ever came to giving a clear and unequivocal answer to the problem of philosophy's relation to politics occurs in a public exchange late in life with his friend Jacob Klein. Strauss regarded Klein, along with Alexandre Kojève and

Hans-Georg Gadamer, as his oldest philosophical friends, a group who, despite their philosophical differences, remained committed to the idea of philosophy as a way of life. In a revealing sentence Strauss noted that on the basis of his reading of Maimonides he came to attach a much greater significance to the tension between philosophy and morality than had Klein. "Mr. Klein and I differ regarding the status of morality," Strauss said. He then goes on to clarify his meaning as follows:

> Now let me explain this. That the philosophic life, especially as Plato and Aristotle understood it, is not possible without self-control and a few other virtues almost goes without saying. If a man is habitually drunk, and so on, how can he think? But the question is, if these virtues are understood only as subservient to philosophy and for its sake, then that is no longer a moral understanding of the virtues. . . . If one may compare low to high things, one may say similarly of the philosopher, *what counts is thinking and investigating and not morality.*[33]

It has sometimes been argued that Strauss's defense of philosophy as a way of life has led to the creation of an inward-looking elite that exempts itself from the moral principles applicable to the rest of humanity. This assertion of the priority of the philosophic over the political life did not lead Strauss to neglect, much less to despise morality or virtue. To the contrary, Strauss was deeply concerned with the steady erosion of democracy into a form of mass culture. "Democracy," he wrote, " is meant to be an aristocracy which has broadened into a universal aristocracy."[34] By this he meant a regime in which education—liberal education—had become the prerogative of every citizen. Democracy as originally understood was, in a word, liberal democracy. But this classical conception of democracy as an aristocracy of everybody has slowly degraded into a form of "really existing" democracy. Modern democracy is today a form of mass rule, but mass rule does not mean rule directly by the masses so much as rule by mass culture, a culture manipulated by marketing techniques and other commercial forms of propaganda. "Are we not crushed, nauseated, degraded," Strauss asks rhetorically, "by the mass of printed material, the graveyards of so many beautiful and majestic forests?"[35] It remains today the task of liberal education to act as a "counterpoison" to the effects of mass culture and to recall citizens to the meaning of democracy as it originally was meant.

Strauss once described himself as a "friend of liberal democracy." This was clearly intended to be ambiguous. A friend of liberal democracy is not the same thing as a liberal democrat. So what kind of friend was he? Strauss was not a liberal in any orthodox sense of the term, but there is such a thing as Straussian liberalism. He was certainly not a partisan of the hardcore Right, although some of his students have been. Strauss's politics, such as they were, had more in common with cold-war liberals of his generation— Isaiah Berlin, Lionel Trilling, Walter Lippmann, Raymond Aron—than with any of the major conservative figures of the same period. What Strauss brought to liberalism was a kind of "Tocquevillian" sensibility that regarded the freedom of an educated mind as the best antidote to the pathologies of modern mass politics. Contrary to the views attributed to him by many of his friends and virtually all of his enemies, Strauss regarded himself as a teacher of moderation. "Moderation," he wrote, "will protect us from the twin dangers of visionary expectations from politics and unmanly contempt for politics."[36]

The Current Volume

The essays included in this volume attempt to sketch out a range of topics central to the understanding of Strauss. They have all been written—and in some instances rewritten—in a manner that, I hope, will be of use to both longtime readers of Strauss and relative newcomers hoping to discover for themselves what all the hoopla is about. These essays do not purport to be exhaustive, although they do attempt to canvass Strauss's views on some of the most significant and controversial topics as well as to put him into conversation with a number of his most important contemporaries.

This collection is divided into two unequal sections that broadly capture the bipartite nature of the theologico-political question. The first section, titled "Jerusalem," deals with Strauss's views on religion and particularly on Jewish themes and thinkers; the second, titled "Athens," presents his views on a variety of strictly philosophical and political topics. To be sure, these two parts are more intimately linked than any cut-and-dried division between them would suggest. Jerusalem is not only the name of the holy city, the city of faith, but is simultaneously the political center of the Jewish people; likewise Athens is not just the place of an often contentious democratic polity, but—as Strauss's own writings on Aristophanes, Thucydides, and Plato indicated—a city saturated with concern about piety and the gods.

The theme of the first essay, "How Jewish was Leo Strauss?" explores the tension between Jerusalem and Athens as the two conflicting poles of human loyalty and aspiration. This essay takes its theme from Strauss's 1957 lecture "Jerusalem and Athens: Some Preliminary Reflections," a

theme to which he continually returned throughout his writings, notably in
his lectures on "Progress or Return" and the "Preface to Spinoza's Critique
of Religion." The issue to which Strauss drew his readers' and his listeners'
attention was whether Judaism understood as a body of revealed law was
compatible with the requirements of citizenship in a modern liberal democracy. Can one be both a Jew and a citizen in the fullest sense of those terms,
especially if one chooses to live in one of the lands of the diaspora?

The second essay is a comparative study of Strauss and one of his greatest contemporaries, Gershom Scholem, the founder of the modern historical study of kabala or Jewish mysticism. Strauss's relation with Scholem
went back to the 1920s in Berlin. The two maintained a friendship and correspondence virtually until the end of Strauss's life; only recently have
some of those letters been published. It was under Scholem's sponsorship
at the Hebrew University of Jerusalem that Strauss gave his famous lecture
series "What Is Political Philosophy?" during the academic year of 1954/55.
One finds between these two giants of twentieth-century Jewish thought a
dialogue of the highest kind, carried out with great mutual respect, with
Strauss the defender of a kind of Maimonidean rationalism on the one hand
and Scholem the great anti-Maimonidean defender of the role of the mystical, irrational, and antinomian sources of Jewish life and thought on the
other. The essay concludes with an examination of the implications of their
historical studies for their understanding of Zionism and modern Israel, to
which they were both passionately, albeit not unambiguously, attached.

The third essay, "Strauss's Spinoza," considers Strauss's relation to the
figure he once described as "the greatest man of Jewish origin who had
openly denied the truth of Judaism and had ceased to belong to the Jewish
people without becoming a Christian."[37] Spinoza was the subject of
Strauss's first book, *Die Religionskritik Spinozas*, published in 1930, and
the figure who continued to haunt his studies throughout the rest of his
life. Spinoza represented for Strauss the high point of modern rationalism,
to which, as a young man, Strauss was reluctantly committed, although
later he came to regard Spinoza's critique of such traditional Jewish beliefs
as revelation, prophecy, and the law as resting on a set of hypothetical
premises that could not be proved. I try to show that Strauss's critique of
Spinoza was filtered through the great figures of the German Counter-
Enlightenment, notably F. H. Jacobi, who was the subject of Strauss's doctoral dissertation. From these figures, as well as others, Strauss came to see
that the rationalist critique of orthodoxy rested on beliefs about the power
of reason that on closer inspection turned out to be either circular or self-
contradictory. Strauss, I suggest, like some of the great philosophical

"fideists" of the past—Montaigne, Pascal, Wittgenstein—regards the alternatives of reason and revelation as resting on an act of choice or faith.

The section of the book devoted to "Athens" begins, appropriately, with an essay on "Leo Strauss's Platonic Liberalism." Plato was *the* figure to whom Strauss returned again and again throughout his writings; but what, exactly, did Plato represent to him? In contrast to the earlier orthodoxies that regard Plato as one of the chief enemies of the "open society" or that regard his theory of Ideas as the basis of modern metaphysics with its "forgetfulness of being" (Heidegger), Strauss continually emphasized the dialogic, open-ended, and ultimately skeptical character of the Platonic dialectic. The dialogue form was not for Plato merely the medium, Strauss argued; it was the message. Most importantly, the famous Platonic theory of Ideas was not a system of metaphysical absolutes, but something like the permanent problems or questions of life to which thoughtful men and women would always, but inconclusively, return. It was precisely the *aporetic* character of the Platonic dialogues Strauss fastened on, and that focus allowed him to develop a distinctively liberal Platonism. The essence of Strauss's Platonic liberalism was a radical questioning of all utopias or final solutions in political life that purport to put an end to philosophical reflection.

It is only fitting that Strauss's reflection on the greatest ancient political thinker be paired with his analysis of the greatest modern thinker. "Destruktion or Recovery?" puts Strauss into conversation with Heidegger, the figure he called "the only great thinker of our time" and the "highest self-consciousness" of modern thought.[38] Strauss met Heidegger in 1922 during a postdoctoral year in Freiburg, where Strauss had gone to study with Edmund Husserl, the founder of the phenomenological school. It was during this year that he heard Heidegger's lectures on Aristotle's *Metaphysics,* which led him later to remark that his earlier philosophical hero, Max Weber, appeared as an "orphan child." Strauss remained fascinated, one might almost say obsessed, with Heidegger, especially with the latter's claim to have carried out a "Destruktion" of the Western philosophical tradition. By a "Destruktion" Heidegger meant both an uprooting of the ultimate presuppositions of thought and a radical historicization of thought, the relativization, as it were, of being and time. Strauss's work as a whole, I argue, especially *Natural Right and History,* in which Heidegger's name never even appears, can and should be read as an attempt to overcome Heideggerian "Destruktion" through a recovery of the tradition and its conception of philosophy. In particular Strauss was deeply concerned about the way Heidegger's thought proved inseparable from his support of Nazism not only before, but even after World War II. What was it about Heideggerian "Destruktion" that led it not merely to acquiesce to, but to actively support Hitler's revolution of 1933? Strauss's attempt to recover the classical grounds of what he called natural right was part of an elaborate stratagem to provide the rational grounds for resistance to tyranny.

The theme of tyranny is the subject of the next chapter, on "Tyranny Ancient and Modern." Strauss's *On Tyranny*, originally published in 1948, was the first of three books he would write on the political philosophy of Xenophon, and the first book he would write in America. Writing shortly after the conclusion of World War II, Strauss, like many political scientists of the era, was interested in understanding the nature of modern tyrannies like Nazi Germany and Soviet Russia. Rejecting the idea that these represented some new and unprecedented kind of regime unknown in all previous history, he argued that the roots of tyranny, ancient and modern, are better accounted for by a little-remembered dialogue of Xenophon's entitled *Hiero or On Tyranny*.

Of course, Strauss's commentary on this dialogue would scarcely be remembered today were it not for his subsequent exchange with the Russian émigré philosopher Alexandre Kojève. Kojève and Strauss were old friends who produced a sizeable body of correspondence between them. By the time of their exchange over Strauss's study of tyranny, Kojève had become a senior official in the French Ministry of Economic Affairs. He was also an ardent defender of the "progressive" function of modern tyrannies, especially the Soviet Union, which he saw as hastening the advent of a global state that would extend universal recognition to free and equal men and women. Their exchange focused on the Hegelian-Marxist idea of an "end of history" that has recently been taken up again by Francis Fukuyama in his book of the same name. At the core of the debate was the question of whether the phenomenon of tyranny is better understood by the presuppositions of classical political philosophy or by the modern doctrines of history and progress.

The last two chapters in this work both deal with Strauss's relation to his adopted home. "Strauss's America" is an attempt to unearth Strauss's subtle but controversial treatment of the American regime. At issue is whether Strauss believed America has its roots in some combination of the classical and biblical tradition or whether it belongs mainly to the world of the Enlightenment and modern philosophy. The answer is clearly in some respects both, but there is no doubt in my mind that the preponderance of the evidence supports the "low but solid" foundations of the American republic in early modern political philosophy. Strauss's writings on America, I argue, follow the pattern he detects in all careful writers. This consists of a pious and patriotic teaching at the beginning and end of a discourse and a more cautiously expressed but subversive teaching in the middle or in other out-of-the-way places. For reasons already indicated, Strauss was deeply reluctant to criticize publicly the land that offered him safe haven from European tyranny, but his sense of loyalty and obligation did not blind him to some of the underlying pathologies at work in modern thought and culture to which America was not immune. His solution was to offer a reform of the teaching of modern political science that in its desire to become scientific had lost sight of the distinction between tyranny and freedom.

The final chapter, "WWLSD; or, What Would Leo Strauss Do?" addresses the widely held opinion that Strauss has served as the inspiration for a group of foreign-policy hawks in or around the Bush administration. It is not my purpose in this chapter to assess the wisdom of the war in Iraq or to try to attribute responsibility on the basis of who studied with whom (always a risky and questionable exercise). I am interested instead in teasing out what, if anything, Strauss had to say about foreign policy in order to find out what bearing his thought might have on our current predicament. To make a long story short, Strauss was a great admirer of strong leadership and gave some of his highest marks of approval to those great statesmen who either founded or preserved regimes, especially in times of war. In particular he claimed that extreme measures are necessary when the very existence or independence of society is at stake. At the same time, I suggest, Strauss would have been deeply skeptical of the current rhetoric of a "war against evil." Strauss wrote frequently about evil; it is a term that recurs throughout his work. But his purpose is always to show that evil is inseparable from the human situation and therefore that our expectations must be moderate rather than the reverse.

PART ONE

Jerusalem

CHAPTER ONE

How Jewish Was Leo Strauss?

> But while being compelled, or compelling myself, to wander far away
> from our sacred heritage, or to be silent about it, I shall not for a mo-
> ment forget what Jerusalem stands for. — *Leo Strauss, "What Is Political
> Philosophy?"*

Harold Bloom, the Yale literary critic, once described Leo Strauss as
"political philosopher and Hebraic sage."[1] This always seemed to me
unusually prescient. For Strauss is most frequently understood as an interpreter and critic of a number of thinkers, both ancient and modern, who
belong to the history of political philosophy. But he is far less often regarded
as a contributor to Jewish thought. It is neither as a historian nor as a
philosopher, but as a Jew that I want to consider him here.

At first blush this approach to Strauss seems relatively unproblematic.
Even a superficial perusal of his major works show that Jewish themes were
a continual preoccupation from the earliest times onwards. His first book,
Die Religionskritik Spinozas (1930), was written while he was a researcher
at the Akademie für die Wissenschaft des Judentums in Berlin.[2] His second
book, *Philosophie und Gesetz* (1935), looked to Spinoza's most illustrious
predecessor, Moses Maimonides, and his conception of law.[3] Furthermore,
a number of later essays and lectures return to these early themes, especially his Frank Cohen lecture on "Jerusalem and Athens."[4] Finally, in a
semi-autobiographical introduction to the English translation of his book
on Spinoza, Strauss spoke in no uncertain terms about the various currents
of neo-orthodoxy and of political and cultural Zionism within which he
came to maturity.[5]

Jewish themes have not, however, always been regarded as central to
Strauss's *oeuvre*. His most widely read book, *Natural Right and History,*

makes scarcely a reference to any of the thinkers of the ancient or modern Jewish tradition. Here his interest is in recovering the ground of natural right from the rise of the German historical consciousness. He makes it appear as though the greatest problem affecting post–World War II America has been the influence of Max Weber on American departments of social science. In addition, there is not so much as a nod toward the two most significant events of twentieth-century Jewish history: the Holocaust and the creation of the state of Israel. Strauss seems intent on downplaying his Jewishness even as his silence underscores it. If one were to ask Strauss the same question he put to others—namely, had he written a Jewish book or a philosophical book—the answer, I think, would be obvious.

Yet this cannot be the whole story. At best it belongs to what Strauss elsewhere calls "the sociology of knowledge."[6] It does not go to the heart of the matter. For a writer who taught his students to read "between the lines" and for whom what is left unsaid is as important as what is repeated ad nauseam, it should not be surprising if the Jewish Question were to turn out to be Strauss's major concern. A recent review in the *Times Literary Supplement* by George Steiner captures something of this:

> If, in the traditional pairing which Strauss adopts, the life-long labors turn around Jerusalem and Athens, it is the former which, at the last, radiates at the center. It is in the light or dark of Jewish identity and history, made dramatically intense by the twentieth century, that Leo Strauss, Hermann Cohen's dissenting successor in the development and tragedy of German Judaism, reads, that he "lives" the interactions between classical Greek, Islamic, Renaissance, and Judaic views of the meaning of man. Everywhere the declared topic is outwardly remote from Judaica, in the somewhat strange book on Aristophanes and Socrates, for example, we need, as Strauss himself would have it, to read between the lines. The Hebrew characters are never far off.[7]

To say that Strauss is not just a historian but also a contributor to Jewish thought presupposes that there is some meaningful sense in which we can speak of something called Jewish political thought. But what, for instance, does the thought of men such as Akiba, Rashi, Judah, Halevi, and Maimonides have in common with the thought of such "non-Jewish Jews" as Spinoza, Heine, Marx, and Freud? What is Jewish thought? Is it the iconoclastic naturalism of Spinoza? The rationalist universalism of Mendelssohn or Cohen? The Zionism of Hess and Herzl? The neo-orthodoxy of Soloveitchik and Leibowitz? Or the redemptivist nationalism of Rav Kook and the Gush

Emunim? What can such names possibly mean apart from their inclusion on a list of Jewish thinkers, no different from books and magazines that include names of famous Jewish movie stars and sports figures (Did you know that Cary Grant . . . ?). It gets us no closer to defining the thing in itself.

While there might be some reason to believe that the political problems faced by Jews are no different from those faced by any other peoples, even a moment's reflection reveals that this is emphatically not the case. At the risk of arbitrariness, I would suggest that Jewish political thought is uniquely marked by a preoccupation with such themes as exile, homelessness, and marginality. Since for much of its history Judaism has existed as a "despised religion" (Judah Halevi) among non- or even anti-Jewish peoples, the aspirations for assimilation and the assertion of separateness are the twin polarities within which Jewish thought has developed.

The position of the Jews in modern, enlightened, liberal society is only the most tangible contemporary expression of the theologico-political problem. Strauss traces his own preoccupation with this problem back to his experiences as "a young Jew born and raised in Germany." The Germany to which he alludes here is Weimar Germany, the Germany that came into being in that all-too-brief period between the Treaty of Versailles and the Reichstag fire. Weimar was, of course, a liberal democracy, one that could trace its name back not only to the residence of Goethe, but to a preference for things Western and, above all, French and English. The Weimar Republic was of a "moderate, nonradical character," determined to maintain "a balance between the dedication to the principles of 1789 and the dedication to the highest German tradition."[8] This Germany offered both unusual opportunities and dangers for the Jews.

On the one hand, liberal democracy traces its origins in continental Europe back to the French Revolution's claim to be entirely neutral on the religious issue. Liberalism, as articulated in the philosophy of such men as Locke, Montesquieu, and Kant, to say nothing of such official documents as the American Declaration of Independence and the French Declaration of the Rights of Man and the Citizen, was based on a universal morality of natural rights that was blind to the difference between Jews and Gentiles.[9] Liberalism was thus the first European political settlement to offer the Jews "emancipation" from the tyranny of state-sponsored religious intolerance.

On the other hand, the emancipation of the Jews was conceived by liberalism along the lines of assimilation. Jews would henceforth forgo their claims to exclusivity and adherence to a specific tradition and become one with the non-Jewish majority. Even Zionism of the type sponsored by Herzl and Pinsker did no more than offer a political or civil solution to the so-called Jewish Question. It promised the Jews a state of their own that, like the modern European states, would be a liberal state that is indifferent to or above religion. Strauss described as "blasphemous" the very suggestion that liberalism or Zionism could be regarded as the solution to the Jewish Question. He could write in 1962 that

> The establishment of the state of Israel is the most profound modification of the Galut which has occurred, but it is not the end of the Galut: in the religious sense, and perhaps not only in the religious sense, the state of Israel is a part of the galut. Finite, relative problems can be solved; infinite, absolute problems cannot be solved. . . . From every point of view it looks as if the Jewish people were the chosen people, at least in the sense that the Jewish problem is the most manifest symbol of the human problem insofar as it is a social or political problem.[10]

The Jewish problem, then, is of interest because it is "the most manifest symbol of the human problem." But what is the human problem of which the Jewish problem is but a symbol? In a phrase, it is the problem of the universal and the particular, the one and the many. It is a problem with many branches and tributaries. But in purely social or political terms it presents itself as a conflict between universalistic commitments and particularistic identifications. For Strauss, this problem became a conflict between assimilation and eventual absorption in a universal humanity, or the assertion of a stubborn loyalty to a particular tradition. When the particular tradition in question claims divine or revealed origins, as Judaism does, this conflict is made all the more difficult. It was precisely his choice to stand outside of or above this conflict as a sort of mediator between reason and revelation that constitutes the uniqueness of Strauss's answer to the Jewish Question.

Jerusalem or Athens

The core of Strauss's thought is the famous "theologico-political problem," a problem, he said, that "remained *the* theme of my studies" from very early on.[11] The question *quid sit deus*, first raised in his study of Spinoza, was later described by him as "the all-important question" of philosophy, "although the philosophers do not frequently pronounce it."[12] This problem reveals a number of distinct aspects that must be untangled.

In the first place, the theologico-political problem represents for Strauss the "core" or "nerve" of the West. The conflict between biblical faith and

Greek philosophy is said to be "characteristic of the West" and "the secret of its vitality."[13] This conflict, symbolized by the eternal archetypes of Jerusalem and Athens, indicates the two great antitheses of the Western tradition. The Bible and philosophy represent two fundamentally different "codes" or ways of life that defy final reconciliation. In the final analysis one can be either a philosopher or a theologian but one cannot be both, even though Strauss argues that each should be open to the challenge of the other.

What exactly is that challenge? Philosophy, as Strauss claims, is the attempt to replace opinion about all things with knowledge about all things.[14] By its nature, philosophy is the effort to understand the whole or cosmos by means of one's unaided reason alone. Philosophy must submit, and submit ruthlessly, everything to the bar of its own critical rationality. It was their relentless emphasis on reason, their own reason, that led the philosophers to believe that contemplation, *theoria*, is the highest or best life for a human being. Biblical thought, by contrast, begins not from the experience of intellectual curiosity about all things, but from a sense of sacred awe or fear of the Lord. According to the Bible, human life is characterized not by self-sufficiency but by a radical sense of our dependence upon God. Not contemplation but piety, obedience, and the need for divine mercy are what is most characteristic of us.[15]

This conflict, then, between revelation and reason, the Bible and philosophy, took on from the beginning a predominantly secular or political character. Philosophy, as represented in the person of Socrates, finds its natural home in the city. Philosophy presupposes a context of urbanity, wealth, and leisure to sustain it. By contrast, the life of simple piety and humble awe, as extolled by the Bible and its most authoritative interpreters, is unequivocally in favor of the rustic or pastoral life. According to the Bible, the first murderer was also the founder of the first city and of the arts necessary for civilized life. It is no accident that it was not Cain, the tiller of the soil, but Abel, the keeper of the sheep, who found favor in the eyes of God.[16]

But this secular conflict has another dimension as well. The conflict between philosophy and the Bible is ultimately a conflict about how political and ecclesiastical authority should be divided. In earlier times communities were held together by powerful moral and legal codes said to be derived from God or the gods. The *theos nomos*, divine law, is said to constitute the foundation of all society. Accordingly, the ideal regime was a theocracy governed by priests or kings claiming priestly authority. The problem is the conflict, or potential conflict, between divine laws.

Over time this monopoly of power was challenged by those philosophers seeking to carve out a sphere of freedom of thought and opinion over which clerics should have no say. Strauss attaches enormous significance to this fact. Apparently belief in the gods or religion is found wherever humans live together. Philosophy, by contrast, is a late and relatively rare phenomenon. Philosophy was made possible only with the discovery of "nature." There is, Strauss likes to remind his readers, no word in biblical Hebrew that approximates the Greek term *physis*. The Hebrew *mishpat* meaning "way" or "custom" is at best a pre-philosophic anticipation of nature.[17] To inquire into nature is to seek for principles or first causes. However, the discovery of nature was only a necessary and not a sufficient condition for the possibility of political philosophy. It was only when Socrates applied the idea of nature to the study of the human and political world that political philosophy proper was born. It is, again, no coincidence that Plato's *Republic*, the greatest work of ancient political philosophy, culminated in the claim that there would be no cessation of evils until kings became philosophers or philosophers became kings.

Despite the obvious and important differences between biblical thought and classical philosophy, Strauss was not blind to their areas of agreement. In particular, he points to two. First, there is broad agreement regarding the place of morality in the overall economy of human life. Both Greek philosophy and the Bible agree that the locus of morality is the patriarchal family, which is the basic cell of society. And second, both agree that the core of morality is justice. By justice is meant primarily obedience to law. Law is understood here to mean not just civil law, but divine law, law with some transcendent sanction.[18] Strauss is not altogether clear about the precise content of justice or the penalty for its transgression. However, it entails a fundamental intuition about certain restraints upon our behavior or, as he put it, "a kind of divination that not everything is permitted."[19] Indeed, Strauss claims that what Plato says about the power of divine retribution in the *Laws* is "literally identical" with certain verses of Amos and Psalm 139.[20]

The conflict or tension between the Bible and philosophy that has been the "nerve" of the Western world seemed, at the time when Strauss wrote, to be on the verge of extinction. While many would, no doubt, regard this as a sign of progress, Strauss takes it as symptomatic of a "crisis." The "crisis of the West," as Strauss sometimes calls it, is a direct result of a new kind of philosophy, the philosophy of the Enlightenment, which is based on the idea of progress.[21] The heritage of this idea is neither clearly Greek nor clearly biblical. Unlike the biblical prophets who chastised their contemporaries by invoking an earlier time of piety and obedience, the modern philosophers, beginning with Machiavelli, Descartes, and Hobbes, turned away from the past and looked toward the future. Between the past and the future one could discern progress understood as the conquest of nature for the relief of man's earthly estate. Strauss even toys with the idea that the Enlightenment conception of science as a universal technique was known to the ancients but rejected by them in advance as "unnatural" or "destructive of humanity."[22]

The cause of this crisis can be discovered in the attempt of the Enlightenment to abolish or truncate the roots of the West. Whatever the differences between ancient philosophy and the Bible alluded to above, pre-Enlightenment thought was "conservative" in the sense that it did not seek a solution to the human problem through unaided human effort. The best city of the *Republic*, just like the messianic kingdom of Isaiah, was to be an object of fervent wish or prayer but not of political activism. This awareness served to impose some limitations on what was deemed politically possible. It was ancient political philosophy's understanding that "evil cannot be eradicated" from the soul and that "one's expectations from politics must be moderate" that allowed it to escape the "fanaticism" of destruction.[23] All of the revolutionary movements of our day, on both the Left and the Right, can be traced back to the Enlightenment's forgetfulness of this and other such pieces of prudential advice. The French Revolution's demand to establish justice here and now was just the first act in a political drama that would seek to overcome all otherworldliness or transcendence.[24] It is no accident, then, that the Enlightenment appears in Strauss's thought as nothing less than unprecedented "propaganda" seeking to advance itself through a combination of ridicule and intimidation.[25]

The crisis of the West reveals itself today as the attempt of modern philosophy or the Enlightenment to vanquish, once and for all, the claims of revealed religion, or what Strauss calls simply "Orthodoxy."[26] At the core of orthodoxy—whether Christian, Jewish, or Muslim—is a belief in the revealed or mysterious character of the law. Even later claims regarding the natural law represent a falling away from the standards of strict orthodoxy by suggesting that law can be understood or discovered by unaided human reason. Obviously, the attack upon orthodoxy is as old as philosophy itself. The official charge brought against Socrates by the court of Athens was that he was *atheos*, a disbeliever. What Strauss disputes is that any premodern thinker ever seriously doubted the necessity of religion as a prerequisite for social order.[27] The belief that God or the gods are in some sense "first for us" and that consequently the city is subservient to divine or revealed law constitutes the original form of political self-understanding.[28]

It is only with the modern Enlightenment that we find for the first time the intransigent demand that philosophy replace orthodoxy as the foundation for social order. "Political atheism," Strauss remarks, "is a distinctly *modern* phenomenon."[29] Accordingly, the claims of religion were reviled in the works of the Enlightenment as productive only of error, distortion, and superstition.[30] The underlying premise of the Enlightenment was that the truths of philosophy were "harmless," that is, beneficial to society as a whole, and that henceforth philosophers should be regarded not as threats to, but as benefactors of the public good.[31] To be sure, the early founders of the Enlightenment wrote works like Spinoza's *Theologico-Political Treatise*, Locke's *The Reasonableness of Christianity*, and Kant's *Religion within the Limits of Reason Alone* precisely to defend themselves from allegations of political atheism. The early or moderate Enlightenment still regarded some kind of rationalized religion as a necessary basis for securing a just and stable social order. However, it became part of the modern demand for "probity" that religion, just like politics, defend itself in the court of reason.[32] For later, more radical thinkers like Marx, Nietzsche, and Heidegger the terrors and harshness of existence or history were to be preferred to the comforts and illusions offered by the religious imagination.[33]

The question Strauss asks us to consider, then, is this. Was the Enlightenment successful in banishing religion or at least pushing it to the very periphery of civilization? Has the progress of culture witnessed an abatement of hostility toward philosophy? Or can we expect to see a "return of the repressed"? Is religion a permanent need of the soul, a permanent response to the human condition, or is it a remnant left over from a pre-rational, pre-scientific age? These are questions to which we shall return.

The Dilemma of German Jewry

Strauss's views on the theologico-political problem did not arise full-blown. Rather, they emerged only gradually in his writings and, according to some interpreters, underwent a profound modification over time.[34] The earliest evidence of Strauss's concern with this problem occurs in a review article of Max Nordau's *Zionism* published in Martin Buber's journal *Der Jude* in 1923.[35] In this article the young Strauss makes clear his differences with the policies of both liberal assimilationists and Zionists. He deplores especially the "self-destructive" tendencies of assimilationist Jews, with their naïve belief in the liberalizing principles of the French Revolution and their willingness to abandon the traditional grounds of Judaism, namely, the idea of chosenness and faith in the Messiah. For Strauss, the experience of the *galut*—the history of the Jews during their Diaspora—has had the positive effect of strengthening the traditional faith. "This is the essence of *galut*,"

Strauss writes. "It provides the Jewish people with a maximal possibility of existence by means of a minimum of normality."[36] The policy of assimilation seeks to reverse the historical relationship of the Jews with their host nations. Its goal could be stated as providing a minimum possibility for existence by ensuring a maximum normality. Strauss considers this policy illusory. It deprives the Jews of "the self-assurance of ghetto life" by promising "the illusionary surrogate of trust in the humanity of civilization."[37]

As for political Zionism, it merely "continues and heightens the dejudaizing tendency of assimilation." This de-judaizing tendency is revealed in Zionism's attribution of the distress of the Jews not to divine punishment for the sins of the fathers, but to "the accumulation of minor political and economic facts."[38] And likewise Zionism understands the amelioration of this distress as having nothing to do with the coming of the Messiah, but everything to do with the secular, political struggle of the Jewish people for a homeland. While for tactical reasons Strauss felt closer to the representatives of German Zionism than to the representatives of assimilation, he recognized that Zionism too was but another form of assimilation based on the belief that the Jews should become a people no different from any other.

In other words, Zionism offers the Jews only another version of the liberal secular state—"a state for a people, for a people without a state." Nordau's particular form of Zionism, with its lofty appeal to a politics of honesty, sincerity, and candor, has no other aim than to appeal to "the Jewish heart which is always susceptible to an appeal to innocent suffering and disappointed idealism."[39] But a Jewish state divorced from traditional Jewish beliefs and practices can be only an empty shell. Consequently, Nordau's quasi-Hegelian belief that European civilization is moving toward a more rational solution to the Jewish problem is itself evidence of a gross philistinism. "Nordau," Strauss writes, "has the attitude of Homais the apothecary [in Flaubert's *Madame Bovary*] who puts his famous scientific knowledge in the service of the public by engaging in the improvement of cider making while constantly emphasizing his virtue."[40]

Strauss's identification of the delusions of German Jewry (or at least its most prominent representatives) led him to search out the roots of this attitude. His book on Spinoza was a result of that search. Spinoza was, after all, the founder of the so-called "higher criticism" of the Bible, with its search for more accurate historical and philological evidence about the dates of composition. But even more importantly, Spinoza gave decisive impetus to the twin currents of Zionism and assimilationism mentioned above. Strauss's book was in large part an answer to Hermann Cohen, the founder

of the Marburg School of neo-Kantianism, who had savagely attacked
Spinoza at a time when the latter's reputation was being rehabilitated
among educated German Jews.[41]

Cohen had attacked Spinoza's *Ethics* periodically throughout his long
career, but it was only when he turned to the *Theologico-Political Treatise*
that his criticism turned hateful. Cohen's attack stemmed from the belief
that Spinoza's entire philosophy represented a kind of "revenge" upon
Judaism for the edict of excommunication he had received from the rab-
binate of Amsterdam.[42] Cohen denounced Spinoza first and foremost as a
"renegade to his people" and an "apostate" who preferred Christianity to
Judaism. Spinoza's cardinal sin was his depiction of Judaism as a purely
political religion that had the function of denying the universalism and ethical idealism of the prophets. Consequently not only did Spinoza willfully
misrepresent Judaism before a predominantly Christian audience, but his
work became a justification for anti-Semitism among those who have taken
his depiction of Judaism as authoritative.[43] For all of these reasons, Spinoza
stood condemned as a "base traitor" to his people, guilty of a "humanly
incomprehensible betrayal."[44]

In an early article titled "Cohen's Analysis of Spinoza's Bible Science"
(1924), Strauss denied that Spinoza's philosophy could be understood simply as motivated by a desire for revenge.[45] He attacked Cohen's psycholo-
gistic method of attempting to explain a text by reference to motives like
hatred or a desire for revenge. In fact, the emphasis Cohen had put upon
Spinoza's excommunication is at best a "conjecture," since the main lines
of Spinoza's biblical criticism had been worked out prior to his expulsion
from the synagogue.[46] Further, Strauss doubted the authenticity of Cohen's
claim that Spinoza's sacrilege consisted in his politicization of Judaism. For
Cohen, the social democrat, it would have have been not "satanic" but
rather "godly" if Spinoza had said that the religion of Moses was the foundation of the socialist state.[47] Finally, Strauss maintained, as he would
almost forty years later, that Spinoza's Bible science was motivated not by
a hatred of Judaism, but by a desire to free philosophy from ecclesiastical
supervision. His critique of the prophets is not "completely incomprehensible" once we realize that it is directed not to any specifically Jewish matters, but to the sect-filled Netherlands of the seventeenth century.[48] Strauss
concludes that Spinoza's Bible science is "adequately motivated" by "objective considerations" and cannot be reduced to the "personal motives"
stressed by Cohen, although he applauds Cohen's efforts to move beyond
the image of Spinoza as a "god-intoxicated man" and therefore to move
beyond both German and Jewish romanticism.[49]

Cohen's reasons for repudiating Spinoza are tied not only to his commitment to Judaism but to his ethical theory and especially the Kantian idea of rational autonomy. Cohen's argument proceeds in two stages. In the first place, he accepted Kant's view that for a moral law to be binding—a "categorical imperative" in Kant's terms—it had to be universal. A universal law is one whose determining ground is the rational will (vernunftige Wille) and not simply the agent's arbitrary whim or caprice (Wilkür). Indeed, for Cohen as for Kant, there can be no other source of law than an individual's practical rationality itself; any other incentive for obeying the law would, strictly speaking, be outside of reason and therefore not a moral justification.

But while Cohen accepted the Kantian demand for universality, he had to reject Kant's specific views on Judaism. For Kant, Judaism was nothing more than a collection of "statutory" laws and therefore "really not a religion at all."[50] Kant accepted Spinoza's view (although he lacked Spinoza's profound knowledge of Jewish law and tradition) that Judaism was a purely political or civil legislation and as such indifferent to the higher moral or spiritual needs of mankind. The religious practices and rituals of Judaism—the entire domain of halakha—are no more than a historical contingency and are thus lacking in moral necessity. Judaism was for Kant a religion of sheer heteronomy, that is, of externally imposed command. Thus did Kant regard the Akedah, the binding of Isaac, as an "illusion" contrary to the moral law.[51]

Cohen's conception of Judaism seemed to owe more to Kant's greatest Jewish contemporary, Moses Mendelssohn. For Mendelssohn, Judaism was the original repository of a rational monotheism. Belief in God, providence, and the immortality of the soul are rational precepts not dependent upon revelation. The beauty of Judaism's ethical monotheism is that it is independent of any special revelation or particular providence, but is available to man as such. After all, did Mendelssohn not write in his Jerusalem that "According to the concepts of true Judaism, all the inhabitants of the earth are destined to felicity; and the means of attaining it are as widespread as mankind itself, as charitably dispersed as the means of warding off hunger and other natural needs?"[52] Did not Talmudic Judaism itself declare that "the righteous of all nations have a share in the world to come?" For Cohen as for Mendelssohn, the essence of Judaism is that it is a "religion of reason" in which all human beings, so long as they are rational, are invited to participate.

This leads to another set of differences between Spinoza and Cohen, namely, their treatment of the messianic theme in Judaism. For Spinoza, the prophets were not philosophers but men with "a more vivid power of imagination" and as such "less fitted for purely intellectual activity."[53] In contrast to Maimonides, for whom Mosaic prophecy was raised above that of all other prophets, Spinoza argued that "it would be hardly likely that men addicted to Egyptian superstition . . . should have had any sound understanding of God" and that the Mosaic prophecy, far from representing a liberation, merely substituted one form of oppression for another.[54] Indeed, the alleged election of the Jewish people had less to do with their wisdom or tranquility of mind than with their social organization and the means by which they acquired and maintained political hegemony. Accordingly, the gift of prophecy was limited to the period of Jewish sovereignty after which it was lost forever.[55]

For Cohen, however, the messianic idea in Judaism is not of a purely national or political character. The Messiah is not just a national savior but a universal redeemer. For Cohen, messianism was tied to the idea of the progress or the perfection of the human race, to be attained not through God's grace, but through the historical process itself.[56] Cohen goes so far as to suggest that the messianic idea of a united humanity living under self-chosen laws was already implicit in the teachings of the prophets. Messianism is only another term for socialism, which envisages a perfect unity of all mankind raised above petty national vanities and rivalries. Indeed, Cohen's passionate attack on Zionism was undertaken out of the belief that the reassertion of Jewish nationalism would only affirm what the anti-Semites had believed all along.[57]

Cohen believed that there was a particular affinity between Germany and Judaism that it was the unique contribution of his work to explore. In a wartime pamphlet titled "Deutschtum und Judentum" he argued that the essence of "Germanism" (Deutschtum) was its "ethical idealism," by which he meant the humanistic culture of Kant, Schiller, and Beethoven. It was also this cosmopolitan (Weltbürgerlich) outlook that informed the prophetic teachings of Judaism. The combination of Germanism and Judaism, then, would bring out the best of both "the nation of Kant" and the people of the book.[58] To be sure, Cohen understood that this "German-Jewish symbiosis" was not yet an actuality. It remained for him an "idea" in the precise Kantian sense of the term, a legitimate object of moral aspiration. For this reason, he feared the over-hasty tendency of many of his contemporaries toward assimilation. Until a cosmopolitan culture had been realized, Jews had an obligation to remain apart, if only because he believed the very future of monotheism was at stake.[59]

While remaining an admirer of Cohen, Strauss did not share either Cohen's rationalistic conception of Judaism or his optimistic assessment of its future in the German homeland. In the first place, he believed there was a kind of unreality in Cohen's conception of Judaism as the religion of reason. This conception depended for its validity upon a distinction between what is rational and hence morally obligatory and what is merely historical and contingent in Judaism. But this distinction is itself a product of the modern Enlightenment and as such is external to Judaism itself. Cohen's method of "idealization" thus led him to distort the very thing he tried to understand and defend.

Strauss's conception of Judaism always remained closer to Cohen's younger partner, Franz Rosenzweig, to whose memory Strauss's Spinoza book was dedicated, and "whose name," he would later remark, "will always be remembered when informed people speak about existentialism."[60] Strauss was especially impressed by Rosenzweig's claim that Judaism is not about law (*Gesetz*) in the Kantian sense of universality but about command (*Gebot*).[61] The mitzvot are commandments in the primordial and most revealing sense of the term: God speaks, we listen. But this emphasis on command did not entail a return to a religion of sheer heteronomy or otherness. God's first command to "love men" is followed by another to "love thy neighbor."[62] According to Rosenzweig, the command to love is superior to the Kantian demand for rational autonomy for two reasons. First, it provides some "content" to the Kantian moral imperative, which Rosenzweig, following Hegel, regards as an "empty formalism."[63] And second, the Kantian emphasis upon formal laws or rules makes unintelligible the highest form of moral action, namely, saintliness which is only possible with the assistance of divine love.[64]

Even here, it must be admitted, Strauss did not find Rosenzweig's reconstruction of Judaism altogether convincing. Rosenzweig himself admitted that he could not believe all the commandments revealed in the Torah. A number of them remained "alien" to him. At the heart of his Judaism, Rosenzweig imposed a conception of free choice that Strauss regarded as contrary to the spirit of genuine orthodoxy. For all of his efforts to avoid the excessive rationalism of the philosophers, Rosenzweig still regarded his work as "a system of philosophy." Despite his claim to be developing a "new thinking" (*neue Denken*) different from both the philosophers and the rabbis, Rosenzweig remained in some sense dialectically dependent upon the thought he tried to supersede.[65] Concerning this point Strauss wrote: "Whereas the classic work of what is called Jewish medieval philosophy, the *Guide of the Perplexed*, is primarily not a philosophical book, but a Jewish book, Rosenzweig's *Star of Redemption* is primarily not a Jewish book, but 'a system of philosophy.'"[66] The failure of Rosenzweig to produce a "Jewish book" merely showed the difficulty of recovering orthodoxy in the face of modernity.

Strauss did not share Cohen's optimistic forecast for an eventual synthesis of Germanism and Judaism. Cohen believed that this synthesis was made possible because of the inherent perfectibility of human nature.

Interpreting Moses' exclamation "Would that all the Lord's people were prophets" (Numbers 11:29) in the light of Kant's perfectibilian philosophy of history, Cohen predicted an eventual end of war and human suffering.[67] In contrast to Cohen's prophetic idealism, Strauss emphasized the constancy of human nature and especially the human propensity for evil. Cohen's belief in progress, which relegated hatred of Jews completely to the past, was itself refuted by subsequent events. Cohen's synthesis of Greek classicism, German idealism, and Jewish messianism did not survive beyond 1933. In his lecture on "Jerusalem and Athens" Strauss devastatingly concluded:

> Cohen's thought belongs to the world preceding World War I. . . . The worst things that he experienced were the Dreyfus scandal and the pogroms instigated by czarist Russia: he did not experience Communist Russia or Hitler Germany. . . . Catastrophes and horrors of a magnitude hitherto unknown, which we have seen and through which we have lived, were better provided for, or made intelligible, by both Plato and the prophets than by the modern belief in progress.[68]

According to Strauss, Cohen sought to replace both historical Judaism and Christianity with a religion of reason. This religion would provide the basis for a new culture that would be secular in its scholarship, democratic in its politics, and individualistic in its ethics. This belief in the redemptive or transformative power of culture reached its high water mark in Germany in the years immediately before and after World War I. At that time "the faith in the power of Western culture to mold the fate of mankind" was considerably greater than it is today. The fact that this kind of culture— modern, secular, and democratic—soon became the object of the murderous hatreds of both the Left and the Right proved to Strauss that the Enlightenment's solution to the Jewish question was deeply flawed.

Strauss's "Maimonidean" Turn

The flaws with the Enlightenment came to light only in the course of Strauss's later studies of Maimonides's *Guide of the Perplexed*, a work, he would say later, that occupied "about twenty five years of frequently interrupted but never abandoned study."[69] What, exactly, were the fruits of this study?

Strauss discovered that the modern Enlightenment of which Spinoza was one of the chief proponents had been preceded by a medieval Enlightenment whose greatest representative was Maimonides. Unlike the modern Enlightenment, which had as its public goal the "Epicurean" intention to banish fear of invisible powers from the religious imagination, the "medieval Enlightenment" was characterized precisely by its esoteric teaching. The medieval philosophers by contrast were, in the original understanding, precisely not Enlighteners. They were less concerned with spreading knowledge than with preventing its misuse.[70]

The difference between modern and medieval rationalism can be traced back to their different views regarding the relationship of reason to civil society. The esoteric mode of utterance was necessary, in the first place, to protect philosophers from the accusations of impiety and atheism that inevitably attend the utterance of unpopular truths. The popular suspicion of philosophy derives from the belief that knowledge is power and that philosophers must aspire to tyranny. Strauss does not believe that this allegation is simply false. It is because, as a practical matter, philosophers lack the power to attain their ends that they are forced to resort to esoteric rhetoric. Esoteric teaching, therefore, was widely practiced as a matter of practical necessity in pre- or nonliberal societies that do not guarantee the absolute right of freedom of speech.

At the same time, esoteric writing was practiced by those writers who wished not just to protect themselves from persecution, but also to protect society from the dangers always inherent in philosophy. Accordingly, premodern thinkers presented a purely edifying teaching that could be grasped by any relatively intelligent reader and another, esoteric teaching wrapped up in enigma, contradiction, and paradox that would have quite another meaning for the philosophers or philosophers-in-training.[71] The distinction between esoteric and exoteric writing is not, as a recent interpreter maintains, simply a convenient medium through which the philosopher can put forward a shocking, nihilistic teaching.[72] There is rather a public or political purpose to this distinction. The distinction is necessary so that the philosopher's proposals for political reform are phrased in a language or rhetoric that his audience will be able to understand. Exoteric writing is a way of exercising political responsibility. "Exoteric teaching is *political philosophy*," as Nathan Tarcov says.[73]

Strauss found ample evidence of the esoteric character of medieval rationalism in Maimonides's *Guide*. In the introduction to the work Maimonides notes that the two main subjects to be taught there, *Maaseh Bereshit* and *Maaseh Merkavah*, the Account of Creation and the Account of the Chariot, are equivalent to physics and metaphysics respectively. Furthermore, he notes that there is a rabbinic injunction against the public discussion of these teachings. "The Account of the Chariot," the injunction reads, "ought not to be taught even to one man, except if he be wise and able to understand himself, in which case only the chapter headings may be transmitted to him."[74] And Maimonides goes on to remark that these teachings will not be set down by him in order but will be "scattered and entangled with other subjects" so that "the truths be glimpsed and then again concealed."[75]

From passages such as these, Strauss became convinced that Maimonides practiced a mode of writing that revealed different things to different people with different abilities. The *Guide*, he tells us, is a book "sealed with many seals" and "an enchanted forest."[76] The exoteric or public premise of the work is that reason and revelation are mutually compatible, but to the careful reader Maimonides indicated that there was a profound, perhaps unbridgeable gulf between them. Thus to vouchsafe the freedom to philosophize Maimonides had to present philosophy as something commanded by the Torah or within the traditional framework of Jewish law. There was, Maimonides argued, a legal obligation to philosophize laid down by Moses "our Master." Only by its presentation within the context of law could philosophy acquire respectability within the community of the orthodox.

Maimonides's attribution of a secret teaching to Scripture and especially to the story of Creation in Genesis 1-3 is scarcely unique in medieval literature.[77] The so-called Gnostic heresy of late antiquity took the account of creation not as a literal story of God's workmanship, but as a tissue of symbols and allegories that had to be properly decoded if Scripture was to reveal its deeper meaning. Christian writers of the second century like Valentinus completely inverted the literal meaning of the story. No longer was the world seen as the creation of the just and loving God; rather, the Gnostic deity was something "wholly other" who stands in no positive relation to the finite, human world. Indeed, thanks to Gershom Scholem we now know that Gnosticism was not just a Christian phenomenon, but had deep roots in early Jewish mysticism as well. The school of Merkabah mysticism incorporated important Gnostic elements in its interpretation of Ezekiel's vision of the throne as a kind of apocalyptic disclosure of God's knowledge of the end of days.[78]

The idea, then, that Scripture contained a deeper, richer allegorical substructure than had been thought had potentially explosive implications. As Hans Jonas, Strauss's friend and colleague from the New School for Social Research, argued, Gnosticism contained latent nihilistic and antinomian movements of thought.[79] For if God is withdrawn from human affairs as the Gnostics assert, then we are permitted an unprecedented freedom to dispose of our powers as we see fit. The paradoxical results, as Jonas demonstrates, are the revolutionary extremes of asceticism and libertinage. The two are equally valid (but also equally groundless) replies to a cosmic order that has been purged of telos and where the only legitimate source of value is the pneumatic self. From here, one can see, it is not far to the infamous doctrine of "redemption through sin" according to which those who have been initiated into gnosis (knowledge) are encouraged to abrogate the laws of the Torah in order to hasten the end of time.[80]

The adequacy of Strauss's interpretation of Maimonides and other medieval writers is obviously too large a topic to be treated here.[81] Suffice it to say that Strauss's attribution to them of an esoteric teaching has important implications for his understanding of the theologico-political problem. For if his reading is correct, it follows that Maimonides regarded the entire history of Jewish law as having only instrumental value. Normative Judaism, like all religion, should be judged by its ability to secure such pragmatic goals as social peace and stability and not by its ability to attain the higher ends of intellectual or theoretical perfection. Indeed, the entire thrust of Maimonides's teaching, according to Strauss, is the subordination of moral to intellectual virtue, the way of the Torah to the way of philosophy. Consequently, exoteric works like the *Mishneh Torah* which are intended as a guide for the regulation and direction of Jewish practice are sharply severed and even depreciated when compared to such esoteric works as the *Guide* which are intended to fashion and reform opinion.

Strauss was aware that this interpretation of the *Guide*, like the *Guide* itself, was rich with paradox. For if the *Guide* contains a hidden teaching, Strauss appears to be violating the first rule of that teaching, namely, discussing publicly what is best left wrapped in silence or enigma. By recovering and publicizing this "forgotten kind of writing," Strauss seems to be in "flagrant transgression" of the law. How does he justify this act?

Strauss is not unaware of this paradox and offers two solutions to it. In the first place he says, "the historical situation today is fundamentally different from that of the twelfth century."[82] This statement suggests that while public opinion at the time of Maimonides was ruled by a belief in the divine or mysterious origin of the law, today this is simply no longer believed. The modern Jew has become a disciple of Spinoza with the belief in the historical or merely contingent character of the Torah. The modern scholar, unlike Maimonides, need not fear persecution at the hands of the Jewish community because both scholar and layman are likely to share similar beliefs. Consequently, Strauss feels justified in transgressing the rabbinic injunction because the law itself no longer has the same hold upon the lives of modern Jews. The esoteric tradition can today become a subject of scholarly research and even public debate because it is a dead tradition, one which, like political philosophy itself, is in a state of "decay" or "putrefaction."[83] Thus what earlier generations could only whisper or hint at through indirection, Strauss feels justified in revealing in the full light of day.

But there is another reason justifying Strauss's apparent transgression of the law. Commentary, even on an esoteric work, need not imply disobedience to the law. There are commentaries and there are commentaries. Strauss himself hints at the possibility of an esoteric commentary on Maimonides.[84] Such a commentary may be today the only way of keeping alive the philosophical tradition of which Maimonides was the greatest representative. It is not inconceivable that Strauss's manner of writing sought to wed modern scholarly research with the function of the traditional commentator as a keeper and transmitter of tradition. Strauss suggests that the historical recovery of works from the past "takes on philosophical significance for men living in an age of intellectual decline."[85] Commentary on an ancient author, then, becomes a way of recovering certain "fundamental problems" or questions, questions like the proper relation of order and freedom.[86] If the author in question is one like Maimonides who operated within a tradition of revealed law, it falls to the scholar to recover the meaning of the law and how it was understood both by the author and by his audience. It is a suggestive possibility that in his emphasis on scholarly commentary and the close reading of texts Strauss was fulfilling, not abrogating, the claims of orthodoxy.

Citizen or Jew?

To return, then, to our original question: how Jewish was Leo Strauss? How does his handling of the Jewish Question help us understand the more general theologico-political problem? Where do we stand vis-à-vis the universal and the particular?

At one level Strauss defends the integrity of Judaism from the skeptical assaults of philosophy. He denies that reason can ever simply refute orthodoxy. The only way one could refute orthodoxy would be to prove that the cosmos is perfectly intelligible without recourse to the workings of a mysterious God. Spinoza and Hegel were in Strauss's view the two thinkers who made the grandest efforts to refute the very possibility of biblical revelation by means of reason alone. But their philosophies reveal themselves, on close examination, to rely on arbitrary premises or on premises no more rational than the claims of revelation. Thus from a strictly epistemological or scientific angle, modern philosophy remains no more certain than the view of orthodoxy that it set out to refute.[87]

On the other hand, however, Strauss seems to believe that orthodoxy is no longer a viable option for ourselves as citizens of the modern enlightened world. By orthodoxy Strauss means such things as the belief in an omnipotent and inscrutable God, the creation of the world *ex nihilo*, and the possibility of miracles. Any modification of these fundamental tenets or "roots," as the medieval Jewish tradition would call them, would be a corruption of the original spirit of orthodoxy. Despite his repeated assertions that we must remain "open" to the claims of both reason and revelation, I do not believe that Strauss considered orthodoxy a feasible alternative in the final analysis. The suspension of critical judgment needed for such things as belief in the resurrection of the dead is no longer a living possibility. Indeed, Strauss himself often warned of the dangers in attempting to reoccupy earlier positions. He remarks that every modern attempt to return to an earlier position has unwittingly resulted in "a much more radical form of modernity."[88] The attempt to restore orthodoxy in its pristine form today can only lead to obscurantism and fanaticism.

The question becomes, then: what posture ought a Jew to take living in a skeptical age? Here Strauss delineated two attitudes. The first was that of Spinoza, the most consistent and uncompromising critic from within Judaism. His was the rationalistic criticism of the Enlightenment that everywhere juxtaposed philosophic detachment or freedom from the tradition of his own people. Spinoza as well as other *Aufklärer* of his age rejected not only Judaism but all tradition as incompatible with the alleged freedom and dignity of man.

The second form of criticism Strauss, following Hermann Cohen, calls "idealizing." Rather than rejecting tradition *in toto*, the idealizing critic begins from a posture of "fidelity" or "sympathy" toward one's tradition. This does not mean uncritical or blind acceptance of tradition, but rather the interpretation of a tradition in the light of its highest possibilities. To idealize is not just to praise or flatter, but to use what one regards as the best or highest aspects of one's tradition as a standard to criticize others. It is this method of criticism that is at the basis of Strauss's oft-quoted remark: "It is safer to try to understand the low in the light of the high than the high in the light of the low."[89] It is this kind of idealizing criticism that Strauss practiced himself in his treatment of the Jewish Question.

At long last this brings us to the relation between Judaism and liberal democracy. Are they compatible? There is surely much evidence for an affirmative answer to this question. It is arguable that the liberal democracies of the West with their guarantee of full civil rights and universal suffrage have provided the only decent solution to what Strauss called the theologico-political problem. The liberal solution to this problem can be described as a combination of legal equality plus private discrimination. Liberalism is based on the distinction between public and private. Thus while the liberal state has by and large eradicated the worst forms of state-sponsored religious bigotry and persecution, it cannot and has not sought to abolish all social hierarchies and private forms of religious and ethnic discrimination. The attempt to use political power as a means of abolishing all private discrimination may result in a cure worse than the disease.

At the same time Strauss believed that it was unconscionable for Jews to abandon their ancient faith for the sake of assimilation to the mainstream. As the early critique of Nordau indicated, the price of assimilation came at the cost of a loss of Jewish self-identity and Jewish pride. The result of assimilation was inevitably "the bog of philistinism . . . a most inglorious end for a people which had been led out of the house of bondage into the desert with careful avoidance of the land of the Philistines."[90] While there is no reason to doubt that Strauss was profoundly grateful to the United States for the opportunities it had bestowed on the Jews to live safe and secure from the worst forms of European anti-Semitism, this by no means blinded him to a frankly realistic assessment of the problem:

> It is very far from me to minimize the difference between a nation conceived in liberty and dedicated to the proposition that all men are created equal, and the nations of the old world, which certainly were not conceived in liberty. I share the hope in America and the faith in America, but I am compelled to add that that faith and that hope cannot be of the same character as that faith and that hope which a Jew has in regard to Judaism and which the Christian has in regard to Christianity. No one claims that the faith in America and the hope for America are based on explicit divine promises.[91]

This brings us close to Strauss's core belief about the essence of Judaism. The core of Judaism is its belief in the reality of a supernatural revelation. The fundamental Jewish experience in history is God's revelation of the Torah on Mount Sinai. This revelation has the function, to some degree, of insulating and protecting the Jews from the cultures of other nations. Unless it can somehow be demonstrated that this revelation demands the unification of all mankind by the overcoming of each particular faith, Jews will be justified in remaining stubbornly attached to their own particularity. To the extent that the liberal Enlightenment has urged the abolition of particular providence, it will always be at odds with Judaism.

CHAPTER TWO

Gershom Scholem and Leo Strauss: Notes toward a German-Jewish Dialogue

> I see again that you are the only antiphilosophic contemporary—for you are consistent enough to be antiphilosophic—from whom I learn something with pleasure. — *Leo Strauss to Gershom Scholem, in a letter dated August 11, 1960*

When someone eventually writes the intellectual history of the twentieth century, it would not be at all surprising if Gershom Scholem and Leo Strauss turn out to be the two most important Jewish thinkers. Their prominence, if not preeminence, among the most important German Jewish thinkers is already secured.[1] Despite their renown and influence in their respective fields of kabala and political philosophy, no comparative study of their work has yet been attempted. This essay represents a first step in that direction.

The biographies of Scholem and Strauss present some striking parallels and contrasts. Scholem was born into a middle-class, assimilated Berlin family, the milieu of which he ridiculed mercilessly in his autobiography, *From Berlin to Jerusalem*. From an early age he was attracted to political Zionism and was active in the German anti-war movement during World War I, something that proved a profound embarrassment to his parents. He studied mathematics and philosophy at the universities of Berlin, Jena, and Bern before deciding to return to Germany to pursue a doctorate on the kabala at Munich. It was during these years that he struck up a friendship with the Marxist philosopher Walter Benjamin that would eventually produce one of the great literary correspondences of this or any other age.[2]

Strauss, by contrast, was born into a religiously observant family in the Hessian village of Kirchhain. He would later describe it as a home in which "the ceremonial laws were rather strictly observed," but where "there was very little Jewish knowledge."[3] He too studied philosophy, natural science, and mathematics before taking a doctorate at Hamburg under the great neo-Kantian Ernst Cassirer. During the 1920s Strauss worked as a researcher at an academy for Jewish studies in Berlin, where, it appears, he and Scholem crossed paths for the first time. While Scholem emigrated to Palestine in 1923, later to become Professor of Jewish Mysticism at the newly established Hebrew University in Jerusalem, Strauss remained in Germany until the early 1930s. In 1932, with the aid of a grant from the Rockefeller Foundation, he left Germany for a brief stay in France, where he established a lifelong friendship with the Russian Hegelian emigré Alexandre Kojève.[4] Strauss emigrated to the United States in 1938, where he taught principally at the New School for Social Research and at the University of Chicago until his death in 1973.

It was only after Scholem's departure for Jerusalem that he and Strauss struck up a correspondence, if not exactly a friendship, that continued well into the 1960s. Their correspondence, which has only recently been collected, expresses on the surface great mutual esteem and regard. Yet this apparent esteem is implicitly undercut by their published works, in which each demonstrates scant attention to or recognition of the work of the other. Scholem's studies make only the most passing nod to Strauss, while Strauss's brief personal statements make no mention of Scholem whatever.[5] To be sure, neither man was prone to excessive praise of contemporaries. Scholem's extensive autobiographical works appear to suggest that he found himself a subject of endless fascination and believed that others should think so too, while Strauss's rather scant use of the personal pronoun testifies to a desire to hide—or perhaps disappear altogether—behind the various texts he chose to interpret.

What is of interest here is not so much what Scholem and Strauss say as what they leave unsaid. Their silences seem to me to go beyond the mere facts of professional rivalry or even a conflict of personalities. Rather, they point to the most profound differences regarding their views on history, modernity, and, perhaps most of all, Jewish identity. It is through a juxtaposition of the views of these two great representatives of *mittel Europa* that we can begin to reconstruct their own German-Jewish dialogue.

The Limits of *Wissenschaft*

For all of their many differences, Scholem and Strauss have one important fact in common: they were both radicals. I do not mean this in the colloquial and uninteresting sense of being either "left-wing" or "right-wing."

I mean it in the philosophic sense of breaking profoundly with the prevailing orthodoxies of their day. Both men were driven by a belief not only that modern scholarship was intellectually flawed, but that it created, rather than removed, grave obstacles to honesty and self-understanding.

Scholem's lifelong antagonist was the school of *Wissenschaft des Judentums*, which, as the name implied, held up the idea of science or *Wissenschaft* as "the summit of values."[6] The so-called science of Judaism was a creation of the early nineteenth century and its attempt to enthrone the new historical consciousness as the queen of the sciences. The *Wissenschaft* school, whose leading proponents were Leopold Zunz and Moritz Steinschneider, sought to comprehend Judaism not as living spirituality but as a historical artifact. Applying to Judaism the Hegelian adage that "philosophy is its time apprehended in thoughts," the idea of the *Wissenschaft* school was to locate Judaism as a historical phenomenon firmly in the past. The purpose of this endeavor, as its founders recognized, was not only scholarly but political. Their project of historicization meant to integrate Jewish studies within the broader context of the development of European civilization.[7]

Scholem found the *Wissenschaft* school defective for at least two reasons. First, the very idea of a science of Judaism seemed from the outset to prejudice the findings of this school in favor of the legal and rationalistic themes of Judaism and against its mystical and antinomian dimensions. Scholem's rehabilitation of kabala was his herculean effort to liberate the "underside" of Judaism from the dead hand of historical positivism and to accord it a living respectability. Jewish mysticism was not for Scholem merely bad theology or some kind of heresy; it was vital to the very development of Judaism as a tradition. Thus rather than depicting Jewish history, as did the *Wissenschaft* school, as the gradual unfolding of the idea of a rational faith, Scholem saw it as deeply torn between conflicting rationalist and antinomian tendencies.[8]

Second, Scholem attacked what he took to be not merely the scientific or scholarly project, but the political and ideological tendencies of this school. By seeking to divest Judaism of its irrationalist and antinomian qualities, the *Wissenschaft* school sought to "normalize" or accommodate Judaism to the cultural mainstream of Protestant Europe. To be sure, the *Wissenschaft* school had come of age during the era of romantic historiography, with its search for the authentic roots of particular national and religious cultures and its aim of achieving pluralism and toleration. But as the century wore on, this aspiration to diversity turned more toward the desire for assimilation. Scholem was fond of quoting Steinschneider's blunt but absolutely revealing remark that "We have only one task left: to give the remains of Judaism a decent burial." Thus while the *Wissenschaft des Judentums* had begun as a project of cultural awakening aimed at the restoration of Jewish pride, by the early twentieth century it had collapsed into a species of self-abnegation and "dejudaization."[9]

Strauss's attack on the core assumptions of modern social science and intellectual history mirrored some of the same presuppositions and motivations that underlay Scholem's critique of the *Wissenschaft* school. Like Scholem, Strauss attacked the *Wissenschaft* ideal in historical studies as identical with the dominant academic positivism. The particular object of Strauss's critique, however, was Max Weber's conception of "ethical neutrality" and "value freedom." Turning the argument for value freedom back upon itself, Strauss argued that it was pre-committed to certain values and beliefs that were hardly neutral. The very idea of a social science presupposes values like open-mindedness, liability to error, and respect for truth. It cannot help but assert, if only implicitly, the superiority of these values to all others. Hence, the demand for strict ethical neutrality in the social sciences, he argued, was a contradiction in terms.[10]

Strauss maintained that the subject matter of the social sciences is by its nature constituted by reference to some good, that is, to some goal or set of goals that people believe to be desirable, valuable, or advantageous for their well-being. To demand that these goals be described in a scientifically neutral language is to distort the very subject matter of our inquiry. For Strauss, for whom the experiences of Stalin's Russia and Hitler's Germany were always at the forefront of his consciousness, this seemed like an abnegation of the purpose of a social science. To describe the goings-on in a concentration camp without reference to such value-laden terms as "cruelty," "inhumanity," or "barbarism" would produce not a more scientifically accurate account but a mockery of truth and clarity. Social and historical studies are, in contrast to the prevailing norms of social relativism, linked not only to description but to judgment and evaluation.[11]

Furthermore, in the study of political ideas in particular Strauss denied the prevailing orthodoxy, which held that the ideas of a thinker must always be studied as a response to or a reflection of that thinker's immediate time, place, and circumstance. This is not to say that Strauss went to the opposite and equally absurd extreme of believing that an author or text can be studied in isolation from all context or history. Rather, he remained true to the claim that we must seek to understand an author as he understood himself, and to do this we must begin from the author's own indications of how he or she wished to be understood. The attempt of modern intellectual historians to derive an author's thoughts from the economic, cultural, or (as it is said nowadays) linguistic context of the age is to impose an external standard on that author's thought that distorts his perspective from the outset. It is to claim that we know better than the author himself what his thoughts really mean. For Strauss, true historical objectivity requires us to bracket our prejudices and beliefs in order to allow the author's own questions and understanding of his context to guide our inquiry.[12]

Scholem and Strauss were thinkers who were deeply convinced that theirs was an age of crisis, a crisis whose most visible or immediate symptoms were the great wars and upheavals of their time, but whose true causes lay more deeply hidden or sedimented in the traditions they sought to understand. For both, tradition was at once a vital and living source of ideas and at the same time an obstruction to clarity. In order, then, to uncover those causes it was necessary to cultivate a critical attitude toward that tradition, to see better what, precisely, it concealed from view. For Scholem, this meant interrogating—one could almost say deconstructing—the tradition of rabbinic Judaism in order to grasp those theological tendencies it had sought vainly to repress. Scholem's monumental studies of kabala in general and the *Zohar* or Book of Splendor in particular were undertaken with this critical end in view.

For Strauss, the crisis was precipitated not so much by the institutional prejudices of rabbinic Judaism as by modern political philosophy itself. Strauss's rehabilitation of Maimonides as the "classic" of medieval rationalism was intended to aid in our understanding of the progressive destruction of reason by both positivism and historicism.[13] As with Scholem, Strauss's purposes were diagnostic. But here already we can see the beginnings of a quarrel between Scholem and Strauss that affects both their diagnoses of the crisis as well as the direction of their studies. For Scholem, the problem stems precisely from a surfeit of rationalism that has tried to repress everything that does not fit its categories and concepts; for Strauss, it is the abnegation of reason and the denial of possibly true standards that is the root cause of the problem. With this in mind we can begin to see better why Scholem was drawn to a study of the Gnostic and Sabbatian movements within Judaism, while Strauss was drawn to the Platonic and Maimonidean forms of rationalism as antidotes to the problem.

The Lure of Kabala

Scholem's analysis of Jewish mysticism grew out of a practical desire to offset the predominantly rationalistic understanding of Judaism propounded by both the rabbis and the scholarly consensus. However, it would be a mistake to see him as giving up altogether on the project of *Geistesgeschichte*. Unlike other historians (e.g., Salo Baron, who wrote a social history of the Jews), Scholem remained in many ways committed to determining the true or real *Geist* of Judaism. His quarrel was with those who would reduce the *Geist* to some version of rational ethics (e.g., Hermann Cohen). Rather, for Scholem the real *Geist* of Judaism no longer spoke through the authoritative voice of *halakha*, but through the subterranean incantation of the mystics and kabalists. To use Nietzschean language, it was the Dionysian spirit of Judaism that Scholem sought to liberate from its rational Apollonian form.

Scholem's analysis of Jewish mysticism has been the subject of considerable scholarly controversy among students of religion.[14] It is not my purpose here to question the validity or historical accuracy of Scholem's categories, but rather to see how mysticism functions within his overall philosophy of history. It is necessary to observe at the outset that the phenomenon of mysticism constitutes a definite stage within what Scholem often refers to as his "dialectical" theory of history. As Hegel does in his *Philosophy of History*, Scholem regards Judaism as passing through three stages. The first consists of a "naive" or "immediate" stage of religious experience corresponding to the situation of ancient Israel prior to the destruction of the Temple. The second stage consists of a more self-conscious or mediated encounter between the believer and the various myths and legends embodied in the Torah. This stage corresponds historically to the Talmudic period and the beginnings of the legal and halakhic institutions intended to govern life in the diaspora. It is only in the third stage that mysticism comes into play. The mystical stage attempts to recapture the lost spontaneity and innocence of toratic belief, but through the use of a highly abstract, and even esoteric set of categories.

Scholem's account of the mystical stage of religion is best stated in his own words:

> The secret of the success of the Kabbalah lies in the nature of its relation to the spiritual heritage of rabbinical Judaism. This relation differs from that of rationalist philosophy, in that it is more deeply and in a more vital sense connected with the main forces active in Judaism. Undoubtedly both the mystics and the philosophers completely transform the structure of ancient Judaism; both have lost the simple relation to Judaism, that naïveté which speaks to us from the classical documents of Rabbinical literature. Classical Judaism expressed itself: it did not reflect upon itself. By contrast, to the mystics and the philosophers

of a later stage of religious development Judaism itself has become problematical. Instead of simply speaking their minds, they tend to produce an ideology of Judaism, an ideology moreover which comes to the rescue of tradition by giving it a new interpretation.[15]

This is an admittedly cursory account, but it contains all the main themes of Scholem's analysis of mysticism. In the first place, it expresses his view that Jewish mysticism both runs counter to and is superior to the greatest works of medieval Jewish philosophy. Scholem's opposition of kabala to philosophy seems a bit like a distant relative of Plato's famous "quarrel between poetry and philosophy" in book 10 of the *Republic*. While medieval philosophy and the kabala both emerged in response to rabbinic Judaism, Scholem leaves little doubt regarding his preference for the kabalists. This preference appears to be based on the belief that philosophy stands, so to speak, outside of Judaism or at best as an alien growth within it. Its principal questions and problems derive from Plato and Aristotle rather than from within traditional Jewish sources. Philosophy remains, then, disconnected from the main lines of Jewish life and spirituality.

More importantly, Scholem carries over a critique of philosophy that derives at least some of its force from the nineteenth-century romantic attack on rationalism and finds resonance in the works of Benjamin and other members of the Frankfurt School.[16] For Scholem, philosophy always represents the rationalistic attempt to neutralize the content of religion by converting it into a set of bloodless abstractions. Typical here is Scholem's attitude toward Maimonides, whose "negative theology" he sees as demystifying and hence displacing the teachings of the Torah. Mysticism may in some sense be just as abstract as philosophy, but its purpose is to reinvigorate life, to add to it new depths of meaning and purpose that cannot be given purely rational expression. Thus mysticism sought to revitalize Judaism from within, which allowed it to present itself as a form of internal renewal and innovation.

The second feature of Scholem's account is mysticism's esotericism. For the mystics, kabala is an esoteric discipline in two senses of the word. It deals with the most deeply hidden and hence mysterious meanings of the Torah, the so-called "Secrets of the Law"; and it is a knowledge available only to an elite. Scholem traced this tradition of esoteric interpretation back to the Gnostic sects of late antiquity that had already endowed the story of creation in Genesis and Ezekiel's vision of the throne-chariot with great allegorical significance. The Gnostic or esoteric interpretations of these works typically contained elaborate rules for achieving the ascent of the soul from earth through the hostile planet-angels to the Merkabah or seat of divine wisdom. Later Jewish mysticism even established schools and cults with elaborate rites of passage and initiation for those deemed competent to receive gnosis (divine knowledge).[17]

The third and final feature of Jewish mysticism is its antinomianism. From the outset mysticism was related less to contemplation than to action. Its goal was redemptive. The big question was how this redemption was to be achieved. For Scholem, the idea of redemption and the coming of the messiah in rabbinic Judaism took a largely conservative or "restorative" form. It looked to the restitution of Jewish sovereignty but along the lines of the Davidic monarchy of the past. The messianic age or the world to come would not entail any essential rupture with cosmic processes or even with historico-political possibilities. Rather, the early kabalists sought to bring about the coming of the messiah through a scrupulous adherence to the law, which they regarded as immutable, eternal, and absolute. Thus the messianic age could at most be a product of wish or prayer but was certainly not the outcome of anything like historical "progress" or the dynamics of the historical process.[18]

According to Scholem, this largely conservative attitude toward the messianic age changed radically after 1492, the year that witnessed the forced expulsion of the Jews from Iberia. The shock of this expulsion was so great that it seemed to many that the biblical end of days might not be only a distant and remote possibility, but might already be at hand. The person most responsible for affecting this transformation from restorative to "apocalyptic" messianism was the Spanish kabalist Isaac Luria. According to Luria, God created the world through an initial "breaking of the vessels" that produced a scattering of divine sparks throughout the universe. This act of divine self-alienation, mirrored in the fall of Adam and the subsequent exile of Israel, would only be redeemed with the ingathering of the sparks and the restoration of the cosmic order. For Scholem the novelty of Lurianic kabalism was its depiction of the expulsion not simply as an event in secular time, but as part of a cosmic drama of exile and redemption. Luria's emphasis on *tikkun*, or a "mending" of the world, had the function of turning kabalism from an esoteric doctrine intended only for the elite into the basis of a mass movement that shook rabbinic Judaism to its foundations. Luria, Scholem notes, was not himself a radical, although his version of the kabala put an unprecedented emphasis on human activity and on the will as a means of bringing about the end. Lurianic kabalism was apocalyptic precisely because it envisaged a messianic kingdom not as a restoration (or maybe a remembrance) of things past, but as a radical overcoming and break with the normal state of affairs.[19]

Without prolonging this story needlessly, the radical possibilities only latent in the Lurianic kabala were extended by later messianic movements, particularly the appearance of the false messiah Sabbatai Zevi. It was only with Sabbatianism that kabala became an avowedly antinomian movement that maintained that the laws of the Torah became obsolete with the appearance of the messiah. The aim of this movement was nothing short of liberation understood as freedom from the yoke of the law rather than as the traditional freedom to fulfill what the law requires. The Sabbatians first announced the nihilistic doctrine of "redemption through sin," which not only excused but justified antinomianism on the grounds that it would hasten the end. Even Sabbatai's later apostasy was interpreted as evidence that he was the bearer of a new law.[20]

Scholem attributes enormous historical importance to Sabbatianism for preparing the ground for the Enlightenment, "Frankism," and the various forms of secular messianism that have dotted the modern era.[21] It provided some basic unity to the immense transformations of modernity. Though the official movement went into eclipse after Sabbatai's apostasy, Scholem claimed to discern what amounted to a Sabbatian underground exerting tremendous influence. Thus he detected its influence during the French Revolution and the later reform movement in Judaism. He also argued that the kabalistic doctrines of divine immanence that found resonance in Spinoza played a largely unacknowledged role in the rise of modern science with its attempt to control and manipulate the hidden forces of nature.[22]

Mystical Theology or Rational Philosophy

Scholem's philosophy of history contains interesting and important parallels with that of Strauss. Strauss's scholarly project received its practical impetus from a sense of the weakness or vulnerability of German Jewry. He described the dilemma of modern Judaism, torn between fidelity to an ancient faith and entrance into the modern emancipated world, as a "theological-political predicament" that held him in its "grip."[23] This predicament remained the basic theme of his thought from very early on. Like other Weimar Jews, Strauss regarded the return to orthodoxy as impossible, yet he remained skeptical of the various modern alternatives to it. Strauss's "turn" to Maimonides and medieval Jewish philosophy, like Scholem's study of kabala, can be understood as a response to the situation of Jews in modernity.

Strauss's analysis of the "medieval Enlightenment," as he called it, was premised on the contrast it presented to the modern Enlightenment of the eighteenth century. In particular the modern Enlightenment derived its strength from the critique of revealed religion or what Strauss called simply "Orthodoxy."[24] This conflict, at its core, juxtaposed the Enlightenment's faith in reason, our limited human rationality, and the biblical faith in revelation or the prophetic power of the law. Strauss concluded that at its deepest level this conflict could not be resolved in favor of either reason or revelation. Yet rather than producing a sense of despair or cynicism over the permanence of this conflict, Strauss took it to be the "core" or "nerve" of the Western tradition. It was precisely this tension between Torah and philosophy—or, put metaphorically, between Jerusalem and Athens—that was both an invitation to reflection and the secret of the West's "vitality."[25] Already, however, this statement of the problem bespeaks important differences between Scholem's and Strauss's understandings of the philosophical inheritance of the West. Scholem regarded all philosophy as simply of a piece. Its single purpose was for him ultimately to translate mystical theology into a system of rational ethics. Consider the following passage: "Authoritative Jewish theology, both medieval and modern, in representatives like Saadia, Maimonides, and Hermann Cohen, has taken upon itself the task of formulating an antithesis to pantheism and mythical theology, i.e.: to prove them wrong. In this endeavor it has shown itself tireless."[26]

Strauss, by contrast, repudiated the view of a monolithic philosophical tradition stretching from the ancient to the modern world. He emphasized instead the radical differences between ancient and medieval philosophy on the one hand and the varieties of modern thought on the other. These differences stem from their quite different notions of the relation of philosophy to society as a whole. To put the matter crudely, but not altogether misleadingly, modern philosophy beginning with the Enlightenment sought to reform if not to abolish theology, while the ancient and medieval Enlightenments took the problem of the divine law, the Torah, or the new dispensation as a necessary point of departure and asked how philosophy could be justified within its parameters.[27] Strauss's studies of the classics of medieval Jewish thought, such as Judah Halevi and Maimonides, were undertaken in large part to bring to light the deep differences separating them from such typically modern Jewish philosophers as Hermann Cohen and Franz Rosenzweig.[28]

At first glance Scholem and Strauss appear to agree that the very term "medieval Jewish philosophy" is an oxymoron. The term is a hybrid of two historically and conceptually opposed bodies of thought: Greek philosophy and the biblical faith in revelation. Yet within this broad area of agreement, Strauss disagrees entirely with Scholem's curt dismissal of philosophy and his assertion of the superiority of kabala. Contrary to Scholem's claim that "the whole world of religious law remained outside the orbit of philosophical inquiry" and that "to the philosophers, the Halakhah either had no significance at all, or one that was calculated to diminish rather than enhance its prestige in his eyes,"[29] Strauss replied that it was never the intention of philosophy to enhance belief or to find new, more rational grounds for practicing the *mitzvot*. The purpose of medieval philosophy, on Strauss's view, was to provoke a dialectical confrontation between the biblical faith, with its belief in oral inspiration and the revealed character of the Torah, on the one hand, and the sufficiency of the contemplative life on the other. Furthermore, it was by no means clear, in his view, who the winner in such a confrontation would be.[30]

These differences point to even deeper divisions between Scholem's and Strauss's understandings of the relation between kabala and philosophy. Here again both men appear to occupy some common ground in the special attention they accord to the esoteric character of their respective disciplines. For Scholem the *Zohar* represented the flower of kabalistic esotericism with its Gnostic interpretation of Scripture, while for Strauss Maimonides's *Guide of the Perplexed* occupied this position. In a remarkable series of letters to his friend Jacob Klein, Strauss describes Maimonides as possessing "a truly free mind" (*ein wirlkich freier Geist*) and as one who has managed to treat the subject of religion with "an infinite finesse and irony" (*unendlichen Feinheit und Ironie*) worthy of Voltaire.[31] Strauss used Maimonides to recover a "forgotten kind of writing" that he thought typified philosophers prior to the advent of modernity.[32] This kind of writing is political not in the sense that it takes politics as its primary subject matter, but in the sense that it made the author's relation to society into a hermeneutic principle in the interpretation of texts. Politics is, then, an implicit theme of every text insofar as every careful writer must at some level acknowledge the possible influence of his words on the wider social and political context in which they occur. It was precisely Maimonides's use of a rhetoric of caution, indirection, and ellipsis that made him in Strauss's view the political writer *par excellence*.[33]

Unlike Scholem, who made esotericism into the unique province of Jewish mystical theology, Strauss saw it as a fundamentally political act. While every interpreter of Maimonides had to make some acknowledgment of the esoteric aspect of the *Guide*, only Strauss turned it into the key for understanding the work as a whole. The result, paradoxically, was both a more and a less radical Maimonides than had previously been thought. Maimonides came to appear as more radical because of his studied ambiguity regarding such controversial themes as the problem of creation *ex nihilo* versus the eternity of the world, to say nothing of the vexed issue of personal immortality. He seems less radical because of the reaffirmation of such traditional beliefs as the existence of a personal deity, the revealed character of the law, and the centrality of the prophets as the bearers of this divine legislation for the sustenance and political health of the community. It is this dual strategy, pursued by Maimonides as well as other Jewish and Arabic writers, that made the interpretation of their thought so much more difficult than had been previously believed. Further, this hermeneutic procedure produced a much higher degree of interpretive skepticism and uncertainty precisely because of the deliberate ambiguities, contradictions, and anomalies the texts themselves contained.[34]

Scholem's and Strauss's works contain parallel causal accounts of the rise of modernity. Scholem stressed the rise of apocalyptic messianism in the wake of the Spanish expulsions of 1492. Strauss, however, emphasized the pivotal role of Machiavelli in effecting the break with the ancient and medieval tradition. Strauss highlighted three aspects of Machiavelli's thought that prepared the ground for the subsequent development of all modern political philosophy. First, he emphasized Machiavelli's new "realism," his repudiation of the utopianism of the ancients and his desire to bring about a political order more attuned to the often brutal realities of human nature. The classical concern with justice gave way to the concern for survival and stability.[35] Second, Machiavelli's new teaching about virtue sought to reverse the traditional means-ends categories of both pagan and biblical antiquity. No longer would politics serve to promote the moral or intellectual virtues; instead, the virtues were to be instrumental to the collective safety and security of society. The result was an unprecedented "lowering of the standards" of premodern thought.[36] And third, Machiavelli pioneered a new attitude toward nature that came to fruition in the later works of Bacon, Hobbes, and Descartes with their project for the conquest of nature for the sake of human convenience. Nature ceased to be a source for human ends and purposes, as it was in the hands of Aristotle and the Stoics, and became instead the domain of chance or *fortuna* that could be made to reveal its secrets through policies of conquest and domination.[37]

These differences notwithstanding, Strauss's interpretation of Machiavelli is not without a kabalistic dimension.[38] Strauss is the only interpreter of Machiavelli to my knowledge to stress Machiavelli's injunction against the "pious cruelty" (*pietosa crudeltà*) of Ferdinand for his expulsion of the Marranos.[39] Further, Strauss highlights Machiavelli's *Discourses on Livy*, II, 5 where in the context of a critique of the Aristotelian conception of the eternity of the world Machiavelli notes that religions tend to change two or three times every five to six thousand years.[40] This passage, which has struck most commentators as no more than a curiosity, indicates Machiavelli's belief that religions have a typical life span of not less than 1,666 and not more than 3,000 years.[41] But as Strauss surely knew, 1666 was for the kabalistic tradition a number of great mystical significance, and it coincided more or less with the date of the appearance of the false messiah Sabbatai Zevi. This is not to say that Strauss thought Machiavelli was a kabalist, but only someone like Strauss who knew the meaning of kabala could have brought out these themes in his interpretation.[42]

It is at this point, however, that any remaining similarities between Scholem and Strauss begin to break down. Scholem diagnosed the development of modernity as leading to increasingly secular forms of rationality, while Strauss saw Machiavelli's new orientation as leading to new and dangerous forms of irrationalism. Each of the "three waves of modernity" tried, unsuccessfully in Strauss's view, to ground the political order in the ever-shifting sands of the passions. The first wave consisted of proto-liberals like Hobbes and Locke who tried to domesticate Machiavelli and thus find a ground for natural rights in the passions or desire for self-preservation and productive acquisitiveness.[43] The second wave was initiated by Rousseau but culminated in Hegel and Marx, who effected the decisive change from nature to history. For these thinkers, history itself became the source of moral ends operating through the blind and willful play of human passions and interests.[44]

The third phase of modernity began with Nietzsche and culminated in Heidegger's "radical historicism." Nietzsche denied the efforts of those thinkers of the second wave who regarded history as a rational process endowed with some intelligible point or purpose. Their various attempts to find meaning in history seemed but a faint-hearted way of reintroducing theology through the back door. Nietzsche's critique of historical reason thus prepared the way for Heidegger, whom Strauss called the "highest self-consciousness" of modern thought. Heidegger's "fundamental ontology," with its search for the authentic roots of *Dasein*, had the practical function of abandoning the individual to the mercy of fate, chance, or destiny, whatever that might happen to be or wherever it might happen to lead. It was this repudiation of eternity that led the most radical historicist in 1933 to

succumb to "the verdict of the least wise and least moderate part of the
nation while it was in its least wise and least moderate mood."[45]

Ahavat Yisrael

These contrary causal accounts of modernity gave rise in turn to very different assessments of modernity's possibilities and objective tendencies.
Not only did they give different diagnoses of the causes of modernity, but
they offered very different prognoses for its future. Wherein, then, do they
differ?

Scholem saw modernity as leading to the gradual drying up of precisely
those mystical and antinomian currents that had been the traditional life
blood of Judaism. It was, of course, reason—the reason of the philosophers
and the rabbis—that contributed most to the rigidification of this tradition.
For Scholem, the legitimate or dialectical use of reason came not through
its legislative but through its "critical" or "destructive" side. The great religious and ethical systems of the past, he averred, were never the product of
reason alone but of "other forces" that had had "far more outstanding and
decisive successes in construction than Reason."[46]

For Scholem, then, as for the great poets and mystics, reason is ultimately dependent upon a source or sources outside itself. The idea of a
rational ethics was for him always a contradiction in terms. The following
passage speaks to Scholem's skepticism about a purely rational morality of
the kind envisaged by Kant and his modern heirs:

> I don't believe it is possible to build a morality that will be an immanent
> network for Reason. I confess that in this respect I am what would be
> called a reactionary, for I believe that morality as a constructive force is
> impossible without religion, without some Power beyond Pure Reason.
> I do not believe in this possibility. This is an utter illusion of philoso-
> phers, not to speak of sociologists.[47]

It was, then, the critical or dialectical impulses in reason that explained
Scholem's fascination with and attraction for anarchism and various other
antinomian movements. Only anarchism, which he calls a "positive utopianism," is capable today of keeping the messianic vision alive. "Of course,"
he concurred, "from the standpoint of the values of official traditional
Judaism, this conception is negative."[48]

Like Scholem, Strauss's evaluation of modernity also traced the gradual
decay or "putrefaction" of the tradition that he would understand. He was

convinced that his was an age of "intellectual decline" in which only historical studies could substitute for and perhaps even stimulate genuine
philosophic investigation and a recovery of the "fundamental problems."[49]
Further, this decline was directly traceable to the progressive destruction of
reason and the consequent crisis of confidence in the very purpose of the
West. The loss of confidence, Strauss held, was precipitated by Nietzsche
and other radical historicists who attacked the premises of the modern liberal project with its conception of "a universal league of free and equal
nations, each nation consisting of free and equal men and women" enjoying unprecedented peace and prosperity guaranteed by the power of modern
science and technology.[50] It was not only the persistence of evil in the face
of affluence, but the emergence of a new kind of nihilism that denied the
ability to distinguish good and evil that led many late modern doctrines to
question the very humanity of the West.[51]

Strauss was by no means sanguine that this process of decay could be
halted, much less reversed. He seems to have accepted the possibility that
the modern West was evolving toward a new type of human being that
Nietzsche had identified as the "last man." Strauss's cautious defense of
liberal democracy must be seen as an attempt to stave off for as long as possible Nietzsche's hideous vision of a world of test-tube–bred homunculi.[52]
At the same time Strauss regarded the shaking of all traditions as a precondition for a genuine recovery of the central problems of political philosophy. He even speaks of the "accidental advantage" accruing from the decay
of all tradition that makes possible a new understanding of what was previously understood "only in a traditional or derivative manner."[53] It is only
in·an age when God is dead and, literally, all things seem possible that we
might be able to effect a genuine recovery of the past.

I want to conclude with some brief reflections on the role of Jewish
identity for both Scholem and Strauss. Both men were passionate (if somewhat idiosyncratic) Zionists who believed that the establishment of the
state of Israel "procured," in Strauss's words, "a blessing for all Jews everywhere regardless of whether they admit it or not."[54] Scholem's view was
most eloquently stated in a public letter to Hannah Arendt in response to
her analysis of the Eichmann trial and her famous "banality of evil" thesis.[55] Here Scholem accused her of lacking any sense of *Ahavat Yisrael* or
love for the Jewish people.[56] A word about this exchange will be useful.

The exchange over Eichmann both capped and ended what had been an
almost thirty-year friendship between Scholem and Arendt. Both were great
admirers of Walter Benjamin, to whom Scholem dedicated his *Major Trends
in Jewish Mysticism*. And like many Jews from the German Left, they

shared strong reservations about the nationalistic Revisionist wing of the Zionist movement led by Jabotinsky. Scholem was a founding member of the Brit Shalom group (Covenant for Peace), which in the 1920s and 1930s favored a binational solution to the Jewish-Arab conflict in Palestine.[57] For many of the figures associated with this group, which included Hugo Bergman, Ernst Simon, and Judah Magnes, the danger of the Revisionists' demand for immediate Jewish sovereignty was its tendency to conflate Zionism with messianism. The convergence of the two, Scholem wrote, is a "great error . . . for which Zionism might have to pay dearly." Zionism is "a movement within the mundane, immanent process of history." It is not only a conceptual mistake, but a piece of political irresponsibility to infuse politics with messianic expectations of redemption and of bringing about an end of time "within the history of an unredeemed and unmessianic world."[58]

The differences between Scholem and Arendt emerged slowly in response to the Holocaust—Scholem always referred to it as the Catastrophe—and the creation of a Jewish state in its wake. In an essay titled "Zionism Reconsidered" Arendt argued as late as 1944 that the demand for a Jewish state was a part of the orbit of nineteenth-century European nationalism and imperialism. The Jewish leadership was at fault for allowing the nationalist wing of the Zionist movement to trump its socialist and internationalist side.[59] Two years later Scholem responded to her with some reluctance ("I don't have the slightest wish to have a fatal falling out with you"), but making clear his displeasure with her views. "Your article has nothing to do with Zionism," he wrote, "but is instead a patently anti-Zionist, warmed-over version of Communist criticism, infused with vague *galut* nationalism."[60] He accused her of attacking Jewish separatism while at the same time complaining that "when the same Jews make efforts to fend for themselves, in a world whose evil you never cease to emphasize, you react with a derision that itself stems from some otherworldly source." Describing his own political credo as anarchistic, he goes on to state that "I cannot blame the Jews if they ignore so-called progressive theories which no one else in the world has ever practiced."[61]

These differences finally came to a head over the Eichmann trial. Although Scholem had publicly opposed the execution of Eichmann, he refused to acquiesce to Arendt's depiction of Nazi "banality." "This new thesis [the banality of evil]," he wrote bluntly, "strikes me as a catchword: it does not impress me, certainly, as the product of profound analysis."[62] Instead, he opposed this conception to Arendt's own more fruitful analysis of "radical evil" in her earlier book *On the Origins of Totalitarianism*. Stung by her analysis of the role of the Jewish councils (*Judenräte*) as complicit in their own fate and even suggesting some degree of moral equivalence between them and their captors, Scholem cautioned her to adopt a little more interpretive sympathy ("there were among them also many people in no way different from ourselves").[63] It was here that Scholem accused Arendt of lacking *Ahavat Yisrael*. "In you, dear Hannah," he writes, "as in so many intellectuals who came from the German Left, I find little trace of this. . . . In circumstances such as these, would there not have been a place for what I can only describe by the modest German word—*Herzenstakt* [tact of the heart]?"[64]

Part of what was behind Scholem's description of Arendt as a member of the "German Left"—a description Arendt loftily dismissed—is a broader critique of those intellectuals who sought to treat Israel and Zionism as a derivative European, rather than a distinctively Jewish, phenomenon. Scholem regarded Zionism as a modern continuation of certain atavistic, kabalistic energies, with its desire to end the exile and its proud refusal to bow to the pressures of assimilation. His emphasis on the particularity of Jewish identity led him to deny the possibility of any German-Jewish symbiosis. His attack on the very idea of a "German-Jewish dialogue" set him sharply at odds with those Enlightenment universalists who could still maintain that the Holocaust was an aberration and distortion of the essential humanity of Western civilization.[65]

Still, Scholem regarded Zionism as a "calculated risk." True to his dialectical perspective, he interpreted it within the dynamics of modern secularization theory. Zionism was an understandable and legitimate response to traditional Judaism that had accommodated itself to what must have appeared as permanent life in exile. The attempt to establish a home for the Jews in Israel, therefore, met a genuine historical and political need by facilitating the Jewish entry into the modern world. Nevertheless, Scholem did not consider the secular vision of a Jewish homeland to be the last word and saw the slogan that Israel should be "a nation like all nations" as foolish and self-destructive. It was, above all, the fact of revelation that defined the moral center and purpose of Jewish life and made Israel different from the other nations. To deny this value by courting assimilation to the way of the nations would be an unconscionable act of self-liquidation.[66]

In an essay titled "Reflections on Jewish Theology" Scholem provided perhaps his most trenchant remarks on this tension between secularism and revelation and its meaning for the future of Israel:

If we live in a world in which Revelation as a positive possession has been lost, the first question is: Does this not mean the liquidation of Judaism insofar as Revelation is understood as a specific characteristic of the Jewish people, as the shape in which it has presented itself in world history? . . . I am quite convinced that the realization of this slogan ["like all nations"] could only mean the transition to the decline or even disappearance of the Jewish people.[67]

Scholem expressed confidence that despite the dialectical tension between political Zionism and the facts imposed by revelation that a transition to a completely secularized world was unlikely. There was no reason why Zionism and the traditional faith in the one God could not and should not coexist as parts of the same community. As always, however, it was for Scholem the religious dimension of life that was accorded the final say. "If humanity should ever lose the feeling that there is mystery—a secret—in the world, then it's all over with us," he told an interviewer in 1975. "But I don't believe we'll ever come to that," he concluded.[68]

"The Most Profound Modification of the *Galut*"

Likewise, from an early age Strauss expressed deep respect and gratitude for Zionism and its role in helping to maintain a sense of Jewish dignity and self-respect (*Selbstauchtuung*). Zionism meant for him "simple, straightforward political Zionism," the demand of Jews to be politically self-determining. But the desire to be self-determining, he recognized, meant a "radical break" with the principles of the Jewish tradition inasmuch as it substituted reliance on one's own power for the traditional trust in God's providence. Strauss illustrated this point with an amusing anecdote from his youth:

I was myself . . . a political Zionist in my youth, and was a member of a Zionist organization. In this capacity, I occasionally met Jabotinsky, the leader of the Revisionists. He asked me, "What are you doing?" I said, "Well, we read the Bible, we study Jewish history, Zionist theory, and, of course, we keep abreast of developments, and so on." He replied, "And rifle practice?" And I had to say, "No."[69]

Strauss's meeting with Jabotinsky brought home to him a basic truth about politics that he would later have confirmed in his study of Hobbes, namely, that "covenants without the sword are but words." Politics was more than talk. From Weber, too, whom Strauss much admired during this period, he learned that power was central to politics. The state, according to Weber's definition, was characterized by its possession of the monopoly on violence. But it was from Carl Schmitt, whose book *The Concept of the Political* (1927) Strauss both read and reviewed, that he found the theoretical framework within which to locate his Zionism.[70]

Schmitt's book was an effort to define the essence of what he called *das Politische*. Schmitt regarded all efforts to explain the political by reference to economic, social, cultural, or technological conditions as a form of "depoliticization." Politics represented an autonomous sphere independent of all nonpolitical spheres of influence. Just as economics is defined by the distinction between profit and loss, the aesthetic by the categories of the beautiful and the ugly, morality by reference to the good and the bad, so politics is defined by the primordial distinction between friend and enemy.[71] "The political," he writes, "is the most intense and extreme antagonism and every concrete antagonism becomes that much more political the closer it approaches the most extreme point, that of the friend-enemy grouping."[72] For Schmitt, the political meant, above all, that peoples are by nature pitted against one another in a condition of war or readiness for war. The idea of a League of Nations or a body of international law designed to put an end to war was to Schmitt the very negation of the political.[73]

It was from Schmitt that Strauss learned that conflict, not just between individuals, but between states and peoples, is the core of political life. What most impressed him was Schmitt's claim that a world without conflict, a world bent on consensus or the pacification of differences, would be a world that lacked moral seriousness. In such a world "there would be culture, civilization, economic life, morality, law, art, *entertainment*, and so on, but there would be neither politics nor the state."[74] In this passage, the words are Schmitt's but the emphasis is Strauss's. The desire to abolish conflict, to reach agreement at all costs, to avoid risk and danger, would be a world where nothing really matters, where there is nothing worth fighting for. "Hence what the opponents of the political have in mind," Strauss writes, "is to bring into being a world of entertainment, a world of fun, a world devoid of *seriousness* (*eine Welt ohne Ernst*)."[75] Strauss brought something of Schmitt's sense of existential drama and urgency to his understanding of politics. The liberal desire to secure the conditions for life is in danger of obscuring the question about the meaning of life. At the moment "when man abandons the task of raising this question regarding what is right, and when man abandons this question, he abandons his humanity."[76]

Schmitt and Strauss drew fundamentally different conclusions from their understandings of politics. Schmitt's affirmation of the "dangerousness" of human nature led him to endorse a form of Catholic authoritarianism that drew inspiration from the counter-Enlightenment doctrines of Joseph de Maistre and Juan Donoso-Cortes. The essence of the political meant the state of emergency (*Ernstfall*, literally: earnest case) when the rule of law is suspended for the sake of maintaining order. Schmitt wished to invest authority in a *Reichspräsident* who, like Hobbes's Leviathan, stands outside the constitution and has the power to declare the exception.

Strauss drew from Schmitt an awareness of the illusions of liberal cosmopolitanism and a belief that the fate of Jews could not be entrusted to either benevolent governments or the norms of the international community. Strauss took the view that the Jews cannot rely on the good will of others, but must take affairs into their own hands, must use their own "hardware," so to speak. If the Jews are a people, they must start to act like a people and provide themselves with more "natural conditions of existence." In the diaspora Jews have lived as a *Luftvolk*, a people without land or real estate. Zionism showed the emptiness of the promise of emancipation or assimilation, which "takes away from the Jews the self-assurance of ghetto life and gives them instead the illusory surrogate of trust in the humanity of civilization."[77] It is necessary to replace "the helotry of assimilation" with "the Spartan spirit of Zionism." This will only happen after the displacement of "teleologism" (i.e., providence) by a "manly causalism."[78]

Strauss reaffirmed the positive role of Zionism thirty years later after spending the academic year of 1954-55 at the Hebrew University. In a rare public intervention he wrote an angry letter to the editors of the *National Review* protesting the magazine's "anti-Jewish animus." In his letter Strauss defended Israel as "the only country which as a country is an outpost of the West in the East" and "in which a single book absolutely predominates in the instruction given in elementary schools and in high schools: the Hebrew Bible." The spirit of Israel he declared to be one of "heroic austerity supported by the nearness of biblical antiquity." Further, Strauss defended Zionism for restoring Jewish dignity and Jewish pride when "the moral spine of the Jews was in danger of being broken by the so-called emancipation which in many cases had alienated them from their heritage" while supplying nothing more than "merely formal equality."

Whatever the problems with political Zionism, Strauss concluded, it deserves our lasting gratitude for "what it achieved as a moral force in an era of complete dissolution."[79]

Strauss's views on Zionism did not significantly alter over time, but he came to emphasize that politics and statehood alone could not solve the "Jewish Question." In the remarkable preface to the English-language edition of *Spinoza's Critique of Religion* published in 1965 Strauss stated in no uncertain terms that the future and survival of the Jews as Jews could not be guaranteed by political means alone but required something more. That something was the simple faith that had sustained them throughout the centuries of diaspora. Zionism was at best a partial solution to the problem of Jewish survival in a predominantly non-Jewish, even hostile world. Thus Strauss could say that the creation of the state of Israel was "the most profound modification of the Galut which has occurred, but it is not the end of the Galut." The survival of Judaism remained a problem that could never be solved by human, political means alone: "From every point of view," he wrote, "it looks as if the Jewish people were the chosen people in the sense, at least, that the Jewish problem is the most manifest symbol of the human problem as a social or political problem."[80]

Whatever other differences might have been between Scholem and Strauss, they were both prepared to admit that profound obstacles stood in the way of their prognoses for the future of Jewish identity. Each of their alternatives seems fraught with danger. Scholem's reassertion of theological antinomianism courted the dangers of the religious nihilism that he so powerfully diagnosed. It was by no means clear that the kind of secular mysticism about which he spoke could serve as a catalyst to ensure Jewish continuity and tradition. His passion for kabala centered on its antinomian and apocalyptic dimensions, which seem more suitable to a people in exile than to those who face the concrete exigencies of statecraft and political life.

Strauss was also a critic of the dangers of assimilation, but for whatever reason he found it easier than Scholem did to make peace with a life in exile. For Strauss, the practices and institutions of Western liberalism, with their tacit endorsement of public toleration of and private discrimination against Jews, seemed preferable to any of the going alternatives. However, Strauss's guarded defense of liberalism coupled with his preference for the Maimonidean form of rationalism with its self-professed esotericism will seem to many inconsistent with the demand for "intellectual probity," the supreme value of modern life.[81] Judaism would thus come to serve the same function as a Platonic noble lie or a Machiavellian civil religion intended to ensure a sense of Jewish pride and self-respect, but void of truth content or redemptive grace. This essay does not even attempt to answer the question which of these alternatives may be correct. It is enough for now to have opened up this neglected *Dialog unter Abwesenden*.

CHAPTER THREE

Strauss's Spinoza

The Jewish people and their fate are the living witness for the absence
of redemption. This, one could say, is the meaning of the chosen people;
the Jews are chosen to prove the absence of redemption. — *Leo Strauss,
"Why We Remain Jews"*

Introduction

In an essay from 1932 titled "Das Testament Spinozas" Leo Strauss
observed that the reception of Spinoza has undergone various stages, from
condemnation as a soulless atheist and materialist, to canonization by the
German romantics who saw him as a mystical pantheist and "God intoxi-
cated man," and finally to neutrality by scholars who had come largely to
accept the results of his historico-critical approach to the Bible.[1] The
official reception of Spinoza was possible, Strauss writes, only once the
famous *querrelle des anciens et des modernes* had been decided in favor of
the moderns and the legitimacy of modern thought had been accepted. It
was this that permitted Spinoza to enter "the small band of superior
minds" that Strauss, following Nietzsche, refers to as the "good
Europeans":

> To this community belong *all* the philosophers of the seventeenth cen-
> tury, but Spinoza belongs to it in a special way. Spinoza did not remain
> a Jew, while Descartes, Hobbes, and Leibniz remained Christians. Thus
> it is not in accordance with Spinoza's wishes that he be inducted into
> the pantheon of the Jewish nation. Under these circumstances it seems
> to us an elementary imperative of Jewish self-respect that we Jews
> should at last again relinquish our claim on Spinoza. By so doing, we by

no means surrender him to our enemies. Rather, we leave him to that distant and strange community of "neutrals" whom one can call, with considerable justice, the community of "good Europeans."[2]

The question posed by "Das Testament Spinozas" is whether Spinoza and the principles of modern thought have come to triumph too easily. What does this community of "good Europeans" represent and what does it mean for the future and possibility of Judaism and especially what he calls orthodoxy? The question is not whether the principles of modern philosophy have triumphed, but whether they deserve to have done so.

The very legitimacy of modernity is the issue addressed in Strauss's first book, *Die Religionskritik Spinozas*, the most profound work of Spinoza scholarship written in the twentieth century.[3] The book was published under the aegis of the Akademie für die Wissenschaft des Judentums, where Strauss was then a fellow and whose co-founders were Hermann Cohen and Franz Rosenzweig.[4] The work carries a dedication to the memory of Rosenzweig, an early benefactor and confidant of Strauss, who had died the year before its publication and whose name, Strauss would later remark, "will always be remembered when informed people speak about existentialism."[5] Strauss's book is an attempt to situate Spinoza's "Bible science" (*Bibelwissenschaft*) within the tradition of the critique of theology from Epicurus to Hobbes. His aim was to cast doubt on the new scientific study of Scripture that Spinoza had done so much to influence and in doing so help to reopen the ancient question of reason and revelation, Athens and Jerusalem.

From early in his career Strauss realized that the issue at stake was not merely the status of Spinoza's philosophy, but the problem of the Enlightenment. Spinoza's philosophy stands or falls by its claim to have refuted the authority of biblical orthodoxy with its belief in such things as the creation of the world *ex nihilo*, the revealed character of the Law, and the possibility of miracles. The comprehensive goal of his work was to replace the God of Abraham with the light of reason as the authoritative guide to life, to replace the opening chapters of the book of Genesis with the opening definitions and axioms of the *Ethics* as the definitive account of the nature of the universe and our place within it. Spinoza's philosophy is poorly understood, or rather it is not understood at all, unless it is seen as casting the initial broadside in the Enlightenment's war against orthodoxy.

In attempting to come to terms with the Enlightenment's critique of orthodoxy, Strauss was not flying solo. In the 1965 preface to the English translation of *Spinoza's Critique of Religion* Strauss gives an oblique acknowledgment of his intellectual debts. The "formal reception" of Spinoza into Germany was effectively accomplished in 1785 when F. H. Jacobi "made public the fact that in Lessing's view there was no philosophy but the philosophy of Spinoza."[6] The subsequent canonization of Spinoza through the influence of German idealism was to continue until the twentieth century, when Strauss set out to rethink the Enlightenment tradition which Spinoza himself set out to found.

This bare reference to Jacobi conceals the fact that Strauss had written his doctoral dissertation in 1921 on *Das Erkenntnisproblem in der philosophischen Lehre Friedrich H. Jacobi* at the University of Hamburg under the direction of Ernst Cassirer.[7] Although he later disparaged this work as a "disgraceful performance," and although Jacobi is hardly ever mentioned in his later works, Strauss's indebtedness to the Jacobian critique of reason is evident up to and including the autobiographical preface just mentioned.[8] Yet it would be premature to identify Strauss entirely with the intellectual tradition of the German Counter-Enlightenment of which Jacobi was a part. Strauss's purpose, as we shall see, is not to vouchsafe the primacy of faith, as Jacobi's was, but to defend the idea of the Law as understood by Judaism. If Strauss's critique of Spinoza should reveal the essential limitations of the Enlightenment, this would require not an embrace of irrationalism but a reconsideration of orthodoxy.[9]

Jacobi's Affirmation of Faith

The first person to indicate the problematic status of Spinoza's rationalism was F. H. Jacobi. Jacobi was a minor figure of the German Counter-Enlightenment who, along with Hamann and Herder, was the principle instigator of the famous *Pantheismusstreit,* the pantheism dispute that raged throughout Germany in the 1780s and 1790s.[10] The pantheism debate was occasioned by the rehabilitation of the reputation of Spinoza in Germany in the last quarter of the eighteenth century. Although he had been anathema for approximately a century after his death, the fortunes of Spinoza took a dramatic turn once it was revealed that Gotthold Lessing had been a secret admirer and even a closet Spinozist for much of his life. The subsequent debate took place between Jacobi and Moses Mendelssohn, who sought to defend his friend from what was regarded as a dangerous slur and accusation. The pantheism debate, however, was much more than a dispute over the reputation of Spinoza or over Lessing's alleged Spinozism. It was at bottom a debate about the authority of reason.

Jacobi and the romantics were not simply opposed to reason, as they are often made out to be. They were opposed to the Enlightenment's conception of sufficient reason. By the principle of sufficient reason is meant the belief that for any possible state of affairs there are reasons capable of explaining it. To accept the principle of sufficient reason is, then, tantamount to accepting Spinoza's view that everything that is happens for a reason and that to understand that reason is to see that events could not have happened otherwise. It is ultimately equivalent to accepting some form of determinism according to which for every event, A, there must be some prior event, B, that is sufficient to explain A. Whether this is an accurate depiction of Spinoza's understanding is not the issue. The point for the romantics is that accepting the principle of sufficient reason meant denying that we are free and responsible agents who can choose to do this rather than that on the basis of our free will and understanding. The romantic critique of reason was, therefore, less an epistemological than a moral one. Its aim was ultimately to save the possibility of morality from all forms of determinism.

In the romantics' crusade against the Spinozist principle of sufficient reason, they acquired an unlikely ally in David Hume.[11] In the *Treatise of Human Nature* Hume had demonstrated that reason has a far more restricted scope than the Enlightenment had alleged. Applying reason to itself, Hume contended that there are no necessary or causal relations between events. That we see the sun rise in the morning and set at night is not a necessary truth of reason. It is at most an observed regularity, but there are no sufficient reasons capable of explaining it. At most what we believe to be universal and necessary laws are no more than judgments made on the basis of habit, custom, and experience. The truths of reason may be applicable to limited areas of thought like mathematics and logic, but to the vast areas of human experience there are no necessary consequences following from the nature of things, only loosely associated sequences of events. The most we are entitled to say is that it is probable that events will occur in the future as they have in the past; there is no necessity for them to do so. In some respect these claims seem modest enough, but for the romantics, Hume's deconstruction of the claims of reason came as a liberation. They extended his claim to mean that the way we perceive and understand the world is the product not of reason, but of faith.

Jacobi achieved notoriety after publishing his *Letters to Herr Moses Mendelssohn Concerning the Doctrine of Spinoza* (1785).[12] The *Letters* took the form of a series of conversations between Jacobi and Lessing in which the latter allegedly professed to being a disciple of Spinoza.

According to the account of these conversations, not published until after Lessing's death, Jacobi told how he journeyed to Wolfenbüttel to discover Lessing's opinions on a range of philosophical and theological topics. Among the topics the two men discussed was a copy of Goethe's then-unpublished poem, "Prometheus." After reading the poem Jacobi reports the following exchange.

JACOBI: Do you know the poem?

LESSING: The poem I have never seen before; but I think it is good.

JACOBI: It is good in its kind, I agree; otherwise I would not have shown it to you.

LESSING: I mean it is good in a different way. . . . The point of view from which the poem is treated is my own point of view. . . . The orthodox concepts of the Divinity are no longer for me; I cannot stomach them. *Hen kai pan*! I know of nothing else.[13]

Jacobi professed to express surprise at Lessing's endorsement of the philosophical principle of pantheism (*Hen kai pan*) or the belief that God is immanent in the world. When the two spoke again the next day, Lessing continued his defense of Spinozism as follows:

LESSING: I have come to talk to you about my *hen kai pan*. Yesterday you were frightened.

JACOBI: You surprised me, and I may indeed have blushed and gone pale, for I felt bewilderment in me. Fright it was not. To be sure, there is nothing that I would have suspected less, than to find a Spinozist or a pantheist in you. And you blurted it out to me so suddenly. In the main I had come to get help from you against Spinoza.

LESSING: Oh, so you do know him?

JACOBI: I think I know him as only very few can know him.

LESSING: Then there is no help for you. Become his friend all the way instead. There is no other philosophy than the philosophy of Spinoza.[14]

The issue of Lessing's Spinozism is hardly the point. At issue is Jacobi's belief that a pantheistic system, a religion of divine immanence, leads not only to atheism, but to a radical determinism with no room for human freedom and agency. The result is to turn human beings into passive effects of a system of immanent causality rather than self-governing agents capable of initiating new chains of causality. Jacobi takes this to mean that in Spinoza's world there can be no "I" who acts or thinks, but only a conjuncture of forces governed by the same laws that govern everything. Jacobi expresses this opinion in a lengthy rejoinder:

> The whole thing comes down to this: from fatalism I immediately conclude against fatalism and everything connected with it. If there are only efficient, but no final, causes, then the only function that the faculty of thought has in the whole of nature is that of observer; its proper business is to accompany the mechanism of the efficient causes. The conversation that we are now having together is only an affair of our bodies; and the whole content of the conversation, analyzed into its elements, is extension, movement, degree of velocity, together with their concepts, and the concepts of these concepts. The inventor of the clock did not ultimately invent it; he only witnessed its coming to be out of blindly self-developing forces. So too Raphael, when he sketched the School of Athens, and Lessing, when he composed his *Nathan*. The same goes for all philosophizing, arts, forms of governance, sea and land wars—in brief, for everything possible.[15]

Jacobi's point is that if Spinoza and the principle of sufficient reason are correct, then the inevitable result is not only determinism but fatalism and atheism, in other words a complete denial of human agency and freedom. Once again, this is not intended to be simply an attack on Spinoza's *Ethics*; rather, it calls into question all systems of rationalistic metaphysics. While Hume had chastised reason in order to show that our moral beliefs were rooted in certain preexisting natural sentiments, Jacobi and the romantics limited reason in order to make room for faith (*Glaube*). No more than Spinoza did Jacobi mean by faith belief in the God of Scripture. Faith meant for him simply the place at which all rational demonstration came to an end. *Glaube* refers to certain pre-rational "givens" that were simply the primary data of experience that could not be questioned. All argument rests on certain assumptions and beliefs about what counts as true or valid. My belief that a glass of water is on the table is possible because of certain assumptions I make about the veracity of perception and the nature of physical reality. But these assumptions cannot in turn be justified in terms of the beliefs they validate without falling into circularity. Reason is incapable of establishing its own premises. This means for Jacobi that all of our assumptions—the assumption that everything is determined no less than the assumption that we possess free will and choice—rest ultimately on an act of faith. Jacobi's answer to Spinozistic determinism is his concept of the *salto mortale*, a death-defying leap of faith confirming a belief in freedom and individual moral responsibility.

Jacobi's brief against Spinoza is ultimately carried out in defense of morality. Spinozistic determinism, like all systems of philosophical rationalism, undermines faith, the sole basis for morality, Jacobi believed. Jacobi's case was not directed at Spinoza *ad hominem*, but rather against all philosophical systems, of which the *Ethics* was simply the limiting example. The *Ethics* had taken the rationalism of all philosophy and simply pushed it to its outer limits. Rationalism can only lead to a loss of faith and hence to skepticism and indecision, a moral posture he was the first to call *Nihilismus*.[16] Although Jacobi carried out his critique of rationalism in the name of Christianity, he ultimately saw it as applicable to all forms of moral belief. Moral beliefs and commitments require faith, not reason. Reason can analyze and criticize, but morality requires belief, at a minimum belief in human freedom and individual responsibility. Jacobi is not saying that morality can dispense with reason. He is not an irrationalist, although he sometimes looks like one. He is arguing rather that reason presupposes faith or choice and that choice presupposes the primacy of ourselves as moral agents. The difference between freedom and determinism is not a theoretical matter, a question of truth; it is a moral question, a matter of choice between two competing systems. We can choose to affirm our freedom through a leap of faith or we can deny it. The one thing we cannot do is to ignore it altogether.

The Modern Impasse

The issues raised in Jacobi's *Letters* form the intellectual background to Strauss's critique of Spinoza and the Enlightenment. Strauss well understood the challenge to rationalism posed by the Jacobian critique of reason, but unlike Jacobi he was less concerned with defending the possibility of faith than with what he termed orthodoxy. The claims of orthodoxy—revelation, miracles, the immutability of the Law—had all been shaken by Spinoza and the radical Enlightenment he helped to launch. The challenge to orthodoxy posed by Spinoza was turned by Strauss into nothing less than the fate of modern Judaism torn between a fundamental choice: either join the party of Spinoza and the radical Enlightenment or return to orthodoxy and all that it entails. Nothing less was at stake.

This challenge was addressed at length in the preface to Strauss's second book, *Philosophy and Law*, a study of Maimonides and his predecessors.[17] The title of the book already reveals an important difference between

Jacobi and Strauss. As we have seen, the central concept of Jacobi's critique of Spinoza was *Glaube* in the dual sense of faith and belief. Strauss, however, takes as his point of departure not the primacy of faith but that of Law, that is, the objective experience of revelation. The major disjunction for Jacobi is between faith and knowledge, between what we can know and what we are, perforce, compelled to believe, while for Strauss it is between *Philosophie und Gesetz*, between the claims of reason and the revealed character of the Law. The difference is crucial for an understanding of how Strauss differs from the romantic critique of the Enlightenment.

Early in the work Strauss presents Spinoza as the source of the "radical Enlightenment." By the Enlightenment he understands not just an attempt to purify religion from the stain of priestcraft and corruption, but a wholesale repudiation of the very pillars of the law, the "roots" of the faith, as it were. At issue is nothing less than the choice between Enlightenment and orthodoxy:

> If . . . the basis of the Jewish tradition is belief in the creation of the world, in the reality of biblical miracles, in the absolute obligation and the essential immutability of the Law as based on the revelation at Sinai, then one must say that the Enlightenment has undermined the foundation of the Jewish tradition. The radical Enlightenment (Spinoza comes to mind) did just this from the beginning, with full consciousness and full intent.[18]

The attempt of the radical Enlightenment to overthrow orthodoxy met with a number of responses. Among them were various efforts, undertaken in all good faith, to mediate between or mitigate the twin poles of orthodoxy and Enlightenment. The work of Moses Mendelssohn comes most immediately to mind. Mendelssohn was the greatest exponent of a "moderate Enlightenment" that attempted to construct a Judaism amenable to philosophy, a rational Judaism, a "religion of reason from the sources of Judaism" as Hermann Cohen would later call for. Mendelssohn refused to go down the path of either Spinoza or Jacobi by maintaining that a natural religion of reason could hold together the two alternatives of metaphysics and faith.[19]

In part because of what he believed to be the failed example set by Mendelssohn, Strauss showed himself hostile to all such efforts at mediation, at defending religion before the tribunal of philosophy. Every third way or affected synthesis could do no more than obscure the fundamental differences between reason and revelation, philosophy and the law. The

Enlightenment described this third way as natural religion or natural theology. "It must necessarily remain the case," Strauss writes, "that not just
every compromise but also every synthesis between the opposed positions
of Orthodoxy and Enlightenment proves to be untenable."[20]

Strauss was deeply suspicious of all efforts to bridge the gap between
philosophy and revelation in part because the result could not but distort
the original claims of each. Learning from both Jacobi and Spinoza that philosophy and revelation stand on totally different foundations, Strauss
regarded the attempt to synthesize the two as leading either to the subordination of philosophy to theology ("the queen of the sciences") or the
transformation of religion into a faith, that is, a matter of conscience and
private belief, something quite different from the authoritative character of
law. The result of this transformation of orthodoxy into a matter of inner
faith could be nothing less than theological asphyxiation. The effort to
divest religion of its public, that is to say, its legal character could not but
be a victory of the Enlightenment over orthodoxy. "These reconciliations,"
Strauss avers, "always work ultimately as vehicles of the Enlightenment,
not as dams against it."[21]

The situation described in these passages is the dilemma shaped by the
Enlightenment but only fully developed or made explicit under conditions
established by Nietzsche and Weber with their demand for probity and intellectual honesty (Redlichkeit) at all costs.[22] While earlier thinkers and earlier
times were certainly familiar with the conflicting loyalties engendered by
the claims of Jerusalem and Athens, only the modern Enlightenment has
made necessary the choice between fidelity to the Law (Torah, Talmud,
Midrash) and acceptance of an unqualified this-worldliness or political atheism. This existential impasse has clarified the situation, but as such admits
of no way out. It offers a choice but not a solution, or at least not a solution
that even Strauss himself seems willing to accept. In an unusually self-
revealing passage he admits the cul-de-sac in which he finds himself:

> For a Jew who cannot be orthodox and must hold unconditional politi-
> cal Zionism (the only possible "solution to the Jewish problem" on the
> basis of atheism) to be a highly honorable but in the long and serious run
> unsatisfactory answer, the situation created by that alternative, the con-
> temporary situation, seems to allow no way out.[23]

This awareness of an irreconcilable conflict between Jerusalem and
Athens was central to Strauss's analysis in Natural Right and History.
Although there is little in this book that directly acknowledges this matter,

Strauss alludes to it obliquely in the context of his treatment of the sociology of Max Weber.[24] Contrary to certain reigning views of Weber as a scientific positivist, Strauss treated him as a kind of existentialist who had shown the plurality of "value systems" and made plain the necessity of choosing between them. In his methodological writings Weber could not help but identify the chasm that exists between life and science. Life is based on ideals. Ideals require commitment and dedication and this is in the last instance a question of faith and moral belief. But science is based on reason, on what we can know either empirically or causally. Science requires the suspension of belief or at least neutrality toward the conflicting ideals that constitute life. It is this awareness of the irreconcilable split between life and science that raised what was for Strauss the "fundamental question":

> The fundamental question . . . is whether men can acquire that knowledge of the good without which they cannot guide their lives individually or collectively by the unaided efforts of their natural powers, or whether they are dependent for that knowledge on Divine Revelation. No alternative is more fundamental than this: human guidance or divine guidance. The first possibility is characteristic of philosophy or science in the original sense of the term, the second is presented in the Bible.[25]

"The dilemma," Strauss goes on to say, "cannot be evaded by any harmonization or synthesis":

> For both philosophy and the Bible proclaim something as the one thing needful, as the only thing that ultimately counts, and the one thing needful proclaimed by the Bible is the opposite of that proclaimed by philosophy: a life of obedient love versus a life of free insight. In every attempt at harmonization, in every synthesis however impressive, one of the two opposed elements is sacrificed, more or less subtly but in any event surely, to the other: philosophy, which means to be the queen, must be made the handmaid of revelation or vice versa.[26]

The situation described in these passages forms the ground of what Strauss would later call his "theologico-political predicament," which he addressed directly in the preface to the translation of *Spinoza's Critique of Religion.*

Strauss's "Theologico-Political Predicament"

In the preface to the English translation of his Spinoza book, Strauss describes himself as "a young Jew born and raised in Germany who found himself in the grips of a theologico-political predicament."[27] The most immediate and urgent manifestation of this predicament was the tenuous situation of the Jews in Weimar. Weimar was a republic, a liberal democracy that came into being in that brief period between the Treaty of Versailles and the Reichstag fire. Weimar was a product of the French Revolution and the Enlightenment, but was also connected to the home of Goethe and the tradition of German idealism that contributed to its "moderate, nonradical character." As such Weimar struck a balance between dedication to the principles of 1789 and dedication to the highest German tradition.[28]

The problem with Weimar was in the first instance its weakness and instability. The weakness of Weimar became most evident not with the economic crisis of 1929—other democracies faced similar economic problems—but with its inability to protect the Jews. This dilemma was made all the more acute because the Jews of Germany, more than the Jews of any other nation, had put their faith in liberal democracy to provide a solution to the "Jewish Question." Liberal democracy was understood as the regime devoted to ending persecution not only of Jews, but of all religious and ethnic minorities. It was the first political regime to grant full citizenship and equal rights to Jews while recognizing their right to remain Jews. If for this reason only, the assassination of Walter Rathenau, the Jewish Minister of Foreign Affairs, in 1922 proved a moment of profound crisis.[29]

The dilemma of modern Jewry has a long genealogy going back before Weimar to the time of Spinoza. Spinoza was to Strauss and many of his generation the first example of the modern Jew. Spinoza not only championed a break with orthodoxy and the burdens of the ceremonial law; he was also the first Jewish thinker to endorse liberal democracy in something like its modern form.[30] Although Spinoza had been ostracized by the Jewish community of Amsterdam, he was subsequently canonized by generations of Jewish modernists who celebrated him not only for showing the way out of the ghetto, but for establishing a new kind of secular religion and culture based on the highest aspirations of the educated middle class. Spinoza is depicted by Strauss as nothing short of the prophet of a new kind of ethical culture:

> He thus showed the way toward a new religion or religiousness which was to inspire a wholly new kind of society, a new kind of Church.

He became the sole father of that new Church which was to be universal in fact, and not merely in claim as other churches, because its foundation was no longer any positive revelation—a Church whose rulers
were not priests or pastors, but philosophers and artists and whose flock
were the circles of culture and property.[31]

In particular Spinoza opened the door to liberal democracy, a society
that was neither Christian nor Jewish but above or impervious to each.
Central to the liberal solution to the theologico-political predicament was
the distinction between public and private and the belief that religion
belonged exclusively to the private sphere of life. Henceforth religion
would be deprived of the tools of force and coercion and turned into a matter of conscience and private belief, something quite different from the normative function of the law. This effort to divest religion of its public
character was to have far-reaching consequences:

> The millennial antagonism between Judaism and Christianity was
> about to disappear. The new Church would transform Jews and
> Christians into human beings—into human beings of a certain kind:
> cultured human beings, human beings who, because they possessed sci-
> ence and art, did not need religion in addition. The new society, consti-
> tuted by an aspiration common to all its members toward the True, the
> Good, and the Beautiful, emancipated the Jews in Germany. Spinoza
> became the symbol of that emancipation which was to be not only
> emancipation but secular redemption. In Spinoza, a thinker and a saint
> who was both a Jew and a Christian and hence neither, all cultured fam-
> ilies of the earth, it was hoped, would be blessed.[32]

This utopian vision of a world beyond sectarianism and strife was not,
of course, Spinoza's (he remained far too realistic); rather, it belonged to
mid-nineteenth century German Jewry, which had come to regard him as a
messianic figure promising some kind of secular redemption.[33]

Strauss's critique of Spinoza is twofold: Jewish and philosophical. As a
Jewish thinker, Strauss regards Spinoza as "the greatest man of Jewish origin who had openly denied the truth of Judaism and had ceased to belong
to the Jewish people without becoming a Christian."[34] He takes issue especially with Hermann Cohen, who had attacked Spinoza as guilty of a
"humanly incomprehensible betrayal" of the Jewish people. "He [Cohen],"
Strauss remarks, "condemned Spinoza because of his infidelity in the simple human sense, of his complete lack of loyalty to his own people, of his

acting like an enemy of the Jews and thus giving aid and comfort to the many enemies of the Jews, of his behaving like a base traitor."[35] Strauss adds that "in some respects" his own case against Spinoza is even stronger than Cohen's. The God of Spinoza was certainly not the God of orthodoxy, but neither was it the God of the German romantics. Spinoza's God is that of "the hardhearted pupil of Machiavelli":

> The biblical God forms light and creates darkness, makes peace and creates evil; Spinoza's God is simply beyond good and evil. God's might is His right, and therefore the power of every being is as such its right; Spinoza lifts Machiavellianism to theological heights. Good and evil differ only from a merely human point of view; theologically the distinction is meaningless. The evil passions are evil only with a view to human utility; in themselves they show forth the might and right of God no less than other things which we admire by the contemplation of which we are delighted.[36]

In the same paragraph this "Machiavellian" deity is in turn given a "Nietzschean" twist: "All human acts are modes of the one God who possesses infinitely many attributes each of which is infinite and only two of which are known to us, who is therefore a mysterious God, whose mysterious love reveals itself in eternally and necessarily bringing forth love and hatred, nobility and baseness, saintliness and depravity, and who is infinitely lovable not in spite but because of His infinite power beyond good and evil."[37]

Strauss does not reject out of hand the Spinozist conception of God. If Spinoza offered the possibility of emancipation in a secular liberal society, so too did he hold out the possibility of reconstituting a Jewish state. The Torah, he taught, just like all ostensibly revealed works, is in fact a human book. The Torah is not "from heaven," but is a product of the Jewish mind or the Jewish nation. Judaism, like all religions, is a human invention designed to secure worldly happiness and well-being. Moses was not a prophet to whom God spoke, but a statesman and political leader who used prophetic language to found and maintain a nation. The Jewish religion was thus from the beginning a political religion founded by Moses to create order and instill obedience to law. Spinoza holds out the possibility that what Moses did in the past can under new circumstances be done again. Strauss quotes from the third chapter of Spinoza's *Theologico-Political Treatise* to indicate his call for an independent Jewish state: "Indeed, if the foundations of their religion did not effeminate their hearts, I would absolutely believe that some day, given the opportunity, they will set up their state again and that God will choose them anew, so changeable are human affairs."[38] On the basis of this sentence alone, Strauss assigns to Spinoza an honored role among the founders of political Zionism.

In a number of places Strauss alludes to the fact that he was a political Zionist in his youth and until the end of his life regarded it as a highly "honorable" (be-kavod) solution to the Jewish Question.[39] However, the appropriation of Spinoza for the cause of political Zionism could not but prove doubtful from the standpoint of orthodoxy. Spinoza's advice is to cease waiting for a world-to-come and to take affairs into one's own hands. As the passage just quoted indicates, Zionism ascribes responsibility for establishing a state not to prayer or patient waiting for the messiah, but to force of one's own arms, fighting, and military hardware. It turns responsibility for the security and even the redemption of the Jewish people into a purely human, political problem. Furthermore, he does not say that such a state would have to be reestablished in the historical land of Israel. Unlike Judah Halevi, Spinoza attaches no particular significance either to the Hebrew language or to the soil of Israel. A Jewish state could as easily be located in Canada or Katmandu from his point of view.[40]

Strauss regards the influence of Spinoza as prominent in works like Herzl's *Judenstaat* and Pinsker's *Autoemanzipation* that understood the fate of the Jews as having to do not with divine promises but with power politics pure and simple.[41] The use of human, even crudely political means to attain an end previously reserved for God is a further example of Strauss's complaint that Spinoza raised Machiavellianism to "theological heights." The Zionist solution to the Jewish Question appears to preserve Jews even at the expense of Judaism, something Strauss calls "a most dangerous game":

> Spinoza may have hated Judaism; he did not hate the Jewish people. However bad a Jew he may have been in all other respects, he thought of the liberation of the Jews in the only way in which he could think of it, given his philosophy. But precisely if this is so, we must stress all the more the fact that the manner in which he sets forth his proposal—to say nothing of the proposal itself—is Machiavellian: the humanitarian end seems to justify every means; he plays a most dangerous game; his procedure is as much beyond good and evil as his God.[42]

In the final analysis Strauss felt obligated to repudiate the Zionism and Spinozism of his youth as an honorable but flawed solution to the Jewish

Question. Like his early hero Franz Rosenzweig, Strauss came to regard the problems of Judaism as ultimately beyond history. For both thinkers, the essence of Judaism—the commanding voice of revelation—is, literally, above time and impervious to political solutions. Strauss learned from Rosenzweig that the modern Jew is torn between two competing home-lands (*Zweistromland*), as it were, between faith and reason, law and phi-losophy, *Deutschtum* and *Judentum*.[43] This is why Strauss could regard the foundation of the Jewish state from his lofty vantage point as merely a "modification" of the exile. From the metaphysical or theological point of view it changed nothing. He may have expressed deep admiration and grat-itude for a Jewish state, but he denied to it any deeper redemptive signifi-cance. As he put it in a passage cited earlier, the Jews were the people chosen to prove the absence of redemption.

The specifically Jewish critique of Spinoza points to a second, more broadly philosophical critique that cuts to the core of the ancient problem of faith and reason. The *Ethics* is based on the assumption that human rea-son alone can give a theoretically and practically satisfying explanation of nature, of everything that is. This is the principle of sufficient reason, that there is nothing in the world (or outside of it) that escapes the powers of human rationality. The question is whether the *Ethics* proves this claim or merely begs the question. Strauss appears to doubt whether the premises of orthodoxy have been or ever can be refuted by reason alone. "The *Ethics*," he writes, "thus begs the decisive question—the question as to whether the clear and distinct account is as such true and not merely a *plausible hypothesis*."[44] The merely "hypothetical" character of the *Ethics* would seem to cast doubt on its claims to provide the one true or necessary account of the whole.

The apparent failure of Spinoza to refute orthodoxy stems in large part from the incommensurability of their premises. "The genuine refu-tation of orthodoxy," Strauss writes, "would require the proof that the world and human life are perfectly intelligible without the assumption of a mysterious God."[45] But the assumption of an unfathomable mysterious God, whose ways are not our ways, is "irrefutable" at least by reason. The Enlightenment's recourse to such devices as mockery and ridicule in its critique of religion provides an "indirect proof" of the failure to penetrate the bridgehead of orthodoxy. The difference, then, between Spinoza and even the most fundamentalistic orthodoxy is based not on truth, but on an act of will or faith. The conflict between faith and reason, Jerusalem and Athens, is in the final instance not a theoretical but a moral choice:

Spinoza's *Ethics* attempts to be the system, but it does not succeed; the clear and distinct account of everything which it presents remains fundamentally hypothetical. As a consequence, its cognitive status is not different from that of the orthodox account. Certain it is that Spinoza cannot legitimately deny the possibility of revelation. But to grant that revelation is possible means to grant that the philosophical account and the philosophic way of life are not necessarily, not evidently, the true account and the right way of life: philosophy, the quest for evident and necessary knowledge, rests itself on an unevident decision, on an act of will, *just as faith.*[46]

The critique of philosophy contained in the above passage is far-reaching. There is no proposition more central to the *Ethics* as a whole than the famous *Deus sive nature*, that the mind can aspire to knowledge of God (= nature) and therefore that there is nothing in nature that is not susceptible to a rational explanation. This is the principle of rational sufficiency. However, philosophy that aspires to provide a rational account of nature, of everything that is, itself rests on an act of will, on an "unevident decision." Philosophy that attempts to explain everything cannot explain or account for itself. The idea that philosophy or reason rests on a prior act of faith is obviously not damaging to the standpoint of orthodoxy that assumes the choice between good and evil rests on a decision whose origin is in the will. The standpoint of philosophy (or at least of the *Ethics*) that attempts to make will and choice subordinate to reason and necessity is compromised, perhaps fatally, by this awareness.

There is ultimately a "Pascalian" or Jacobian flavor to Strauss's claim that rational philosophy rests on a mysterious leap of faith. The implication is that philosophy is inferior to faith because philosophy is unwilling to recognize that it rests on faith, on an act of will. In this respect philosophy fails the test of "intellectual probity" that Strauss, following Nietzsche, defines as "the willingness to look man's forsakenness in its face, being the courage to welcome the most terrible truth."[47] Apparently philosophy is unwilling to look itself in the face and consider the most terrible truth. Spinoza's claim to overcome orthodoxy cannot overcome the fact that the basis of his critique rests on an act of will, of arbitrary subjectivity. There appears to be no critical necessity for philosophy, only critical necessity within philosophy. At the root of all philosophy stands a stark epistemic abyss where reason simply comes to an end. Strauss here appears to endorse the view of Wittgenstein, another one of the great philosophical "fideists" of modernity—not, to be sure, the Wittgenstein of the *Philosophical*

Investigations but of the Spinoza-inspired *Tractatus Logico-Philosophicus,* which concludes with the Delphic utterance, "Whereof we cannot speak, thereof we must keep silent."[48]

A Return to Orthodoxy?

What, then, is Strauss's final will and testament on Spinoza? Does he believe that Spinoza's philosophy is refuted by the claim that reason itself rests on a set of undisclosed premises that reason cannot adequately know? Has he rescued the possibility of orthodoxy from the grip of rationalist metaphysics? Or does his critique of Spinoza follow Jacobi down the slippery slope to irrationalist and existentialist affirmations of faith unbounded by reason?

Like Jacobi, Strauss argued that our situation is one of radical existential choice, either for orthodoxy (in the sense of revealed law) or for resolute atheism. There is no third way. In the conflict between faith and reason, Jacobi clearly took the side of faith. Only a radical leap of faith could affirm freedom and our status as moral agents. But the subordination of philosophy to theology or, what comes to the same thing, reason to revelation, was not for Strauss, as it was for Jacobi, a cause for celebration. Strauss regarded the conflict between these two alternatives as the source of a genuine paradox. "The victory of orthodoxy through the self-destruction of rational philosophy," he wrote, "was not an unmitigated blessing."[49]

Throughout his writings Strauss remained deeply cognizant of the potential for conflict between philosophy and morality. Spinoza's critique of religion represented an attack not just on Jewish orthodoxy, but on the necessity of revelation for the moral life. Strauss makes this connection explicit in the context of a discussion of Judah Halevi's *Kuzari.* He regards Halevi as a kindred spirit precisely for his awareness that philosophy represents a challenge not just to Judaism but to the very possibility of morality:

> In defending Judaism, which, according to [Halevi], is the only true revealed religion, against the philosophers, he was conscious of defending morality itself and therewith the cause, not only of Judaism, but of mankind at large. His basic objection to philosophy was then not particularly Jewish, nor even particularly religious, but moral.[50]

Strauss's case is that a purely rational or natural morality, a morality from the sources of reason alone, can never be a sufficient ground for genuine morality. Rational morality can do no more than provide a rationale for collective selfishness or, what comes to the same thing, the morality of a gang of thieves. Only revelation can provide a satisfactory basis for the moral life: "One has not to be naturally pious," he writes, "he has merely to have a passionate interest in genuine morality in order to long with all his heart for revelation: moral man as such is the potential believer."[51]

For all of his talk of a return to orthodoxy, Strauss surprisingly has little to say about the substance of orthodoxy either as a set of beliefs or as a way of life. Is it even possible to speak of orthodoxy as if it were all of one piece? Some orthodox, like the Mizrachi, are willing to work with other Jews and their organizations, while others, like the Agudat Israel, stay apart from non-practicing Jews even as they have representatives in the Knesset. Still others, like the Satmar Hasidim living in the Boro Park section of Brooklyn or the Naturei Karata ("Watcher of the city of Jerusalem") in Israel, have never even recognized the Jewish state and stay as far away as possible from contamination by the outside world. To be sure, all of these sects are examples of orthodoxy, but the great variety in terms of belief, ritual practice, and even dress shows how misleading it is to speak of orthodoxy with an upper-case "O."[52]

In fact Strauss's peculiar conception of orthodoxy has nothing to do with the black hat Haredi community, but consists of a "Maimonidean" strategy that combines outward fidelity to the community of Israel with a private or "esoteric" commitment to philosophy and the life of free inquiry. To be sure, Strauss did not adopt this position in order to undermine Judaism, but to sustain it as a form of political theology. This dual strategy allows one to maintain respect for, even love of, the tradition as a prophylactic to the alternatives of atheism and assimilation, while denying orthodoxy any truth value. The doctrine of the double truth remains the only way of preserving the viability of Judaism in a post-Nietzschean world that demands intellectual probity at all costs.

Strauss's response to the Nietzschean demand for probity is an embrace of orthodoxy, but an orthodoxy of a very particular sort. His adoption of a "hyper-Maimonidean style," as Rémi Brague has observed, has the function of turning the substance of the law into a fiction in the precise legal sense of the term.[53] To be sure, this operation was not peculiar to Maimonides, but was adopted by him from Alfarabi and the Islamic Falasifa and has even carried over into modern forms of civil religion. Strauss himself gave credence to this view in his lecture "Why We Remain Jews," where he refers to Judaism as a "delusion," even a "heroic delusion." "What is a delusion?" he asks:

We also say a "dream." No nobler dream was ever dreamt. It is surely nobler to be a victim of the most noble dream than to profit from a sordid reality and to wallow in it. Dream is akin to aspiration. And aspiration is a kind of divination of an enigmatic vision. And an enigmatic vision in the emphatic sense is the perception of the ultimate mystery, of the truth of the ultimate mystery.[54]

People who live in glass houses should not throw stones. Strauss, who took evident pleasure in exposing the hidden atheism of early modern philosophy, cannot in good conscience complain when the same trick is played on him. The statement that Judaism represents a "heroic delusion" is as close as he ever came, I think, to expressing in his writing that orthodoxy is a kind of Platonic noble lie that must be preserved in order to maintain standards of decency and public civility, to say nothing of Jewish pride and self-respect. Gershom Scholem had it exactly right when he wrote to Walter Benjamin about Strauss's bid for a chair in Jewish thought at the Hebrew University that "only three people at the very most will make use of the freedom to vote for the appointment of an atheist to a teaching position that serves to endorse the philosophy of religion."[55]

In the final analysis Strauss's difference with Spinoza is not with what he said, but with how he said it.

PART TWO

Athens

Leo Strauss's Platonic Liberalism

> Socrates . . . never belonged to a sect and never founded one. And even
> if the philosophic friends are compelled to be members of a sect or to
> found one, they are not necessarily members of one and the same sect:
> *Amicus Plato.* — *Leo Strauss, On Tyranny*

The conjunction of the terms "Platonic" and "liberalism" may seem to
verge on oxymoron. The most influential interpretation of Plato in the
second half of the twentieth century held him to be an intransigent enemy
of liberalism and the "open society."[1] His harsh proposals for a closed caste
system and for the censorship of poetry and literature, his radical measures
to eliminate the family and private property, and his investiture of political
authority in an all-wise and all-powerful philosopher-king must strike even
a sympathetic reader as radically opposed to liberal beliefs in freedom of
thought and expression, a robust sphere of civil society and private life, the
importance of limited constitutional government supported by a system of
checks and balances, and a skeptical disposition toward the rule of experts.
As if this were not enough, Plato's belief that the Forms or Ideas can provide a ground for something like absolute certainty for such terms as justice, beauty, and goodness seems the very opposite of the open-ended,
skeptical, and inquiring spirit of liberal philosophy.

These objections notwithstanding, there is another reading of Plato that
stands in marked contrast to what one might call the standard interpretation referred to above. This alternative reading of Plato, which I want to call
Platonic Liberalism, is best expressed in the work of Leo Strauss.[2] To call
Strauss's Plato liberal is of course to invite reproach. Strauss's Plato, like
Strauss himself, is widely held to be anti-liberal to the extreme. Strauss
allegedly maintains a radical divide between the philosophers and the

multitude that runs counter to the egalitarian spirit of democratic liberalism. His penchant for indulging in "esoteric" interpretation of texts appears further to cut off the democratic many from imbibing the wisdom that is the property of the few. And Strauss's belief that the philosophical life is the best life humanly possible smacks of intellectual perfectionism and elitism and runs counter to liberal pluralism and skepticism about the human good.

Critics of Strauss's Plato have tended to fall into two camps. Those in the first camp have attacked the methodological premises of Straussian hermeneutics. The method of esoteric reading, taken originally from the Jewish and Arabic Platonists of the Middle Ages, is said to be inherently arbitrary and nonverifiable. Leaving aside the rejoinder that other non-esotericist methodologies have equally failed to achieve anything like consensus on key issues, Strauss's reading of central figures in the tradition is said to ignore what the texts manifestly say for what an author may only allude to or not mention at all. The result is to place interpretation outside the realm of debate and falsification.[3]

The second line of criticism is mainly political. Strauss famously regards the *Republic* as anti-utopian, a work setting out "the limits of justice."[4] However, many readers take this to mean that Strauss believes the *Republic* shows the impossibility of justice and therefore the futility of political reform. Strauss is thus said to insert a conservative, if not reactionary, politics into his reading of Plato under the guise of understanding the author in the same way that the author understood himself. The highwater mark of this political critique was Myles Burnyeat's 1985 article in the *New York Review of Books*, in which Burnyeat depicted Strauss as advocating "in all seriousness" the surrender of the critical intellect to the authority of certain canonical texts, something Burnyeat believed "fits into the psychology of conservatism."[5] Burnyeat's article was followed by a spate of debunking studies depicting Strauss as a megalomaniac bent on dismantling liberal modernity and restoring ancient hierarchies based on rank and authority.[6] This political critique bottomed out almost a decade later with a signed editorial in the *New York Times* depicting Strauss as an implacable enemy of democracy and as the *eminence gris* behind the Republican takeover of the U.S. House of Representatives in November 1994.[7]

In the past few years, however, there is some evidence that a reconsideration of not only Strauss but Plato is under way within the academy. The ruling dogmas and even name-calling that once characterized the debates are undergoing a reevaluation. A recent work by Charles Kahn on *Plato and the Socratic Dialogue* has made the issue of the dialogic form and Plato's notorious secrecy and reluctance to speak in his own name central to the interpretation of the Platonic corpus.[8] And Alexander Nehamas, in a book titled *The Art of Living*, attempts to recover the Socratic view of philosophy not only as concerned with theory construction but as a way of life.[9] Socrates, Nehamas believes, set out an ironic conception of life that has proved an irresistible model to thinkers as different from one another as Montaigne, Nietzsche, Thomas Mann, and Michel Foucault. Underlying both these books is a sense that contemporary Platonic studies have misleadingly neglected the literary, dramatic, and characterological aspects of Platonic philosophy. While neither of these works acknowledges Strauss's Plato (for all I know, the authors of these studies may well recoil at the thought of the association), I want to suggest that if a reconsideration of Plato is on the agenda, a reconsideration of Strauss should not be far behind.[10]

None of these works is especially interested in Plato's political philosophy, although they do open up a way of reading him that goes beyond the standard "Plato as Fascist" trope. In part due to the influence of Strauss, we are coming to appreciate a new Plato, less monolithic, less absolutist, and less dogmatic than the totalitarian virtuecrat he has been made out to be by many of his enemies and even a few of his friends. Strauss's Plato is in the first instance a skeptic, a "zetetic" philosopher, whose thought is characterized by an awareness of the limits, the incompleteness, of human knowledge. One corollary of this reading is a warning against the attempt to force a marriage of philosophy and politics that cannot but have untoward results, as the *Republic's* repeated recourse to compulsion, lies, and politically necessary myth would suggest. His denial of the possibility of achieving the just city is designed not only to protect philosophy from the inevitable corruption of political power, but also to protect politics from the potential tyranny exercised by intellectuals and other self-appointed guardians. By emphasizing the always partial and incomplete nature of knowledge, Strauss returned to Plato and classical philosophy as a possible resource for, rather than an enemy of, political liberalism.

Strauss's Literary "Occasionalism"

One thing that most clearly distinguishes Strauss's Plato from the standard interpretation concerns his manner of reading. On the standard view the *Republic* is a proposal for a radical utopia, the first full-scale design for an ideal state. Plato is regarded here as a political reformer who set out a variety of proposals that existing polities ought to implement if they are to be well-governed. The result of such a reading is to regard a Platonic dialogue as setting forth a series of definitions about justice, about the proper organization of a city, and the proper ordering of the appetites and dispositions of the soul. Discussing Plato turns, then, on his various recommendations, prescriptions, and prohibitions for achieving justice. One may, of course, consider how practicable, desirable, or logically consistent these proposals are, but there is relatively little attention given to what Plato's intentions were.

In contrast to the standard view, Strauss presents a more elusive and open-ended Plato. This derives from the centrality he attributes to the dialogue as a distinctive literary form.[11] Strauss refuses to regard the dialogue as merely the external dross in which the philosophical nuggets are concealed. Rather, he believes that the dialogue is the teaching itself. For many readers, this attention to the question of literary form seems perverse or at most of marginal interest when considered next to the philosophical arguments of the *Republic*, but for Strauss the medium is the message. Perhaps "the most valuable feature" of this attention to the dialogue, G.R.F. Ferrari writes, "is simply Strauss's refusal to gloss over or minimize the extent of Plato's literariness."[12]

Why Plato wrote dialogues has been recently and fruitfully debated.[13] That he wrote in dialogue form no one disputes; how much weight to attribute to that fact is a question of potentially great importance. The question that pervades Strauss's reading of Plato is that of authorial anonymity, the fact that Plato is the author of everything we read but is nowhere present in any of his dialogues. Until we figure out the proper relation between author and text, every other question must be put on hold. Strauss puts this question at the very outset of his essay on the *Republic*, stating that "one cannot understand Plato's teaching as he meant it if one does not know what the Platonic dialogue is" and then goes on to remark almost apologetically that "one must postpone one's concern with the most serious questions (the philosophical questions) in order to become engrossed in the study of a merely literary question."[14] Whether Strauss ever moves beyond this "merely literary question" to consider "the most serious questions" will be considered later.

There are, of course, many reasons why an author might wish to conceal his beliefs behind the cloak of anonymity, some of which may be political, theological, or even pedagogical. Strauss himself is guided by Plato's remarks in the *Seventh Letter*, according to which his written work merely conveys his "exoteric" teaching while his true beliefs are conveyed through

well-placed hints and intimations (341d-e). But even if one chooses to dis-
count the authenticity of the *Seventh Letter*, there are still Socrates's own
statements from the *Phaedrus* (275d-e), where he defends the superiority of
oral to written communication. From this point of view it might seem that
Platonic writing is a degenerate form of Socratic conversation. The dialogue, Plato's chief form of philosophical communication, is something
that stands halfway between Socratic oral communication and the systematic treatises of Aristotle. A dialogue is a form of writing that comes closest to the "flexibility" and "adaptability" of actual speech. A good dialogue,
like a good conversation, may say different things to different people. It
argues *ad hominem*. Plato's dialogues contain no assertions, demonstra-
tions, or proofs of Plato's. Rather, they depict conversations addressed to
different kinds of people with a range of abilities, aptitudes, and predilec-
tions who either fail or succeed in becoming philosophers. We cannot
assume, then, that we know what Plato's teaching is in advance of any particular dialogue. Rather, Strauss admits that "the Platonic dialogue is an
enigma . . . one big question mark."[15]

The centrality Strauss attributes to the dialogic form certainly is not
intended to put the text beyond the ken of rational debate or to dissolve it
into an endless play of signifiers. It means only that the interpreter of a
Platonic dialogue must "fall back on his own resources . . . for discovering
the decisive part of the argument by himself."[16] Far from encouraging a
mindless subordination of the interpreter to the text, Strauss emphasizes
that "Plato composed his writings in such a way as to prevent *for all time*
their use as authoritative texts."[17] Yet the difficulty of unraveling the
meaning of a dialogue does not result in a kind of total epistemological
abstinence. In fact, a close reading of the dialogues will reveal that Plato
indicates "very specific hermeneutic rules" about how to read a dialogue.
Strauss states these rules as follows:

> For presenting his teaching Plato uses not merely the "content" of his
> works (the speeches of his various characters) but also their "form" (the
> dialogic form in general, the particular form of each dialogue and of each
> section of it, the action, characters, names, places, times, situations and
> the like); an adequate understanding of the dialogues understands the
> "content" in the light of the "form."[18]

Strauss concludes that Plato provides his readers with at most "decisive
indications" of his most "serious teaching" rather than "ready-made
answers to [his] ultimate and most important questions."[19]

The dialogues, he says, are "dramas in prose."[20] The literary problem posed by the interpretation of a dialogue is not extraneous to its philosophical purpose. Rather, the dialogue may present puzzles of a literary kind, but which are intrinsically connected to the philosophical problems proper. One must read the *Republic* as one would any work of dramatic literature, that is to say, one must consider the words and speeches of any character within the context of the work as a whole. This is simple common sense. But the result of reading Plato in this way is to shift the burden of proof away from the speeches of the characters to their actions and personalities as revealed in the larger dramatic context of the dialogue. The meaning of the dialogues is more likely to be revealed through an examination of the context of particular utterances with particular individuals at particular times. By removing Socrates from the center of things, Strauss wants to look at what takes place between Socrates (or the Eleatic or Athenian Stranger) and his various interlocutors. It is the "action" as well as the "argument" that counts in any Platonic dialogue. Not surprisingly, the only book-length study Strauss ever devoted to a Platonic dialogue is called *The Argument and Action of Plato's Laws*.

Straussian hermeneutics, then, inscribes an essential indeterminacy in the understanding of Plato. We can never claim to have understood what is meant, especially when the presentation of any interpretation can be refuted or confounded by passages occurring in other dialogues. Strauss takes "the undying controversy about the theory of the idea of the good" to serve as evidence for the tentative and provisional character of all Platonic interpretation.[21] The aporetic character of the Platonic dialogues must infuse our ability to interpret those dialogues. For some readers, this openended, skeptical reading is a symptom of the frustration of Straussian hermeneutics. If the dialogues remain "one big question mark," how can we ever hope to reach an understanding of what they mean? Has Strauss eliminated a dogmatic reading of the Platonic texts merely to inscribe his own version of the uncertainty principle? Was Strauss a "postmodern" *avant la lettre*? No.

Strauss does not infer that because the dialogues remain aporetic we can say nothing at all about them. He argues rather that "the rules governing the interpretation of Plato's books are much stricter than the rules governing the interpretation of most books."[22] He wants only to instill a sense of interpretive perplexity that is aware of its own limitations. In a letter to Hans-Georg Gadamer regarding *Truth and Method*, Strauss explicitly distinguishes his own experience as a reader of Plato from any general or universal hermeneutic theory:

It is not easy for me to recognize in your hermeneutics my own experience as an interpreter. Yours is a "theory of hermeneutic experience" which as such is a universal theory. Not only is my own hermeneutic experience very limited—the experience which I possess makes me doubtful whether a universal hermeneutic theory which is more than "formal" or external is possible. I believe that the doubt arises from the feeling of the irretrievably "occasional" character of every worthwhile interpretation.[23]

It is Strauss's insistence on the "occasional" character of each Platonic dialogue that radically distinguishes his from the standard interpretation. Rather than ascribing the various dialogues to the different "stages" in Plato's development—the famous early, middle, and late periods of Plato's thought—he prefers to see them each as articulating a part, but only a part, of the many-sidedness or heterogeneity of being. The dialogue is the form of writing that most closely imitates the openness of inquiry and the limitations on human understanding. In language that owes much to Heidegger, Strauss says that the dialogues "awaken us to the mystery" of being and "assist us in articulating that mystery."[24] The Platonic cosmos, rather than a rational ordered whole, contains a deep sense of mystery and uncertainty that is imitated by the aporetic character of the Platonic dialogues as a whole.

Justice and Necessity

No aspect of the *Republic* highlights the differences between the standard interpretation of Plato and Strauss's more than their readings of the allegory of the cave and the role of the philosopher-king. The importance of the philosopher-king for the "third wave argument," as it is called in the literature, is generally agreed by all schools to be central to the *Republic*.[25] The majority of interpreters agree that Plato's considered view is that philosophers should rule, that human well-being is achievable only with the union of philosophy and politics, and that the just city set out in the *Republic* is the standard or paradigm against which all other cities should be judged. Opinions differ within the majority view over whether Plato regarded the *kallipolis* as both desirable and possible or merely desirable but not possible. Thus when Strauss contends that the proposal for the philosopher-king is neither desirable nor possible, the standard response is to complain that he is not playing by the rules. "The *Republic*," he maintains, "conveys the broadest and deepest analysis of political idealism ever made" and as such contains "the most magnificent cure ever devised for every form of political ambition."[26] How can the text be made to say the opposite of what it manifestly appears to say? These issues get to the very core of the possibility of a Platonic liberalism.

Strauss turned to Plato's image of the philosopher and the cave in order to illustrate the character of what he sometimes referred to as the "natural" or "common sense" understanding of the world, but also to study the moment at which philosophy emerged from within and in conflict with this prescientific world. His return to the Greeks, and especially to Plato, to clarify the presuppositions of what the phenomenologists often call the life-world has sometimes been likened to Heidegger's use of the ancients in order to recapture the most rudimentary features of Being.[27] But Strauss's return to Plato is different from Heidegger's in at least two crucial respects. First, the cave represents the city, even the best city (kallipolis). It is a fundamentally political rather than an ontological category. The cave is in turn decorated with a variety of "images," that is, opinions. Opinion, Strauss maintains elsewhere, is "the element of society."[28] As such opinion stands in contrast to philosophy, which seeks to replace opinion with knowledge. The question the Republic considers is whether philosophy and society must remain mutually antagonistic or whether philosophy can be made to penetrate the cave to bring about a more rational or enlightened form of society.

Second, Strauss differs from Heidegger in his understanding of the obstacles to the recovery of the world of prescientific opinion. Heidegger described this obstacle in terms of a "forgetfulness of Being," wherein the problem of Being seems simply to have disappeared from memory. But for Strauss the first and most fundamental obstacle to such a recovery has been the emergence of the "historical consciousness" or the belief that all thought is necessarily tied to a specific historical situation.[29] This new, unprecedented form of historical understanding must regard as illusory or misguided any attempt to liberate thought from the cave of its historical situatedness. Thus in addition to such natural obstacles to philosophy as stem from the imaginative and affective aspects of human nature, we must contend with such "artificial" obstacles as arise from the historical consciousness of our time. As early as 1931 Strauss described this situation by using a Platonic metaphor of his own making as a "second cave," or a cave beneath the cave of our common sense understanding:

> Bearing in mind the classical representation of the natural difficulties involved in philosophizing, in other words, the Platonic figure of the

cave, one can say that today we are in a second, much deeper cave than the fortunate ignorant persons with whom Socrates was concerned. We need history first of all in order to climb up into the cave from which Socrates can lead us to the light. We need a propaedeutic, something the Greeks did not need, that is, book learning (*lesenden Lernens*).[30]

Strauss's answer to the problem posed by the modern historical consciousness is precisely "book learning," learning by reading. His purpose in returning to the *Republic* is not merely to recover Plato's thoughts, but the thoughts that Plato thought about. These are not easily recoverable today, not only because of the great expanse of time separating us from Plato, but because our world is so much a product of science and historical understanding that it is difficult even to imagine a world where this was otherwise. Before we can even think about ascending to the lofty heights of philosophy, then, we must struggle hard just to find our way back to the cave that is the natural presupposition of philosophy. "If one of [Plato's] descendants," Strauss wrote, returning to this metaphor, "desired to ascend to the light of the sun, he would first have to try to reach the level of the natural cave, and he would have to invent new and most artificial tools unknown and unnecessary to those who dwelt in the natural cave."[31] Our path to philosophy must necessarily be more circuitous than Plato's because we cannot assume the existence of the natural cave he took for granted.

One feature of the natural cave Strauss seeks to recover is the deep, perhaps even intractable hostility between philosophy and the city. This hostility has been abated in modern times due in part to the influence of Christianity, which from an early time appropriated key aspects of Platonic doctrine, but even more importantly because of the Enlightenment, which sought to make a home for philosophy by rendering it useful to legislators and statesmen. Strauss's reading of the *Republic* focuses on just this issue, raised initially in Book V with the assertion that there will be "no rest from the ills for the cities" until "the philosophers rule as kings or those now called kings and chiefs genuinely and adequately philosophize" (473d).[32] The philosopher-king is proposed as the completion of *kallipolis*, the crowning moment that brings together reason and political rule.

Strauss asks under what circumstances philosophy and political power might be made to coincide. He admits that such a coincidence, while "very difficult to achieve," maybe "very improbable," but is by no means an impossibility.[33] Such a coincidence could come about if the city, that is, the multitude of non-philosophers, could be persuaded to accept it. Plato does not rule out, and neither does Strauss, the possibility that an entire people could be persuaded to accept the rule of a philosopher-king. However, due to popular prejudice against philosophy such a possibility is not very likely. It is only possible if the philosophers can first persuade the people to persuade them to rule.

But persuading the people to accept the rule of the philosophers is only the first step in the creation of *kallipolis*. It is necessary not only to persuade the people, but to persuade the philosophers, who, Socrates tells us, have an extreme reluctance to accept political responsibility. While the standard line maintains that it is just their reluctance to rule that guarantees the philosophers' impartiality and dedication to justice, Strauss focuses on the injustice done to the philosophers in compelling them to rule. "Why are the philosophers unwilling to rule?" he asks.

> Being dominated by the desire, the *eros*, for knowledge as the one thing needful, or knowing that philosophy is the most pleasant and blessed possession, the philosophers have no leisure for looking down at human affairs, let alone for taking care of them. They believe that while still alive they are already firmly settled far away from their cities in the "Islands of the Blessed." Hence only compulsion could induce them to take part in public life in the just city, i.e., in the city which regards the proper upbringing of philosophers as its most important task.[34]

From the philosophers' unwillingness or reluctance to rule, Strauss infers that *kallipolis* can only come into being through force or necessity. If the philosophers cannot be persuaded, they must be compelled (499b–c, 500d, 539e–540a). But who will do the compelling? It is absurd to believe that the non-philosophers will compel the philosophers to rule. The only alternative seems to be that the philosophers could compel themselves through the force of argument. But what argument could convince the philosopher to abandon philosophy and take on the responsibilities of public life? Strauss denies that any such argument could be compelling. The passage cited above continues:

> Having perceived the truly grand, the philosophers regard the human things as paltry. Their very justice—their abstaining from wronging their fellow human beings—flows from contempt for the things for which the non-philosophers hotly contest. They know that the life not dedicated to philosophy and therefore even political life at its best is like life in a cave, so much so that the city can be identified with the Cave.[35]

Rather than demonstrating the union of philosophy and politics, the *Republic* demonstrates the opposite. The "true reason" that makes *kallipolis* "extremely improbable" can now be stated: "philosophy and the city tend away from one another in opposite directions."[36]

Strauss highlights *Republic* 519c–20d to demonstrate the importance of the dialectic of persuasion and compulsion. He deliberately underscores those aspects of the dialogue that refer to such terms as compulsion, constraint, and necessity (*ananké*). As opposed to the standard view that "the dramatic action of the *Republic* is a sustained exercise in the power of persuasion,"[37] Strauss emphasizes the weakness of persuasion and the limitations of rational argument in creating a city. He delights in bringing out the breakdown of reasons and the resort to compulsion and necessity. The opening scene of the *Republic* is a good case in point. Here returning from the Piraeus at dusk with Glaucon, Socrates is accosted by a band of young men led by Polemarchus who demand that Socrates stay with them. Socrates asks if Polemarchus and his friends can be persuaded to let them leave; the latter responds, not if they refuse to listen. The failure of persuasion to overcome superior power becomes the context for the discussion of justice that occupies the rest of the dialogue. "We owe then the conversation on justice to a mixture of compulsion and persuasion," Strauss concludes. "To cede to such a mixture, or to a kind of such a mixture, is an act of justice."[38]

The recognition of the role of necessity is captured dramatically in Strauss's treatment of the place occupied by Thrasymachus in the *Republic*. After the initial exchange with Polemarchus at the Piraeus, Thrasymachus is the first to introduce the theme of force into the conversation about justice. Thrasymachus, who is described as savage and like a "wild beast," identifies justice with "the advantage of the stronger" (338c). But while Thrasymachus's thesis appears to have been defeated by the end of Book I, Strauss makes clear that this is only an appearance. Thrasymachus's argument has not been defeated, but deferred. Only when he considers the possibility of the philosopher-king is Thrasymachus reintroduced. "Without 'Thrasymachus,'" Strauss avers, "there will never be a just city."[39] Why is this?

Thrasymachus must be rehabilitated because he represents the art of popular persuasion that Socrates appears to lack. The art of Socrates is adequate for ruling a conversation among a group of cultured Athenians before dinner, but as the *Apology* demonstrates, it is manifestly inadequate for ruling a city. Thrasymachus is a rhetorician, and despite (or perhaps because of) his tough talk, he attributes to speech extraordinary powers of persuasion. It is a typical failing of the Sophists that they overstate the power of their art. This is not to say, however, that Thrasymachus is useless. Strauss notes with a certain irony that Homer and Sophocles must be expelled from *kallipolis* but Thrasymachus is welcomed back in.[40]

Thrasymachus is said to occupy the "central place" among the interlocutors of the *Republic*. He and Socrates stand dramatically disconnected from Cephalus and Polemarchus, the father and son, and Adeimantus and Glaucon, the two brothers. Socrates and Thrasymachus are mirror images of each other and as such require one another's help. By the dialogue's end Socrates and Thrasymachus have become friends even though Socrates says they had never really been enemies (498c–d). Each is a necessary component of justice. The way of Socrates is appropriate for dealing with the political elite, the way of Thrasymachus for dealing with the many and the young. Justice, it appears, consists of combining the "way of Socrates" and the "way of Thrasymachus" and thus managing to avoid the fate of Socrates.[41]

Strauss's view that justice consists of an admixture of persuasion and coercion, freedom and necessity, is intended to dampen the idealist, even revolutionary fervor that the *Republic* might inspire. The *kallipolis*, the "city in speech," represents one side of justice—the yearning for freedom—but abstracts entirely from the context of necessity out of which that yearning arises. Accordingly, the idea that "there will be no rest from ills for the city" until kings become philosophers and philosophers become kings is evidence for Strauss that the best city is "against nature."[42] The effort to bring *kallipolis* into being is tantamount to the effort to abolish evil from the human condition. Strauss regards this as a violation or an effort to transform the very premises of human nature. "The proximate premise of [Strauss's] political thought," Victor Gourevitch argues, "is that there are 'evils which are inseparable from the human condition,' this is to say that there are evils that are, in one sense of the term, natural, and hence cannot be eliminated."[43]

The argument for the persistence of evil is based in part on the empirical observation that attempts to abolish evil have always had to resort to evil means. It is also based on a passage from Plato's *Theaetetus* (176a) in which Socrates argues that we can only know a thing in terms of its opposite, so that we can only understand the good in terms of the persistence of evil.[44] Evil, it seems, is as much a part of human nature as good, and to seek to abolish it is to attempt to transcend human nature itself. The desire to conquer evil, to abolish necessity, while a part of justice, even "the most outstanding" and "practically most important" part, is not the whole of justice.[45] A part of justice is a recognition of the limits of justice. The desire to conquer nature must necessarily lead to the abolition of the family, private property, and all of those things rooted in *eros* or the "erotic necessities" of life. The *Republic* becomes, then, an object lesson in the dangers of efforts at utopian social engineering. By demonstrating what is required in order to conquer necessity, the *Republic* tries to enhance our awareness of the role of necessity and hence the "essential limits" of politics.[46]

What strikes many readers as perverse, even willfully perverse, is not just Strauss's conclusion that the coincidence of philosophy and politics is "extremely improbable"—everyone agrees with that. It is rather Strauss's argument that the union of philosophy and politics was always a non-starter. To force the philosopher to rule is to commit an injustice against him. *Kallipolis* is said to be impossible because its foundation rests upon an act of injustice. But what entitles Strauss to that conclusion? Where in the text does Plato say that? "The reader who asks where exactly in the text of the *Republic* Socrates makes this turn will be hard-pressed for an answer," Ferrari notes. "It is not a turn made in the *Republic*; it is the turn that makes the *Republic*."[47]

Strauss believes that the lack of sufficiently compelling reasons for the philosophers to accept the burden of political office is enough to prove the disjunction of philosophy and politics. But doesn't Socrates give reasons why the philosopher should accept the responsibilities of public life? In answer to Glaucon's objection that it would be unjust to force the philosopher back into the cave, Socrates replies:

> My friend, you have again forgotten . . . that it's not the concern of law that any one class in the city fare exceptionally well, but it contrives to bring this about for the whole city, harmonizing the citizens by persuasion and compulsion, making them share with one another the benefit that each class is able to bring to the commonwealth. (519e-20a)

Strauss clearly finds this line of reasoning unpersuasive; or, more accurately, he finds it persuasive for helping the war-like Glaucon accept the burdens and responsibilities of political life. Justice entails compulsion or a "mixture of compulsion and persuasion." In this context, Strauss cites the Introduction to Kant's *Metaphysics of Morals* to show that reasons to behave justly toward others do not cease to be compulsory or coercive because they are self-imposed.[48]

Strauss does not raise the issue of compulsion in order to impugn the view of morality as obedience to law, even self-imposed law. He raises the issue rather to illustrate the gap between the citizen's view of justice as dedication to the common good and the philosopher's quest for wisdom as the highest aspiration of the human soul. The difference between Kant and Plato is the difference between someone who believes that the highest good is to be found in the moral realm of obligation and duty and someone who believes that only the examined life is worth living. The necessary and inevitable conflict between morality and philosophy is the key to Strauss's Plato. The very title of Strauss's book *The City and Man* is a stand-in for these two most comprehensive alternatives, the moral life and the philosophical life. The *Republic* as a whole is nothing less than an object lesson in their incommensurability.[49]

Socratic Skepticism

A final characteristic of Strauss's reading of Plato concerns his novel interpretation of the Forms or Ideas. For most readers, the theory of Ideas constitutes "the basis for any adequate interpretation of the *Republic*."[50] It is the point of conjunction among Platonic politics, ethics, and metaphysics. To defenders of this view, the Ideas represent Plato's attempt to find some stable ground for our moral, political, even aesthetic standards of judgment that can withstand the corrosive blasts of skepticism, relativism, and subjectivism. On this view, the Ideas provide the ultimate ground of intelligibility without which the world would collapse into chaos. For critics, it was just Plato's search for some ultimate ground of certainty that led him to dangerously absolutist conclusions. The Ideas provide the metaphysical support for the closed, hierarchical, and illiberal society defended in the *Republic*. On this reading, the dangers of absolutism far outweigh those of skepticism. In either case, however, neither party doubts the priority of the theory of Ideas as constituting the essence of Platonism.

Strauss's Plato stands in stark contrast to the standard view for its notable silence on the doctrine of the Ideas and other ontological themes. In his commentary on the *Republic* in the *City and Man* only about two pages out of eighty-eight are devoted to the theme that occupies center stage in most other interpretations. When Strauss does confront this doctrine, he declares it to be "utterly incredible." The proposition that there are Ideas independent of their phenomenal manifestations, he says, "appears to be fantastic."[51] Without further explanation, he remarks that no one has ever yet been able to give a satisfactory account of this doctrine. This apparently dismissive attitude toward what is seen as Plato's most important legacy has met with a certain righteous indignation. "There is much talk in Straussian writings about the nature of 'the philosopher,'"

Burnyeat angrily retorts, "but no sign of any knowledge, from the inside, of what it is to be actively engaged in philosophy."[52]

This last statement is clearly false. While Strauss has turned his attention away from the metaphysical to the political side of Plato, the view that he avoids the larger philosophical themes is grossly exaggerated. What Strauss offers is a quite heterodox reading of what the doctrine of the Ideas means for Platonic thought. The Ideas cease to be self-subsistent metaphysical absolutes and become something like the "permanent problems" of philosophy. This open-ended view of the Ideas "departs markedly from that usually found in the mouth of Socrates in the Platonic writings," Richard Kennington observes. But this does not mean that the term is not used "with economy and precision."[53] What, then, is Strauss's new reading of the Platonic Ideas?

In *Natural Right and History* Strauss provides a reading of the Ideas consonant with his own understanding of philosophy "in its original Socratic sense," that is, knowledge of what we do not know or knowledge of the limits of knowledge. In answering the historicist claim that all thought is relative or specific to time and place, Strauss counters that "the fundamental problems, such as the problems of justice, persist or retain their identity in all historical change, however much they may be obscured by the temporary denial of their relevance or however variable or provisional all human solutions to these problems may be."[54] The Ideas are not a class of separate entities independent of human thought and experience, but are "the fundamental problems and, therewith, . . . the fundamental alternatives regarding their solution that are coeval with human thought."[55]

These reflections on the Platonic Ideas are amplified in Strauss's exchange with Alexandre Kojève in *On Tyranny*. Strauss contends here that "the only possible justification of philosophy" is "zetetic," or, he adds parenthetically, "skeptic in the original sense of the term."[56] Socratic skepticism—knowledge of one's own ignorance—provides a third way out of the sterile alternatives of dogmatism and relativism. In his most important passage devoted to his understanding of philosophy, Strauss writes:

> Philosophy as such is nothing but genuine awareness of the problems, i.e., of the fundamental and comprehensive problems. It is impossible to think about these problems without becoming inclined toward a solution, toward one or the other of the very few typical solutions. Yet as long as there is no wisdom but only quest for wisdom, the evidence of all solutions is necessarily smaller than the evidence of the problems.

Therefore the philosopher ceases to be a philosopher at the moment at which the "subjective certainty" of a solution becomes stronger than his awareness of the problematic character of that solution. At that moment the sectarian is born.[57]

In other words, what distinguishes the "philosopher" from the "sectarian" (or ideologist) is an awareness that there are certain permanent or fundamental problems that make up the natural horizon of being. Of course, one would scarcely be human if one did not feel a pull or attraction toward one solution and not others to the problem of, say, justice. The peculiar heroism of the philosopher consists in refusing to "succumb" to one or another of the various solutions and instead keeping alive an awareness of the problems as things that defy permanent solution. If philosophers are members of a sect, their sectarianism amounts to a refusal to consider anything other than the interests of philosophy, what Strauss calls "the highest interests of mankind."[58]

Strauss's interpretation of the Ideas as the fundamental problems has drawn relatively little notice and has even led some to believe that Strauss is uninterested in the traditional problems of philosophy. This is, I suspect, because of the extremely heterodox nature of his account of the Ideas. The mainstream of Platonic interpretation has historically grown out of Hellenistic and early Christian appropriations of Plato. What has been central to this tradition is Plato's severe two-world doctrine, his depreciation of the body and the senses as belonging to a corrupt and irredeemable material reality, and his Idea of the Good as an anticipation of the God of the New Testament. It was clearly this Plato who was taken up with a vengeance by Nietzsche and who makes an appearance in Heidegger's "Plato's Doctrine of Truth" as well as in the work of such recent commentators as Martha Nussbaum.[59]

The alternative to this Hellenistic and Christian Platonism is Strauss's skeptical or zetetic Plato, a Plato that also has deep roots in classical antiquity, but whose influence has been more muted. This Plato begins with Socrates' famous profession of ignorance in the Apology (23a). Crucial to this tradition of skeptical Platonism are not the various doctrines regarding such things as the immortality of the soul or the theory of knowledge as recollection, but the Socratic elenchus, the method of question and answer, the experience of aporia where beliefs once held dogmatically or unreflectively are shown to be less than satisfactory, and even the Platonic manner of writing dialogues as a way of stimulating discussion rather than stipulating answers.[60]

Strauss's Plato is skeptical not so much about the existence of the problems as about our ability to answer them. What ultimately connects this skeptical Plato with such medieval Platonists as Alfarabi and Maimonides is an awareness of the political context of philosophy and the problems for society posed by a consistent and radical skepticism. It is this awareness that led Strauss to regard Plato not just as a political, but as a politic writer who engaged in the "esoteric" strategy of giving to each of his interlocutors what is good for them while only faintly tipping his own hand.[61] What we can learn from Plato, then, is not a doctrine or set of doctrines, but the permanent situation of philosophy vis-à-vis society. How different writers choose to address this problem will vary over time and place, but that they must address it is a precondition for having anything to say at all. Strauss's Plato shows us, then, not only through the words, but through the deeds of his Socrates what philosophy is and what the obstacles are to its recovery.[62]

Strauss's reading of Plato still leaves many questions unanswered. He offers an interpretation of the Platonic Ideas as "fundamental problems," problems that are "coeval with humanity." Strauss mentions in passing such problems as the conflict between justice and necessity and between freedom and authority, and, most importantly, the "theologico-political problem," but there is relatively little discussion of what constitutes such a problem. What makes a fundamental problem fundamental? Can such problems ever be solved? and, if not, how does Strauss know that? Can new problems ever arise? These are questions raised but not settled by Strauss's analysis of the Platonic Ideas.

A further difficulty arises from Strauss's derivation of the Ideas or fundamental problems. Strauss's Plato is characterized above all by his turn away from the first principles of Being to the opinions or arguments that are said to be directly constitutive of political life. These opinions about such things as good and bad or about just and unjust are said to constitute the "natural horizon" of the citizen and the city. But how do we ascend from this natural or "common-sense" world of opinion and belief to an intuition of the truly fundamental and comprehensive problems?[63] To answer this question one would need to consider more closely the relation between what Heidegger calls the ontological and the ontic realms, between Being and beings, than Strauss seems willing to do. "Strauss's aversion to direct engagement with ontological questions," Ian Loadman writes, "leaves one unsatisfied with the result of the relation between zetetic thought and the problems."[64] The relation between the problems that are "fundamental and comprehensive" and the thought about those ideas is never fully satisfied.

What Is Platonic Liberalism?

It is an oddity of academic mythology that Strauss is viewed as a *bête noir* of liberalism. According to one critic, his writings carry the permanent stigmata of Catholic counter-Enlightenment figures like Joseph de Maistre and Carl Schmitt.[65] For others, he was a Nietzschean immoralist who only lacked the courage of his master to declare openly that God is dead.[66] And for still others his thought was driven by a hatred of the Enlightenment and all modern ideas coupled with a desire to sacralize the existing inequalities of the status quo.[67] How can so many be so wrong?

To be sure, some of the blame for these negative images must be laid at Strauss's door. There's no smoke without fire. Many of these assessments grew out of Strauss's penchant for presenting his recovery of Plato in terms of a gigantic struggle between the ancients and the moderns. Modern thought is understood as consisting of so many "waves," beginning with Machiavelli and Hobbes, who initiated the break with antiquity by self-consciously "lowering the standards" of natural right; the second wave was instituted by Rousseau and the German idealists and was finally completed by Nietzsche and Heidegger, the greatest thinker of the third wave, whose kind of "radical historicism" did most to prepare the way for the Holocaust and the other moral and political evils of the twentieth century. Except for those who perversely see him as a closet Nietzschean secretly celebrating these developments, Strauss has been conventionally understood as taking the side of Plato and the ancients against the moderns. Strauss often claimed to be doing no more than reopening the famous quarrel between the ancients and the moderns, but he frequently wrote as if the issue had been decided by him in favor of antiquity.[68]

Yet Strauss's alleged preference for ancient natural right, as something opposed to modernity, has sometimes been overstated even by him.[69] He often writes as if there is a vast chasm separating antiquity from modernity, but in more cautious moments he recognizes that this break has often been less than complete.[70] For instance, he describes his return to classical political philosophy as no more than "tentative and experimental" and denies that it can provide us with "recipes for today's use."[71] He cannot help but admit the way classical sources have insinuated themselves into and even inspired much of modernity. While acknowledging that only "we living today can possibly find a solution to the problems of today," Strauss goes on to affirm that "an adequate understanding of the principles as elaborated by the classics may be *the indispensable starting point* for an adequate analysis, achieved by us, of present day society."[72]

To describe either Strauss or Plato as any kind of liberal is, of course, deeply counterintuitive. One cannot find in any of their writings an unequivocal defense of such cherished liberal principles as individual rights or human equality. Nevertheless, Strauss typically described himself as a "friend" of liberal democracy who, precisely because he was a friend, did not permit himself to be a "flatterer."[73] Further, he claimed to find in the basic premises of ancient political philosophy new sources of support for liberal democracy rather than the reverse. "Liberal democracy," he wrote, "derives powerful support" from "the premodern thought of the Western tradition."[74] What he seems to be alluding to is the belief that liberal democracy shares with the ancient idea of the mixed regime a balance between the extremes of aristocracy and democracy, the rich and the poor. Liberal constitutional government is better able to balance the radical demands of the few and the many than any other that has yet been devised. Platonic liberalism bespeaks a Churchillian defense of democracy as the worst except for all the alternatives.

None of these views should be sufficient to characterize Strauss as a full-blown liberal, but they should allow us to begin to outline a defense of liberal democracy along Socratic-Platonic lines. First, the Platonic dialogues appeared to Strauss to exhibit the qualities of toleration, open-mindedness, and skepticism, all liberal values on anyone's reckoning. His reading of the ironic and *aporetic* character of the dialogues is fully in accord with no less an authority than John Stuart Mill, for whom "the title of Platonist belongs by far better right to those who have been nourished in, and have endeavored to practise Plato's method of investigation, than those who are distinguished only by the adoption of certain dogmatical conclusions."[75]

Platonic liberalism reveals an intensely skeptical cast of mind consonant with a free and inquiring spirit. In contrast to the standard view of Plato as a thinker driven by an overpowering (some might even say pathological) need for certainty, Strauss highlights the Platonic dialogue as the form of communication most consistent with the fundamentally indeterminate nature of Being. Strauss finds in the dialogue form just the kind of openness that liberalism has most admired. The doctrine of the Ideas is presented by Strauss not as a body of moral absolutes immune to criticism, but as a set of permanent questions or problems that each person must think through for themselves. Far from trying to insulate these ideas from criticism and the give-and-take of democratic deliberation, Strauss goes out of his way to make an awareness of the inadequate character of all human solutions essential to the problems themselves. There are no ultimate answers in the Straussian universe; rather, there is marked disagreement even among the greatest authorities over their answers to the fundamental problems. All that is required in facing these problems is an open mind and a willingness to listen and weigh the alternatives.

Second, in a little-noted passage Strauss gives greater prestige to the Platonic account of democracy than is conventionally done. The virtue of democracy is its ability to foster the greatest variety of ways of life, among which must be included the philosopher, who "can lead his peculiar way of life without being disturbed."[76] This regime is "sweet" because it affords people the political liberty to do as they like, thereby making possible Socrates and Socratic-style conversations. The *Republic* mentions specifically that only in a democracy can a discussion of the city and the various ways of life begin to take place (557d-e). Strauss even draws on Plato's *Seventh Letter* (324d), written after the destruction of Athenian democracy, as evidence that such a regime comes closer than any other to the Hesiodic "golden age." He wonders why Socrates did not assign it "the highest place among the inferior regimes" or even "the highest place simply," given its openness to philosophy.[77] Plato is said to have "deliberately exaggerated" the faults of democracy in order to moderate the excessive Athenian devotion to democracy. As a recent scholar said of Tocqueville: "To love democracy well, it is necessary to love it moderately."[78]

Contrary to a widespread perception, Strauss regards Plato as a support for, not an alternative to, liberal democracy. His sharp and sometimes misleading distinction between ancients and moderns is often refuted by a profound awareness that our fundamental experiences, if not necessarily our ruling ideas, are deeply indebted to classical political thought. His appeal to Plato and the ancients is often used as a part of an effort to prevent liberal democracy from degenerating into "mass democracy." By democracy in its original form he meant an aristocracy that has become universal, that is, a society where every person has had the benefit of a liberal education.[79] Democracy is an aristocracy of everybody. Liberal education represents the "counterpoison" to the corrupting effects of mass culture on democracy. It inculcates certain virtues, certain capacities of mind and heart, that are required if liberal democracy is to be viable in the long run. "Liberal education," Strauss avers, "is the ladder by which we try to ascend from mass democracy to democracy as it was originally meant."[80]

Platonic liberalism is characterized by skepticism toward utopianism and every form of political idealism, a view shared by such anti-utopian liberals as Judith Shklar and Isaiah Berlin.[81] Yet unlike many of his émigré colleagues, Strauss saw Plato as an important source of resistance to tyranny. Platonic liberalism is the regime most consonant with the partial, incomplete, and even contradictory nature of knowledge. Above all, Strauss agrees with such aristocratic liberals as Tocqueville and Mill that freedom of thought and opinion is currently endangered by the degeneration of liberal democracy into mass democracy.[82] It is not economic freedom, or equal rights, or democratic deliberation that most excites Strauss, although these are not goods to be despised. It is the freedom to philosophize that is his highest value. At a time when he saw independence of mind being either ruthlessly or subtly suppressed by the various collectivisms and group identities of the modern age, Strauss returned to Plato and his circle in order to discover "the elementary and unobtrusive conditions of human freedom."[83]

CHAPTER FIVE

Destruktion or Recovery?
On Strauss's Critique of Heidegger

One of the unknown young men in Husserl's entourage was Heidegger.
I attended his lecture course from time to time without understanding
a word, but sensed that he dealt with something of the utmost importance. . . . On my way home I visited [Franz] Rosenzweig and said to him
that compared to Heidegger, Max Weber, till then regarded by me as the
incarnation of the spirit of science and scholarship, was an orphan child.
— Leo Strauss, *"A Giving of Accounts"*

Introduction

Of his numerous legacies, Leo Strauss's influence on the study of German
philosophy frequently goes least mentioned. Apart from some early reviews
and other occasional pieces, Strauss left no major work on any German
thinker of note.[1] With the exception of the chapter on Max Weber in *Natural
Right and History* and a short essay on Nietzsche's *Beyond Good and Evil*
written near the end of his life, there are no works on such giants of the
German *Aufklärung* as Mendelssohn, Kant, and Hegel to rival his studies of
other seminal figures in the history of political thought.[2] Why, for example,
did Strauss not write a *Thoughts on Kant* to parallel his study of
Machiavelli, or *The Argument and Action of Hegel's "Philosophy of Right"*
to complement his commentary on the *Laws* of Plato, or *The Literary
Character of Nietzsche's "Zarathustra"* modeled after his essay on
Maimonides's *Guide of the Perplexed*? In any case for a thinker like Strauss
who has emphasized that what a person does not say is almost as important
as what he does, such a startling omission calls for comment.

The one partial exception to Strauss's generally curt treatment of
German philosophy is, of course, Martin Heidegger.[3] One could almost say

that Heidegger is the unnamed presence to whom or against whom all of Strauss's writings are directed. Strauss's acquaintance with Heidegger went back to the early 1920s. He described how upon hearing Heidegger in 1922, he slowly came to recognize that Heidegger was preparing a "revolution" in thought the likes of which had not been experienced since Hegel.[4] Heidegger brought to the study of philosophy a "passion" for the problems that showed up the "lostness" and emptiness of the then regnant academic orthodoxies, including that of his erstwhile dissertation adviser, the neo-Kantian philosopher Ernst Cassirer. The famous confrontation between Heidegger and Cassirer at Davos in 1929 confirmed this fact for anyone with "sensitivity to greatness."[5]

At the same time that Heidegger commanded Strauss's highest respect, he also elicited many of his sharpest criticisms. Heidegger accepted Nietzsche's proposition that human life and thought are radically historical. The meaning of Heidegger's "radical historicism" was not void of political consequences.[6] Heidegger was not the only thinker but certainly the greatest thinker to embrace Hitler's 1933 revolution. Since the publication of Victor Farias's *Heidegger and Nazism* in 1989 the now infamous "Heidegger problem" has become something of a public scandal.[7] Strauss pointed to this scandal long ago. "One is bound to misunderstand Heidegger's thought radically," he wrote, if one does not see its "intimate connection" to the events of 1933.[8] Heidegger may have surpassed all his contemporaries in terms of "speculative intelligence," yet he was "at the same time intellectually the counterpart to what Hitler was politically."[9] Indeed, Strauss notes that Heidegger, who had never praised any other contemporary political movement or leader, refused to repudiate National Socialism even long after Hitler had been "muted."[10]

It is one thing to trace the influence of Heidegger on Strauss, quite another to evaluate it. Does Strauss's confrontation with Heidegger provide the reader with a critical perspective on some of the problems of modernity not available to those operating within a more standard liberal democratic framework? Or does his appropriation of certain Heideggerian tropes lead to dangerous anti-liberal doctrines crucially at odds with modernity? The latter possibility has been argued at considerable length by the French critic Luc Ferry in his book *Rights—The New Quarrel between the Ancients and the Moderns*.[11] Here is the most impressive case to date alleging Strauss's indebtedness to Heidegger and bemoaning the political consequences of that debt.

The core of *The New Quarrel* is that Strauss took over wholesale Heidegger's critique of modernity, but turned it away from first philosophy or "fundamental ontology" and gave it a more directly political meaning. Ferry asserts boldly that Strauss's *"political* critique of modernity" is "fueled by" the "philosophical presuppositions" of Heideggerian phenomenology.[12] Strauss is said to have "almost literally transposed" Heidegger's "phenomenological deconstruction of metaphysical humanism" to the domain of political philosophy.[13] Ferry notes that unlike Heidegger, Strauss's critique of modernity did not inveigh against rationalism and as such did not lead to the invocation of a new *mythos.*[14] This qualification notwithstanding, Ferry maintains "undeniably" that Strauss's antimodernism is directed by the same "logic" that inspired Heidegger.[15]

The upshot of this "logic" is clear. "The political motivation for a return to classical thinking," Ferry says, "is deeply undemocratic."[16] Strauss's thinking is antidemocratic because it assumes that the political world mirrors or is an imitation of the natural order. Because classical political philosophy "in Strauss's sense" depends upon a teleological cosmology, it is said to follow that Strauss is committed to justifying a political hierarchy where individuals are "destined to occupy different hierarchical stations in the social body." Plato's *Republic* is called "the most striking example" of this point of view.[17] The idea that Strauss attempts to justify political inequality by reading it directly out of classical cosmology is of course palpably false. I will return to this issue later; however, if Strauss's reading of the *Republic* is vulnerable to criticism, it is for exactly the opposite reason—namely, that he minimizes, if not outright denies, the relation between ancient cosmology and political philosophy.

Ferry is not content to aver Strauss's antimodernism. *Natural Right and History,* he maintains, is "one of the most vigorous critiques of the very idea of human rights" ever written.[18] Conceiving human rights along the line of free "subjectivity," Ferry notes correctly that they are "a purely modern invention" with no analogue in the Greek world. Nevertheless Strauss's attack on the idea of rights is said to be consonant with "the neoconservative tendency to sacralize natural inequalities" both "in fact and in law within the social and political hierarchy."[19] Ferry concludes that one cannot be both a Straussian and a liberal without falling into logical "absurdity."[20]

It is not necessary to carry Ferry's critique of Strauss any further, much less to consider his own eccentric defense of modernity. I mention the work at all because it offers an analysis of Strauss's dependence on Heidegger deeply at odds with my own. While appropriating various Heideggerian problems and terminology, Strauss provides a far-reaching critique of Heidegger's antimodernity. To say, as Ferry does, that Strauss simply appro-

priated Heidegger's critique of metaphysical humanism and applied it to
the domain of politics is a non sequitur, for a main thread in Strauss's critique of Heideggerianism is its obliviousness to politics. To turn to the primacy of the political things is not to apply Heideggerian insights to some
new domain of being; it is the basis of Strauss's critique of Heidegger.

The Crisis of Contemporary Liberalism

To start with perhaps the most obvious point: both Heidegger and Strauss
begin their works with a sense of impending crisis or catastrophe.
Heidegger spoke ominously about a "darkening of the world" with its
attendant "enfeeblement of the spirit," while Strauss spoke about a "crisis
of the West" or a "crisis of our time" that he identifies with an encroach-
ing nihilism. How are we to understand these claims?

It is curious to note that despite their alleged similarities, Heidegger and
Strauss offer completely different diagnoses of the current problem. In the
Introduction to Metaphysics Heidegger explains the crisis by reference to
the unique historical situation of Germany. Germany, he claims, is caught
in a "pincers" between the world of Anglo-American democracy to the
west and Soviet communism to the east.[21] The German nation is subject to
"the severest pressure" and is accordingly "the most endangered." Given
these historical pressures, it remains to Germany, "the most metaphysical
of nations," to look inward in order "to wrest a destiny from . . . *within
itself"* (*es in sich selbst*).[22] Heidegger gives as yet no positive indication of
what this destiny will look like, but he gives some clues as to what it will
try to avoid. Heidegger draws on a century-old theme that contrasted
Anglo-French *civilisation* with German *Kultur*, but gives it a new twist.
Germany must resist the pull of modern urban, technological civilization.[23]
"From a metaphysical point of view," and for Heidegger there is no other,
"Russia and America are the same; the same dreary technological frenzy,
the same unrestricted organization of the average man."[24] It is the dominance of this kind of technological political order common to both democracy and communism that Heidegger regards as the root of "the spiritual
decline of the earth" (*der geistige Verfall der Erde*), "the flight of the gods"
(*die Flucht der Götter*), "the destruction of the earth" (*die Zerstörung der
Erde*), and the "hatred and suspicion of everything free and creative."[25]

Heidegger's answer to the problem of an incipient nihilism was, of
course, contained in his famous *Rektoratsrede* of 1933.[26] Whether
Heidegger's embrace of Hitler in this speech constituted a brief and unfortunate "episode" in his career or grew out of the deepest wellsprings of his

thought is a subject that is not likely to be resolved. We do know, however, that at that time National Socialism represented to him just such a third way, an alternative to the two metaphysically indistinct and technologically leveling movements of democracy and communism referred to in the *Introduction to Metaphysics*. Indeed, in the revised edition of the work published in 1953 Heidegger could still speak unabashedly of the "inner truth and greatness" of the Nazi movement, adding parenthetically that this referred to "the encounter between global technology and modern man."[27]

Contrast this attitude with Strauss's understanding of the crisis facing not Germany but liberal democracy. Strauss is less concerned with the problems created by liberal democracy than with those caused by its eclipse. Ferry's statement that *Natural Right and History* is a vigorous assault on "the very idea of human rights" is contradicted by Strauss's opening remarks. In the introduction to the book he begins with a quotation from the Declaration of Independence asserting the universality of equal human rights and warns his readers of the dangers attending the abandonment of this ideal. Without mentioning Heidegger by name, Strauss makes clear that he is troubled not so much by American egalitarianism as by the emergence of the German "historical sense" that today goes under the name of an "unqualified relativism." This would not be the first time in history, he warns his American audience, that a nation defeated on the battlefield had risen up posthumously, as it were, to deprive the victors of "the most sublime fruit of victory."[28] The crisis of the West, Strauss avers, is in the first instance a theoretical one created by the emergence of the German philosophy of history.

To gain critical purchase on this problem, consider Strauss's critique of Isaiah Berlin's famous "Two Concepts of Liberty," which he calls "a characteristic document of the crisis of liberalism."[29] Contrary to what Ferry and others might have us believe, Strauss is by no means an enemy of modern "negative liberty" as such. Unlike Heidegger, who in the *Rektoratsrede* spoke derisively of negative liberty as synonymous with "arbitrariness of intentions and inclination" and "lack of restraint" and celebrated its banishment from the German university, Strauss approves of Berlin's essay, calling it "very helpful for a political purpose" in the struggle against communist totalitarianism.[30]

While recognizing that Berlin's study may be useful for rallying anticommunists, Strauss finds it deficient as a theoretical defense of liberalism against its enemies. The crisis in which liberalism is currently embroiled is, however, not principally political but theoretical. The problem is not that of particular policies but of "the spirit that should inform particular policies."[31] In Strauss's view, Berlin claims to defend "absolutely" a sphere of private, individual liberty while at the same time denying that liberalism rests on any absolute premises and even endorsing the merely "relative validity" of this conviction. It is precisely this contradiction between a maximum defense of individual freedom and complete agnosticism about the foundations of liberty that Strauss finds symptomatic of the current crisis of liberalism. It is "the fact that liberalism has abandoned its absolutist basis" in the philosophy of natural rights "and is trying to become entirely relativistic" that is the cause of the crisis.[32] Not liberalism but a contemporary misunderstanding of liberalism is at the root of the crisis.

In another formulation of the same problem, Strauss contends that "the crisis of the West consists in the West's having become uncertain of its purpose." That purpose has been admirably contained in certain "famous official declarations made during the two World Wars," but more importantly in "the most successful forms of modern political philosophy."[33] These forms—and here Strauss seems to be pointing backward to the founders of modern liberalism—developed a conception of philosophy or science deeply at odds with the pre-modern tradition. The new philosophy would be "active and charitable," devoted to "the relief of man's estate." Rather than serving the interests of a tiny elite, it would enable all "to share in the advantages of society." The new idea of science would ensure progress toward a society extending the benefits of liberty and prosperity to the whole of humanity consisting of "a universal league of free and equal nations, each nation consisting of free and equal men and women."[34]

For Strauss, as we can see from this passage, it is not the crisis engendered by modern philosophy that is at issue, but the crisis engendered by the loss of confidence in it. This loss of confidence is again traceable to the powerful, even consuming influence of Nietzsche and Heidegger, who have made it possible to doubt the essential "humanity" of the West. This doubt or lack of confidence is more than a "strong but vague feeling." Rather, it has received the official sanction of much contemporary social science with its distinction between facts and values, the "is" and the "ought." This feeling, which to some extent explains "many forms of contemporary Western degradation," is at the core of the phenomenon known as nihilism, the condition that obtains when there is no longer believed to be a rational manner of distinguishing ways of life or forms of society.[35] It is the advent not of liberal democracy, but of the modern inability to defend it, that dictated Strauss's return to the classics.

Heidegger and the Problem of Being

Like Strauss, Heidegger's return to the Greeks was motivated by a desire to understand and ultimately overcome the problem of nihilism. This problem is rooted not in any particular moral, political, or even aesthetic mode of perception, but in the very question of Being (*Seinsfrage*). The question of Being, first raised profoundly in Plato's *Sophist*, is not concerned with a particular kind of being, but with the general ground or ordering of beings as such. More specifically, it is concerned with the question of the meaning that beings have and how those meanings are acquired. The inquiry, then, into the meaning of Being is not to be confused with moral philosophy or political science, but takes the forms of a "fundamental ontology" aimed at the very structure of human "being in the world" (*Dasein*).

The problem is that Plato's answer to the question of Being was so successful that it helped to induce a kind of forgetfulness or amnesia about the very question itself. His identification of "to be" with "to be always" established a way of thinking that has forever fixed the history of metaphysics or what Heidegger would later call the tradition of "onto-theology." In *Being and Time* and his later essay on "Plato's Doctrine of Truth," Heidegger demonstrated that the gulf between the sensible and the intelligible, the human and the divine, the thing and the thing-in-itself created a certain "forgetfulness of Being" (*Seinsvergessenheit*) that contains within it the seeds of nihilism.[36] What is more, Heidegger claims that this nihilism is the true fate and destiny of the Western metaphysical tradition. Far from being an aberration or one historical form of modern thought, nihilism has been the secret meaning of the West from Plato onward.

To be sure, Heidegger did not diagnose this problem out of disinterested or antiquarian research. Part of the attraction of *Being and Time* is its sheer bravado, the enormous sense of urgency and risk attending the most apparently abstract metaphysical problems. Hans-Georg Gadamer has noted that "the catchword with which Heidegger approached the tradition of metaphysics at that time was 'destruction'—destruction, above all, of the concepts with which modern philosophy operated."[37] His call for a destruction of metaphysics was offered as a key to our liberation from it.

Heidegger's call for a *Destruktion* of metaphysics was to be carried out in the first instance through a historical investigation into the question of Being. Historical investigation in *Being and Time* was intended not to provide a survey of classical issues or fundamental alternatives, but as a means of bringing to light the various "horizons" within which *Dasein* is interpreted.[38] It is the forgetfulness of the temporal structure of our being in the world that has led to the obscuring or concealment of the question of Being. Only when we see that *"Dasein's* Being finds its meaning in temporality" will we be able to break its hold on us.[39]

Today this hold takes the form of a metaphysical tradition that has become our "master" to such an extent that "it blocks our access to those primordial 'sources' from which the categories and concepts handed down to us have been in part quite genuinely drawn."[40] Heidegger's response to this blockage was to declare that historical analysis be "loosened up" and this "hardened tradition . . . be dissolved."[41] It thus becomes necessary "to *destroy* the traditional content of ancient ontology until we arrive at those primordial experiences in which we achieved our first ways of determining the nature of Being." Heidegger denies that the purpose of his call for a creative destruction is "to bury the past in nullity" (*Nichtigkeit:* nothingness), but the positive purpose it serves remains obscure.[42]

What Heidegger had called a destruction in *Being and Time* was only partially modified in his later works. His later call for an "overcoming" (*Überwindung*) of metaphysics signaled a "going beyond" that is both an acceptance and a deepening. Heidegger spoke of metaphysics in medical terms as a pain or wound that must be gotten over if the health of the patient is to be restored. Thus the *verwindung der Metaphysik* must be regarded as a convalescence in the sense of a *Krankheit verwinden* that is not simply forgotten or overcome, but remains with us like a scar after an operation. The task of the philosopher, then, is less that of a destroyer engaged in a perpetual wrestling match with the power of tradition than it is that of a wary physician or therapist trying to talk us out of some deeply held but long-repressed disorder.[43]

Strauss's Path of Return

Ferry and others are no doubt correct when they remind us that Strauss's return to the Greeks was decisively mediated by the example of Heidegger. Strauss himself admits that "by uprooting and not merely rejecting the tradition of philosophy," Heidegger "made it possible for the first time after many centuries . . . to see the roots of the tradition as they are."[44] The unintended consequence of Heidegger's "uprooting" of the tradition is that it opened up the possibility of "a genuine return to classical philosophy, to the philosophy of Plato and Aristotle."[45]

Heidegger's reading of such works as Aristotle's *Metaphysics* came as a profound revelation to those of Strauss's generation who had been taught to approach the ancients largely along the model of nineteenth-century

Entwicklungsgeschichte as practiced by Wilamowitz-Mollendorff and perfected by his student Werner Jaeger.[46] Heidegger changed all of this by teaching Plato, as had Nietzsche a generation earlier, not as an ancient precursor of modern *Wissenschaft* but as a living and vital contemporary. Consider the following passage from Hannah Arendt's recollections of Heidegger's pedagogy:

> It was technically decisive that, for instance, Plato was not talked about and his theory of Ideas expounded; rather for an entire semester a single dialogue was pursued and subjected to question step by step, until the time-honored doctrine had disappeared to make room for a set of problems of immediate and urgent relevance. Today this sounds quite familiar, because nowadays so many proceed in this way: but no one did so before Heidegger.[47]

Anyone familiar with Strauss's method of "close reading" cannot fail to notice a striking connection to Heidegger's focus on single texts with relatively little concern for developmental history or contextualist background.[48] Similarly, anyone who has pondered Strauss's preference for speaking about a thinker's "teaching" and his aversion to formal "systems" or "doctrines" will also discover a relation to Heidegger's concern for an autonomous domain of human praxis and judgment independent of the pretensions of transcendental philosophy. Yet these similarities mask real differences between Strauss and Heidegger. While Heidegger spoke uncompromisingly of the *Destruktion* of the Western metaphysics, Strauss referred continuously to a "recovery" and a "loving reinterpretation" of the past. These differences are more than merely rhetorical. In what, then, do they consist?

Strauss returned to the ancients not to discover the origins of modern nihilism, but to consider an alternative to it. While Heidegger saw in Plato's theory of the Forms and the Idea of the Good the first and fateful step toward metaphysical nihilism, Strauss turned to the classics, especially Plato's *Republic* and Aristotle's *Politics*, to provide an articulation of the "natural consciousness" or the "common sense" understanding prior to the emergence of philosophy and modern scientific method.[49] The dialogues of Plato as well as the works of his contemporaries (and near contemporaries) Thucydides, Xenophon, and Aristotle make possible a re-articulation of the natural phenomena that have become lost to us. In a particularly striking use of Platonic imagery Strauss speaks about the creation of an artificial pit even below the "natural cave" of our prescientific understanding, a cave beneath the cave, as it were.[50] For Strauss, Plato and the classics showed us first of all our way back to the cave with which philosophy must contend.[51] It is for the reconstruction of the prescientific consciousness and not any specific set of doctrines or systems that Strauss turned to Plato.

This understanding of Plato is very different from Heidegger's. Strauss desired a return to the classics not in order to destroy their conception of truth as "unconcealment" (aletheia), but in order, precisely, to preserve the phenomena. In what Seth Benardete has referred to as Strauss's "golden sentence"[52] we read: "The problem inherent in the surface of things, and only in the surface of things, is the heart of things."[53] In other words, the surface of things constitutes the life world, "the world in which we live and act," which today at least exists in contradistinction to "the world of science." The unnatural or artificial world we now inhabit has been shaped to such an extent that it has become virtually impossible to grasp the nature of the phenomena themselves.

Whereas Heidegger believed it possible to think our way back to the Lebenswelt through what was in fact an ontology of everyday life, Strauss thought that today historical studies are necessary to recapture a public world of pre-scientific meanings. We can no longer make our way back to the phenomena by an examination of the opinions and beliefs, the endoxa, of the world around us precisely because these opinions and beliefs have been partially manufactured by certain "artificial" or unnatural circumstances. Strauss's return to the ancients, then, is motivated by a desire "to grasp the natural world as a world that is radically prescientific or pre-philosophic," and this can only be done via information supplied by classical philosophy and "supplemented by considerations of the most elementary premises of the Bible."[54]

Strauss is fully aware of the objections raised to his project of restoring classical natural right. In particular we have seen Ferry accuse him of engaging in the reactionary project of trying to rehabilitate classical physics and metaphysics as the premise of his understanding of natural right. Since, it is alleged, the modern natural sciences have destroyed the viability of the universe understood as a teleologically ordered whole, Strauss's project necessarily fails. It is doomed to failure either because classical political philosophy is meaningless without its ancient metaphysical underpinnings or because efforts to revive classical cosmology are based on deep ignorance of the modern natural and social sciences.

This criticism misses the point. In Natural Right and History Strauss admits that the emergence of modern natural science has led to two rival conceptions of social inquiry. The first is that the new mechanical physics must be followed up by an equally non-teleological social science à la Hobbes. The other "typically modern" solution favored by certain modern-day Thomists is to establish a dualism between a non-teleological science of nature and a teleological understanding of man. Strauss finds neither of these alternatives adequate. The former is exposed to the "grave difficulties" of attempting to read human ends out of our desires and inclinations purely naturalistically conceived; the latter, while not subject to this criticism, still "presupposes a break with the comprehensive view of Aristotle as well as that of Thomas Aquinas himself." Strauss does not take sides in this contemporary debate, although he notes inconclusively that "an adequate solution to the problem of natural right cannot be found before this basic problem has been solved."[55]

Strauss addressed precisely this "basic problem" from a somewhat different angle in *What Is Political Philosophy*. Rather than posing the problem in terms of a stark either/or, Strauss maintains that classical political philosophy presupposes no specific cosmology or strong teleological commitments. What distinguishes classical political philosophy is its independence from any dogmatic physics or metaphysics. The crucial passage reads thus:

> Whatever the significance of modern natural science may be, it cannot affect our understanding of what is human in man. To understand man in the light of the whole means for modern natural science to understand man in the light of the subhuman. But in that light man as man is wholly unintelligible. Classical political philosophy viewed man in a different light.[56]

Strauss goes on to suggest that Socrates, the founder of classical natural right, was animated not by any cosmology, but by an awareness of the limits of knowledge or "the elusive character of the truth, of the whole." It is here that he restates the view that Socrates "viewed man in the light of the unchangeable ideas, i.e., of the fundamental and permanent problems. For to articulate the situation of man means to articulate man's openness to the whole. This understanding of the situation of man which includes, then, the quest for cosmology rather than a solution to the cosmological problem, was the foundation of classical political philosophy."[57]

Nowhere does Strauss suggest that the rehabilitation of classical natural right requires the restoration of ancient physics. Indeed, he goes to the opposite extreme of denying that one can infer any substantive moral and political conclusions from cosmology which "cannot affect our under-

standing of what is human in man." Strauss appears willing to accord classical natural right a considerable degree of autonomy apart from either
Platonic or Aristotelian metaphysics. Ancient cosmology seems to have
been at most a sufficient but not a necessary precondition for the emergence of natural right.[58]

Strauss describes his attempt to return to classical political philosophy
as necessarily "tentative" and "experimental."[59] While this return may
grow out of the current crisis of liberalism, we cannot expect to find in the
ancients answers to the questions of today. He emphatically denies the old
canard that he seeks to restore directly a "golden age" or a discredited cosmology. "We cannot reasonably expect that a fresh understanding of classical political philosophy will supply us with recipes for today's use."[60]
Instead the "relative success" of modern science and philosophy has created a society "wholly unknown" to the ancients. "Only we living today
can possibly find a solution to the problems of today," he avows. The point
of a return to the ancients is not to find "immediately applicable" answers
to current problems, but to gain clarity about the "starting point" that such
answers would have to address.[61]

The starting point or "principles" alluded to above are precisely the
premises embedded in common sense or the pre-scientific understanding
that have become lost or obscure. Interestingly, Strauss suggests that it is
precisely the crisis of the understanding created by modern relativism and
historicism that has at the same time created a unique vantage point from
which to recover these principles. By throwing all tradition into question,
Strauss even applauds historicism for contributing, if unwittingly, to a "genuine understanding of the political philosophies." Thus Strauss refers to "the
accidental advantage" accruing from the "shaking of all traditions" that has
made it possible "to understand in an untraditional or fresh manner what
was hitherto understood only in a traditional or derivative manner."[62]

Skeptical Liberalism

Strauss's return to the classics in order to preserve the surface of things only
points to a further and more decisive difference with Heidegger. For Strauss,
the natural understanding referred to above comes to light first and foremost as a moral and political understanding. What he calls the "inevitable
problem" of natural right is simply an extension of the common sense or
pre-scientific awareness.[63]

It is the moral and political character of natural right that makes it
absurd to charge Strauss with the simple translation of Heideggerian

insights into the domain of political theory. Heidegger had systematically and deliberately removed ethics from the center of philosophy. One can search in vain for the Heideggerian equivalent of the Aristotelian golden mean or the Kantian categorical imperative. Heidegger rejected ethics because he thought it was one more form of dogmatic rationalism, putting Being in the service of man and not the other way round. The return to the problem of natural right was not, then, an application of Heideggerian ideas, but a radical correction of the blindness of Heidegger to the moral and political dimensions of the human situation. An awareness of the primacy of the political is, above all, what distinguishes Strauss from Heidegger.[64]

Strauss's remarks on natural right make it abundantly clear that he is referring to certain fundamental experiences of right and wrong, just and unjust, that are inseparable from humanity. The two passages from the Hebrew Scripture he uses as an epigraph to *Natural Right and History* seem to be examples of precisely the pre-philosophic experience of natural right he is searching for.[65] Early in the book he refers to "those simple experiences of right and wrong which are at the bottom of the philosophic contention that there is a natural right."[66] Later in the same work he speaks of the "well-ordered or healthy soul" as "incomparably the most admirable human phenomenon" and goes on to suggest that "the rules circumscribing the general character of the good life" may therefore be called the "natural law."[67] The fact that we admire human excellence without reference to mercenary or utilitarian motives is for Strauss evidence that natural right cannot be reduced to materialistic or instrumental considerations.

Elsewhere in the context of his debate with the Hegelian philosopher Alexandre Kojève, Strauss alludes to the experience of natural right as a doctrine of limits and constraints. In contrast to the Hegelian belief that human beings are constituted by the need for recognition from others, Strauss avows what "every reasonably well-brought up child" is said to know, namely that one should not be blinded by the desire for recognition.[68] His summary is worth quoting:

> Syntheses effect miracles. Kojève's or Hegel's synthesis of classical and Biblical morality effects the miracle of producing an amazingly lax morality out of two moralities both of which made very strict demands on self-restraint. . . . Neither Biblical nor classical morality encourages all statesmen to try to extend their authority over all men in order to achieve universal recognition. . . . Both doctrines construct human society by starting from the untrue assumption that man as man is

thinkable as a being that lacks awareness of sacred restraints or as a being that is guided by nothing but a desire for recognition.[69]

Again in *Natural Right and History* Strauss attempts to derive natural right from the fact of human rationality. Rationality gives human beings a freedom of choice in their actions denied to any other species. But this rationality is accompanied by a "sense" that "the full and unrestrained exercise of that freedom is not right." Our freedom is, in our words, accompanied by a "sacred awe" or a "divination" that not everything is permissible. Strauss refers to this primeval sense of restraint or "awe-inspired fear" as equivalent to "man's natural conscience."[70]

Strauss's emphasis on the irreducibly political character of natural right constitutes his most significant disagreement with Heidegger. It follows, therefore, that political philosophy, not fundamental ontology, is the primary means of access to the human world.[71] A further consequence of this difference in perspective is that natural right is said to carry with it certain built-in limitations regarding the efficacy of human action. The standpoint of natural right, rather than demanding the establishment of the one absolutely best regime, culminates in Strauss's insight that the best regime is, for all intents and purposes, unrealizable and that one must know how to make the best out of less than desirable circumstances. Rather than demanding the restitution of the ancient polis or the Platonic *kallipolis*, he warns his readers against the attempt to mandate the best regime or the regime according to nature.

Strauss's teachings about natural right are inseparable from his skepticism about political utopianism and idealism. His expression "the limits of justice" has given rise to the view expressed by Ferry that he is no more than a "neoconservative" attempting to "sacralize" the status quo.[72] This is clearly an example of a critic wanting to have it both ways. Strauss cannot be both a Heideggerian phenomenologist devoted to the wholesale destruction of modernity and a conservative (neo- or otherwise) devoted to preserving existing inequalities "in fact and in law." To see Strauss simply as a conservative bent on defending inequalities of station is to miss the profoundly skeptical temper of his philosophical politics. His endorsement of liberal democracy as the best practicable regime was not only prudential (the best of a bad lot), but related to this skeptical turn of mind. Democracy is the practicably best regime because it makes the fewest epistemic demands on its citizens. It permits philosophy—understood as the Socratic investigation of alternatives—precisely because it does not insist on rigid adherence to dogma or orthodoxy. At the very least Strauss's skeptical defense of liberty gives the lie to the absurd charge that he was a dangerous enemy of democracy.[73]

Strauss's conception of the limits of politics grows out of a serious and principled conception of philosophy and not out of some desire to sanctify existing inequalities. Philosophy consists neither in propounding systems nor in extolling doctrines, but in an awareness of what Strauss calls "the fundamental and comprehensive problems." An awareness of the problems, more than a devotion to one of "the very few typical solutions," is what distinguishes the philosopher from the dogmatic adherents of both the Left and the Right. It is when the belief in the certainty of any solution comes to outweigh our awareness of the problematic status of the solution that the "sectarian is born." Strauss describes this conception of philosophy as "zetetic" or "skeptic in the original sense of the term."[74]

The skeptical disposition, the Socratic awareness that one does not know, is at the core of Strauss's conception of philosophy.[75] A skeptical awareness of the insufficiency of the solutions leads to a reconsideration of the various alternatives. Philosophy is nothing other than an openness to the alternatives, to the fundamental and comprehensive problems. Indeed, Strauss's reading of the *Republic* culminates in an interpretation of the famous Platonic Ideas not as self-subsistent metaphysical certainties (a claim he calls "incredible, not to say . . . fantastic"), but as the permanent problems that beset humanity.[76] It is precisely this sense that the problems resist permanent solution that led Strauss to an appreciation of the dangers inherent in political idealism and other forms of dogmatic certainty.[77]

Strauss's skeptical teaching argues for, rather than assumes, an appreciation of the limits of action and a knowledge of the fact that "evil cannot be eradicated and therefore one's expectations from politics must be moderate."[78] The teaching of natural right is so far from being an encouragement to revolutionary action that Strauss cautions us to limit our expectations to mitigating as far as possible "the evils which are inseparable from the human condition."[79] There are deep-seated reservations against any attempt to mandate or legislate natural right. While Heidegger carried his advocacy of "resolute" action to the point of extremism, Strauss continually enjoins a policy of moderation as the highest lesson of wisdom.[80]

Ultimately, because the natural condition is one of limits and restraints and not simply a set of open-ended possibilities, Strauss urges a recovery, not a destruction, of the tradition of political philosophy. While Heidegger regarded this tradition from Plato to Nietzsche as one of accumulated error culminating in technological nihilism, Strauss regards nihilism not as endemic to the tradition but as a relatively recent phenomenon. Consequently, rather than being a source of the problem, the tradition of philosophy contains the internal resources needed to provide alternatives. The alternative to nihilism is not the "overcoming" of metaphysics, but a return to our recollection of what is presupposed in metaphysics—namely, the experience of natural right.

"Only a God Can Save Us"

No thinker has done more than Heidegger to reawaken a sense of the holy or the divine. Strauss even admits that Heidegger's critique of metaphysics opens up the possibility of non-Western alternatives "one form" of which is the Bible.[81] Heidegger did not, however, return to biblical antiquity as the Ur-form of poetic mythos. Instead he accepted Nietzsche's verdict that God, or at least the God of Judeo-Christianity, is dead and devoted his later writings to hastening the arrival of new gods.[82]

In his post–Being and Time works Heidegger increasingly found in Hölderlin "the poet who points toward the future" and "who expects the god."[83] Hölderlin was to the Germans what Shakespeare was to the English and Homer was to the Greeks. The contemporary of Schelling and Hegel, Hölderlin was deeply troubled by what he perceived to be the end of the Greco-Christian era and the subsequent disenchantment of the world. For Hölderlin, it was not so much men who have lost belief in God as the gods who have deserted the world and gone into hiding ("Aber freund! wir kommen zu spät")[84] Worse, not only have the gods fled, but we moderns are scarcely aware of the loss.[85] The task of the poet who lives in an age of "destitution" is to awaken the sense of possibility that attends the flight of the gods. Heidegger interpreted poetry as preparing a new age of cultural renewal to be achieved through the redemptive power of art and the aesthetic. A state of spiritual destitution may pose grave dangers, but also great possibilities for cultural renewal and redemption. In this context he enjoyed quoting Hölderlin's "Patmos": "But where danger is, grows the saving power also."[86]

In the lectures he gave on Hölderlin during the 1930s Heidegger focused on Hölderlin's "Germania" for its mood of "sacred mourning" (heilege Trauer) at the loss of the gods.[87] Only by adopting an attitude of mourning or affliction for the loss of the gods can men be prepared to receive the "saving power." This saving power Heidegger identified unambiguously with a revivified German "homeland" (Heimat) free from the grip of technological nihilism. This new homeland would mark a different direction in the "path" of history and take the form of a "state rooted in the earth and historical space" (*Staatsgründers der Erde und dem geschichtlichen Raum*).[88] Later on, Heidegger denied that he had used the term "homeland" in a nationalistic or ideologically loaded way. In calling on his countrymen to find their homeland, he claimed not to be invoking the "egoism" of any particular nation. Rather, the homeland in question was a sense of "belongingness to the destiny of the West." The German's true homeland was a historical "nearness to Being."[89]

Heidegger's abandonment of philosophy in favor of a new *mythos* became ever more prominent in his last works. His earlier discussion of *Dasein* gave way to a new poetic of *Gelassenheit* or "letting be."[90] Rather than adopting an attitude of sternness or "resoluteness" as he had in *Being and Time*, in *Gelassenheit* he meant to signify non-interference or simply letting things take their course. This "turn" in Heidegger's thought is sometimes represented as an unspoken repudiation of his Nazi past. In fact it was not so much a repudiation of Nazism as the routinization of it. Nazism, along with communism and "Americanism," became merely one more form of modern thoughtlessness and the "forgetfulness of Being."[91] It was not the inhumanity of the National Socialist movement, but the fact that it remained rooted in Western "humanism" that accounted for its failure to get to the root of "the encounter between global technology and modern man."[92]

The lesson of the Nazi experience, then, showed Heidegger the futility of action in a world dominated by global technology. It is "the planetary movement of modern technology," he told an interviewer in *Der Spiegel* in 1966, as a "history-determining" force that can today scarcely be "overestimated."[93] Political remedies such as democracy, constitutional guarantees of human rights, and so on are but palliatives, "half-way measures" that provide no real confrontation with the world of technology. Heidegger's alternative to the purely functional universe was a new *Bodenständigkeit* or rootedness. "Everything essential and great has only emerged when human beings had a home and were rooted in a tradition," he said.[94] To restore some kind of authentic tradition in a community or a common "destiny" was a constant of Heidegger's thought from *Being and Time* onward.

Heidegger's belated response to the atrocities of the Holocaust was to urge a withdrawal from public life and to adopt an attitude of patient resignation. Instead of attempting to direct or influence action—much less atone for the past—one should prepare for an as yet undisclosed theological dispensation:

Philosophy will not be able to bring about a direct change of the present state of the world. This is true not only of philosophy but of all purely human mediations and endeavors. Only a god can still save us (*Nur noch ein Gott kann uns rennen*). I think the only possible salvation left to us is to prepare readiness, through thinking and poetry, for the appearance of the god, or for the absence of the god during the decline; so that we do not, simply put, die meaningless deaths, but that when we decline, we decline in the face of the absent god.[95]

It was clear that in this context he meant not some personal deity, but rather a new and mysterious revelation of Being that we can do nothing to bring about but for which we must be prepared to wait.

Liberalism without Illusions

Instead of waiting for new gods, Strauss speaks of the "theologico-political problem," a term borrowed from Spinoza that he uses to underscore the relationship between the claims of reason and of revelation. At its simplest level, the theologico-political problem concerns "the all-important question" *quid sit deus*.[96] This question, Strauss claimed, remained "*the* theme" of all his later investigations.[97]

As the expression "theologico-political" implies, the question of God or the gods initially comes to light in relation to the city. Theology is in the first instance political theology.[98] By political theology Strauss understands a teaching whose authority is derived from divine revelation. Religion presents itself in the form of a body of authoritative law whose bringer or interpreter is a "prophet."[99] The task of the prophet, like the Socratic philosopher-king, is fundamentally legislative, the founding of a political community.[100] For this reason, every society, insofar as it is a political society, is based on religion and requires a belief in the sacred or divine character of its laws.[101]

A belief in the divine origin of law is one of those prephilosophic insights that for Strauss is certified by the virtually universal experience of mankind. It is only at specific times and places that this belief comes into conflict with philosophy. At times he suggests that religion is "radically distinct" from philosophy or, to paraphrase his lecture of the same name, that Jerusalem and Athens are founded on fundamentally different principles.[102] Philosophy or the Socratic life is based on the endless quest for knowledge regarding "the whole," whereas biblical thought stresses the ultimate subservience of human reason to revealed law. Philosophy and the

Bible are presented here as "two antagonists" locked in a kind of life-and-death struggle regarding the one right way to live.

Elsewhere Strauss presents the relation between philosophy and religion less as mutually antagonistic than as engaged in a more subtle, even dialectical "tension" with one another. Despite their radically different premises, theology and philosophy are far from incompatible in the manner Strauss sometimes suggests. First, the Bible, along with Plato, remains the most important source we have of the prephilosophic experience of natural right. The belief that God or the gods are in some sense "first for us" and that consequently the city is subordinate to a divine or revealed legislation constitutes the original form of the political self-understanding.[103] Second, at least among the ancient and medieval philosophers there is broad agreement about the necessity of religion for the maintenance of a sound or decent political order. Indeed, premodern writers often developed elaborate esoteric strategies of communication precisely to conceal their atheism—for purposes of self-protection, of course, but more importantly for the health of society.[104]

Finally, Strauss denies that philosophy has or perhaps ever can refute the premises of the Bible. He denies, for example, that modern science and historical criticism has even refuted "the most fundamentalistic orthodoxy."[105] The quarrel between the Enlightenment and biblical orthodoxy has resulted in a standoff where neither party has been able to subdue the other. Strauss comes close to arguing that orthodoxy is in fact impervious to falsification from either experience or the principles of logic. The "genuine refutation" of orthodoxy would require proof that "the world and human life are perfectly intelligible without the assumption of a mysterious God."[106] Strauss doubts that such a proof is forthcoming. Even Spinoza's *Ethics*, the most thoroughgoing attempt to replace the biblical God with modern materialist physics, has failed to show that we are both theoretically and practically the master of our fate. The "cognitive status" of Spinoza's works, to say nothing of all the rationalist explanations that followed, is that they are no different from the orthodox account—that is to say, they remain "fundamentally hypothetical."[107]

Some believe that Strauss's defense of orthodoxy against the Enlightenment constitutes decisive evidence for his radical antimodernism and that his arguments about the political character of religion testify to an antidemocratic elitism. Contrary to the charge of antimodernism, note that Strauss never defends the truth of orthodoxy; he only denies the adequacy of the philosophies that have claimed to refute it. But to say that orthodoxy has not been refuted is by no means to say that it is true or defensible.

Indeed, in his discussion of Franz Rosenzweig's *Star of Redemption* Strauss explicitly points out the dangers and difficulties of trying to reoccupy orthodoxy in the modern world.[108] In another context he warns that every modern attempt to return to an earlier position has only led to "a much more radical form of modernity."[109]

Strauss's warnings are consistent with the skeptical disposition described earlier. His radical "fideism" prevented a final resolution of the ancient quarrel between faith and reason.[110] Because philosophy and religion are incapable of refuting one another, we must remain open or attentive to the arguments embodied in each. The tension between biblical and Greek philosophic understandings has, moreover, been the "core" of the West and "the secret of [its] vitality."[111] Strauss is committed to maintaining the creative "tension" between Jerusalem and Athens rather than providing a final dispositive argument in favor of one of the contestants.

Further, in opposition to Ferry's claim that Strauss's motives were "deeply antidemocratic," Strauss always considered modern liberal democracy with its constitutional separation of state and society the best practicable solution to the theologico-political problem. Far from demonstrating that the linkage of the terms "Straussian" and "liberal" is absurd, I would call Strauss's politics a liberalism without illusions. As a secular Jew, Strauss believed the liberal solution to the theologico-political problem offered Jews a greater degree of freedom and security than was afforded by any other solution. But while Strauss may have embraced this solution as the best practicable one, his endorsement was not unqualified. The constitutional separation of state and society required that religion be depoliticized and confined to the precincts of individual conscience and intellectual persuasion, as had been argued forcefully in Locke's *Letter on Toleration* and Mendelssohn's *Jerusalem*. Yet the separation of religion and politics did not put an end to discrimination; it merely privatized it. The danger of liberal democracy for the Jews was not so much its inability to end social inequality as its creation of "the illusory surrogate of trust in the humanity of civilization."[112] It was precisely this illusion that proved fatal to European Jewry.

Strauss's cautious embrace of the liberal separation of state and society extended also to his endorsement of political Zionism. The state of Israel is "literally beyond praise" and "the only bright spot for the contemporary Jew who knows where he comes from."[113] But even Zionism, with its creation of a modern, secular state, remains an imperfect solution to the Jewish Question. The establishment of the Israeli state may be "the most profound modification of the Galut which has occurred . . . but it is not the end of the Galut" and may in fact be part of the Galut.[114] "Finite, relative problems can be solved," Strauss says, "infinite, absolute problems cannot be solved." As a result "human beings will never create a society which is free from contradictions."[115] In other words, the inability of Zionism to solve the Jewish Question, to put an end to the exile and fulfill the promise of redemption, remains vivid testimony to the permanence of the theologico-political problem.

Strauss's answer to the permanence of the theologico-political problem, then, is not to reconcile, flatten out, or synthesize but to keep alive the contradictory demands made by Jerusalem and Athens. Just as he refused to succumb to the "ire" of those who proclaimed the death of God, so too did he resist the lure of those who promised the creation of new ones. His solution is a kind of unflinching avoidance of two powerful but equally dangerous "charms":

> Men are constantly attracted and deluded by two opposite charms: the charm of competence which is engendered by mathematics and everything akin to mathematics, and the charm of humble awe, which is engendered by meditation on the human soul and its experiences. Philosophy is characterized by the gentle, if firm, refusal to succumb to either charm.[116]

If the Enlightenment in all its varieties represents the charm of competence, Heideggerian *Bodenständigkeit* represented perhaps the more seductive charm of "humble awe."

The Primacy of Political Philosophy

In the final analysis I suggest that Heidegger represented for Strauss an enigma that he never fully resolved. Heidegger's influence on Strauss is incontrovertible down to and including the titles of their two most important works: *Being and Time* and *Natural Right and History*. For Strauss, Heidegger was "the only great thinker in our time" and the "highest self-consciousness" of modern thought.[117] There is today virtually no philosophy apart from Heidegger's. By comparison to Heidegger, "all rational liberal philosophic positions have lost their significance and power."[118] Strauss admits that he may "deplore" this fact, but he cannot bring himself to overlook or ignore it. It will take "a very great effort" to restore "a solid basis for rational liberalism."[119] Liberalism will require a thinker of the stature of Heidegger, but as yet no such thinker has emerged. Instead, the only great or serious thinker of our age was a Nazi, and not merely an unreflective participant, but a willing collaborator in radical evil. What is more, Heidegger's collaboration was, for Strauss, not merely an unfortunate "episode" in an otherwise unblemished life, but intimately connected to his philosophy. How, then, to explain this fact?

Strauss offers two not necessarily consistent or even fully satisfactory answers. At times he maintains that Heidegger's embrace of National Socialism was compelled by his radical historicism. Like Heidegger's student Karl Löwith, Strauss maintains that Heidegger's "renunciation of the very notion of eternity" is bound up with his "submission" to the events of 1933.[120] The result of this renunciation was a deferral to a historical fate or destiny that made "discredited democracy [i.e., Weimar] look like the golden age."[121] It was his contempt for "those permanent characteristics of humanity" that led Heidegger to submit to and even endorse "the verdict of the least wise and least moderate part of his nation while it was in its least wise and least moderate mood."[122]

But is it correct to conclude that the ideas of *Being and Time* are intimately connected to the ideology of National Socialism? Is it not more accurate to say that while Heidegger's thought did not compel surrender to the events of 1933, it provided no principled grounds for resistance to it?[123] It seems that Heidegger's account of historical *Dasein* is at most contingently related to his political choices. The problem with Heidegger's philosophy is not that it is intimately tied to any particular politics, but that it is almost infinitely elastic, capable of adapting itself opportunistically to whatever permutation of *Dasein* happens to come next.

Imagine, for example, the following scenario. Had Hitler come to power in Russia and Lenin and the Bolsheviks in Germany, there is no reason to believe that Heidegger could not have just as consistently become a member of the Communist Party. Under different circumstances, it is just as easy to imagine him arguing that Marxism-Leninism is the authentic fate and destiny of the German nation, which must be defended against Anglo-American democracy and Russian Nazism. One can almost hear Heidegger saying in a hypothetical moment of self-criticism that Stalin's purges and policies of forced collectivization were themselves the result of a misplaced "humanism" with its desire to make man the master and possessor of earth.[124] Indeed, Heidegger's politics, such as they are, have proved remarkably susceptible to manipulation for different ends. Segments of the postwar Left had no difficulty turning his strictures against the dominance of global technology into a critique of capitalist society, and more recently environmentalists have found in his analysis of productionist metaphysics an argument for "green" politics and "deep ecology."[125]

At another point, Strauss suggests that not historicism as such, but Heidegger's virtually exclusive concern with Being blinded him to the real facts of tyranny. His subordination of political philosophy to fundamental ontology created its own forms of moral blindness. It was Heidegger's own curious "forgetfulness" of politics and the primacy of political philosophy that led him to minimize, if not deny altogether, the atrocities of the Holocaust. For Heidegger, the Holocaust remained fundamentally a consequence of technology, not a moral and political problem.[126]

It was Heidegger's indifference to moral phenomena that Strauss ultimately finds inexcusable. In the final sentence of his reply to Kojève (at last fully restored to the English edition), Strauss attacks Heidegger for moral cowardice in the face of tyranny and for lacking the courage to face the consequences of his own philosophy. Here Strauss makes common cause with Kojève for their close attention to the primacy of the political:

> But we have always been constantly mindful of it [i.e., the relation between tyranny and philosophy]. For we both apparently turned away from Being to Tyranny because we have seen that those who lack the courage to face the issue of Tyranny, who, therefore *et humiliter serviebant et superbe dominabantur*, were forced to evade the issue of Being as well, precisely because they did nothing but talk of Being.[127]

Strauss seems to suggest here that it was Heidegger's concern for Being, rather than beings, that led to his indifference to the fact of tyranny. At issue is the very abstractness of Heidegger's articulation of the problem of Being. The extreme artificiality of regarding human beings under the rubric of an anonymous historical *Dasein* could not but anesthetize him to the fate and suffering of actual historical persons. I am not finally convinced that Heidegger's Nazi problem is intimately connected to his analysis of Being, but Strauss's critique enables us to see the high price of Heidegger's forgetfulness of the political.

CHAPTER SIX

Tyranny Ancient and Modern

The tyrant stood at the pinnacle of his power. The contrast between the indomitable and magnanimous statesman and the insane tyrant—this spectacle in its great simplicity was one of the greatest lessons which men can learn, at any time. — *Strauss on hearing of the death of Churchill, January 25, 1965*

Introduction

Leo Strauss's *On Tyranny* was not only his first book written in English; it was his first book written in the United States.[1] The original edition was a mere ninety-four pages plus notes and carried a forward by Alvin Johnson, an economist and the president of the New School for Social Research, where Strauss had taught since 1938.[2] For those interested in such matters, the original edition was dedicated to "CWM"—Clara W. Mayer, the Dean of the Faculty of the New School—and was the last work of Strauss's to carry a dedication. For reasons that are unclear, both Strauss's dedication and Johnson's charming introduction ("On Xenophon and Dr. Strauss") were dropped from the later editions. The brevity of the work is readily understandable. It takes the form of a commentary on Xenophon's dialogue *Hiero or Tyrranicus*, a work that runs to a mere twenty-five pages in Marchant's Greek edition.

The publication history of *On Tyranny* has certainly contributed to the book's continued fascination. The book appeared initially in 1948 unadorned by anything but Strauss's commentary. A French edition under the title *De la tyrannie* appeared in 1954.[3] By this time it included a lengthy critique by the French Hegelian philosopher Alexandre Kojève under the title "L'action politique des philosophes" and a "Restatement" (Mise au

Point) by Strauss responding to Kojève's critique. It was in this form that the book was issued in English in 1963, although by this time it had acquired also a translation of Xenophon's *Hiero*.[4] Almost thirty years later, the work reappeared in a new edition with revised translations and including the collected correspondence between Strauss and Kojève that spanned the years 1932 to 1965. The original edition of less than one hundred pages had morphed into a considerable text of more than three hundred.[5]

On Tyranny was not only the first book by Strauss written in English, it was, so to speak, the first "Straussian" book. Up to that time, Strauss had published three works—*Die Religionskritik Spinozas* (1930), *Philosophie und Gesetz* (1935), and *The Political Philosophy of Hobbes* (1936)—that had been translated from the German. All of these books fall under the genre of what one might call conventional or traditional history of philosophy. They belong to the period Allan Bloom called "the pre-Straussian Strauss."[6] It was only during the late 1930s and the 1940s, after his relocation in America, that Strauss began to discover those themes that would become the earmark of his mature work. *On Tyranny* was the first work to develop such characteristically Straussian themes as the quarrel between the ancients and the moderns, the esoteric-exoteric distinction or what he would later call "a forgotten kind of writing," the contrast between the life devoted to action and the philosophical life, and even the "theologico-political" problem. It constitutes, as it were, Strauss's *Grundrisse*, the work from which all the later themes and ideas follow.[7]

The Title and Its Setting

Strauss opens his book on an apologetic note: "It is proper that I should indicate my reasons for submitting a detailed analysis of a forgotten dialogue on tyranny to the consideration of political scientists."[8] The setting of this book and Strauss's reasons for submitting it is the immediate aftermath of World War II and the onset of the cold war. Strauss's interest in what he calls this "forgotten dialogue" arises from the light it sheds on the present, on the problem of twentieth-century tyranny.

On Tyranny did not arise in a vacuum. It appeared as political scientists were trying to make sense of the experiences of total war and the rise of collectivist tyrannies in both Hitler's Germany and Stalin's Russia. Strauss's book was published originally shortly after Horkheimer and Adorno's famous analysis of the rise of fascism in *The Dialectic of Enlightenment*. It appeared before a wave of books on similar themes, such as Karl Popper's *The Open Society and Its Enemies* (1950), Hannah

Arendt's *The Origins of Totalitarianism* (1951), and Raymond Aron's *Democracy and Totalitarianism* (1965). Strauss's thesis was that modern terms such as fascism, totalitarianism, dictatorship, "Caesarism," and the like all failed to grasp the rudimentary phenomenon of tyranny. In order to grasp this phenomenon in its original or classic form, it is necessary to return to Xenophon's dialogue, the only work of ancient political philosophy devoted entirely to the theme of tyranny.

The failure of studies like the above is indicative of the failure of modern social science to address the fundamental problem of tyranny. Phenomena like communism and fascism are simply species of the genus of tyranny, not new or independent phenomena. At the core of Strauss's analysis is an indictment of modern social or political science: "A social science that cannot speak of tyranny with the same confidence with which medicine speaks, for example, of cancer, cannot understand social phenomena for what they are. It is therefore not scientific" (177). To understand tyranny in its modern form, it is necessary to consider it in its classic form or at least to consider the classical literature on tyranny, of which Xenophon's *Hiero* provides the most "comprehensive analysis."

Note that Strauss is not saying that a reading of the classics is sufficient for an understanding of modern tyranny. There is an "essential difference" between ancient and modern tyranny. Modern tyranny is said to have "surpassed the boldest imagination of the most powerful thinkers of the past" (23). Present-day tyranny is based on present-day philosophy: no modern philosophy, no modern tyranny. In particular, modern philosophy presupposes the existence of science and technology as well as mass ideology. By this Strauss means a conception of science as devoted to the "conquest of nature" imagined initially by early modern thinkers like Descartes and Bacon. Neither Bacon nor Descartes per se gave rise to modern tyranny; rather, it was the popularization and diffusion of the new philosophy that created previously unimagined forms of social domination and control. Strauss even suggests at one point that the possibility of such a universal science was considered by the ancients, but rejected by them as "unnatural" (178).

The specific difference between ancient and modern tyranny was inaugurated not by Bacon or Descartes, but by Machiavelli. *On Tyranny* is the first work where Strauss attributes to Machiavelli this "epoch-making change" in orientation, a change that would only be fully explored a decade later in his *Thoughts on Machiavelli*. Here for the first time, though, Strauss identifies Machiavelli as the *fons et origo* of modernity out of which all the later developments in the social sciences have arisen. What was it, exactly, that Machiavelli achieved?

Strauss's answer is unsatisfyingly brief. Machiavelli's *Prince* stands in fundamental opposition to all the previous "mirror of princes" literature due to its "deliberate indifference to the distinction between king and tyrant" (24). One cannot begin to understand modern tyranny for what it is unless and until one carries out a systematic contrast between the *Prince* and Xenophon's *Education of Cyrus*, the only work on princes that Machiavelli "stoops to mention" and "the fountainhead" of the entire genre. While the *Education of Cyrus* is devoted to "the perfect king," the *Prince* is what one might call deliberately value-neutral.

The differences between Machiavelli and the classical teaching are not exhausted by their views on kingship and tyranny. In his reply to Eric Voegelin's review of *On Tyranny* Strauss alludes to a difference that would later become key to his reading of Machiavelli. Machiavelli's longing for Roman *virtù* is said to be "the reverse side of his rejection of classical political philosophy" (184). In other words, Machiavelli seeks to restore republican virtue on foundations laid by modern philosophy. The modern philosophy of which Machiavelli was in part the creator differs from the ancients regarding his views on "the perfection of the nature of man": "The abandonment of the contemplative ideal leads to a radical change in the character of wisdom: Machiavellian wisdom has no necessary connection with moderation" (184). It is Machiavelli's abandonment of the classical notion of the philosophical life, not any particular teaching about kingship, that appears to constitute the fundamental contrast between ancient and modern perspectives. All virtue is for Machiavelli political virtue. An independent philosophical perspective drops out of the picture.

This is not the end of the matter. One might expect *On Tyranny* to be a stylized contrast between the ancient account of perfect kingship and the modern form of absolute tyranny. But this is not the case at all. After having established the distinction, Strauss then goes on to complicate it. The *Hiero* is hardly a book about perfect kingship. It is a book about the perfect or ideal tyranny. In it a poet is shown giving advice to a tyrant on how to make his tyranny more secure. Hence, "the teaching of that dialogue comes as near to the teaching of the *Prince* as the teaching of any Socratic could possibly come" (24). "The *Hiero*," Strauss concludes, "marks the point of closest contact between premodern and modern political science" (25).

Nevertheless, this "point of closest contact" only serves to reveal certain fundamental differences between the ancients and the moderns. In a footnote to the above passage Strauss clarifies his meaning as follows. Classical political philosophy took its bearings from the perfection of man and hence culminated in a teaching about the best regime that was held to depend largely on chance. Machiavelli, by contrast, took his point of departure from how man actually lives ("the effectual truth of things") and therefore devoted himself to the elimination of chance or *fortuna* as a controlling factor in life. The result was not just a "lowering of the standards of political life," but a belief that the "ideal" could be brought about through worldly action, that is, through "history" (106). It is Strauss's effort to restore something like the classical understanding of the relation between the real and the ideal, the "is" and the "ought," that sets the stage for the debate between him and Kojève that was to follow.

Strauss and Xenophon

A remarkable but little-noted feature of *On Tyranny* is that it inaugurated a lively and often heated debate about the nature of modernity by means of a commentary on a minor dialogue by an author, Xenophon, who had come to be considered by contemporary scholarship as a lightweight. What Strauss referred to as no more than the "temporary eclipse" of Xenophon as a writer of the highest order is due in part to a temporary eclipse of our understanding of the role of rhetoric, especially Socratic rhetoric, of which Xenophon was both student and practitioner. Accordingly, Strauss pays elaborate attention to the characters, the setting, and the action of the *Hiero*.

The text begins with Simonides, a poet and "wise man," paying a visit to the court of Hiero, the tyrant of Syracuse. The reasons for his visit are not indicated by Xenophon, but finding themselves "at leisure" Simonides uses the occasion to press Hiero on the distinction between the tyrannical and the private life. Simonides appears eager to discover the respective merits of the two ways of life from Hiero, who was once a private person but who rose to political power. Each character has reason to fear the other, Simonides because of the jealousy evinced by those who are wise or reputed to be wise and Hiero because of the power over life and death commanded by the tyrant ("The fate of Socrates must be presumed always to have been present to Xenophon's mind"—42).

The first and by far the larger part of the dialogue (sections 1–7) is given over to Hiero listing his complaints about the disadvantages of the tyrant's way of life. This sounds to some degree like the joke about the boy who kills his parents and pleads for lenience on the grounds that he is now an orphan. The principle drawback to the tyrannical life, Hiero avers, is that the greatest goods, namely love and honor, cannot be truly enjoyed because they are always tinged with an admixture of fear and compulsion. The tyrant can never be sure he is being loved or honored for himself alone and not out of either fear of or desire for his power.

Hiero seems to condemn tyranny not because it is unjust, but because it is self-defeating. What Strauss calls the "vulgar opinion" regarding tyranny, that it is bad for the city but good for the tyrant, is shown by Hiero to be false. Tyranny is not only bad for the city, but even bad for the person who exercises it (40). When asked the obvious question—why, if the tyrannical life is so bad, does he not just give it up?—Hiero answers conveniently that he could never atone for all the crimes and injustices that allowed him to acquire power in the first place (15, 57).

The second and by far the shorter part of the dialogue (sections 8–11) consists of Simonides advising Hiero on how to make his tyranny more moderate and thus how the tyrant may be more truly loved. If tyranny is defined as one-man rule over unwilling subjects without the benefit of law, Simonides's burden is to show how this can be transformed into one-man rule over willing subjects without law (68–69). Simonides's picture of the ideal or reformed tyranny sounds suspiciously similar to Plato's formulation of a philosopher-king and has roughly the same chance of realization. Simonides proposes a system of rewards and prizes in the fields of agriculture and commerce that will help to turn Hiero into a beneficent tyrant. Rather than condemning tyranny outright, Simonides finds ways of reforming it in order to make the tyrant's life more satisfying. Even though Strauss believed that the prospects for such a reformed tyranny were slim at best, especially among the Greeks who always identified freedom with the rule of law, the dialogue as a whole is said to reveal "a most forceful expression of the problem of law and legitimacy" (76).

Strauss claims that Simonides's praise of tyranny is in large part rhetorical. The interplay between the two main interlocutors in the dialogue shows that Hiero has reasons for being fearful or skeptical of Simonides's intention. He regards the poet (correctly, Strauss believes) as a competitor for power and influence (43–44). Hence Hiero's long list of complaints about the disadvantages of the tyrannical life is intended to discourage Simonides from setting himself up as a potential rival. At the same time Simonides must show himself to be an ally, not a rival, of Hiero. His praise of tyranny and his proposals for its reform are intended as a means of gaining the confidence of the tyrant in order to press home his real point.

The fundamental teaching of the dialogue is said to be not about the reform of tyranny at all, but about the contrast between the two ways of life represented by the two interlocutors, the political life and the philosophic life, although Strauss admits that this question "does not receive a final and explicit answer" (79). The difference comes down to this: both Hiero and Simonides are driven by a desire for honor as the virtue most characteristic of a "real man" ("no human pleasure seems to be superior to the pleasure deriving from honor"—81). The difference between them is how they conceive this term. Hiero, the political man, desires above all the honor or recognition of his subjects. His desire is essentially demotic; it extends across all classes and boundaries of the city. Simonides, by contrast, desires no such thing. The admiration and friendship of the wise, of the superior few, is all he desires. It is on this basis that Strauss asserts that "the wise man alone is free" (84).

The superiority of the philosophic life derives from its independence from the opinion of others. While the tyrant or statesman is forced to distinguish between citizen and non-citizen and must consider "a streak of cruelty . . . an essential element" of ruling, the philosopher to some degree stands above politics and is incapable of harming anyone. Most importantly, only wisdom is truly self-sufficient because the philosopher is said to serve only himself:

> More precisely: the specific function of the ruler is to be beneficent; he is essentially a benefactor; the specific function of the wise man is to understand; he is a benefactor only accidentally. The wise man is as self-sufficient as is humanly possible; the admiration which he gains is essentially a tribute to his perfection, and not a reward for any services. (90)

The question left hanging by the end of the commentary is why Strauss devotes an entire book intended to lay bare the roots of modern tyranny to the examination of an ancient work that appears to conclude with the praise of "beneficent" tyranny. This hardly seems like condemnation, much less like identifying a political cancer for what it is. One wonders whether Hitler and Stalin could have been so reformed (186). Is the proper role of the philosopher that of an adviser to tyrants—consider Seneca's role in the court of Nero—rather than a rebel or social critic seeking to overthrow the conditions of tyranny? If the creation of a reformed tyranny is merely utopian or theoretical, what function is it intended to play in the dialogue? With these questions in mind, let us now turn to Kojève.

The Politics of Recognition

The Strauss-Kojève debate took place within the context of a long-standing friendship and correspondence that went back to the 1930s. The letters between the two philosophers-in-exile range from the high to the low, from Plato and Hegel to beer and wine to academic gossip. Among other things, we learn of Strauss's pleasure with the English breakfasts ("the hams taste too good as to consist of pork and are therefore allowed by the Mosaic law according to atheistic interpretation")[9] and his low opinion of contemporaries like Eric Weil ("an idle chatterer")[10] and Karl Jaspers ("a well-intentioned North-German Protestant Pastor full of unction and earnestness even in sexual relations").[11] We learn of Kojève's dislike of public lecturing ("I am becoming more and more 'Platonic.' One should address the few, not the many")[12] and Strauss's evident enthusiasm for teaching ("If one wants to see young people who are not mentally in their seventies, one has to come to Chicago").[13]

First, some background: Alexandre Kojevnikov (1902–1968) was a Russian emigré, a nephew of the painter Wassily Kandinsky, who gained fame in Paris during the 1930s for his lectures on Hegel at the École Pratique des Hautes Études.[14] It would be difficult to overstate the influence of these lectures on an entire generation of French intellectuals, from Raymond Aron and Maurice Merleau-Ponty to Georges Bataille and Jacques Lacan. By the time Kojève entered the debate on tyranny with Strauss he had left academia for a post in the Ministry of Economic Affairs under De Gaulle's Fourth Republic, where he became, along with Olivier Wormser, Robert Marjolin, and others, an architect of the future European Union.[15]

It was from the beginning an odd pairing—a white Russian (who turned quite red) and a German Jew—who considered collaborating on a book on Hobbes.[16] The book was never written, but Kojève's Hegel lectures were published in 1947 by his student Raymond Queneau under the title *Introduction à la lecture de Hegel.*[17] These lectures not only sought to provide a comprehensive philosophical account of the foundations of Hegelian thought, but for the first time established a connection between Hegel and Heidegger that would prove a volatile mixture in France after World War II. Kojève remained largely out of sight during his postwar years, devoting himself in the spirit of a good Hegelian civil servant to the task of French public administration while in his private life focusing his energies on writing a series of books on philosophical themes and subjects ranging from the concept of time to commentaries on the pre-Socratics and Kant. [18]

It was alleged that during this period Kojève was a "strict Stalinist" for whom Soviet Russia served as the model for the universal society, or what today goes by the euphemism "the international community." Believing that philosophy had been put in its final form by Hegel, Kojève believed all that remained was to have this vision realized through the political actions of leading statesmen and tyrants. "Like Plato, he wanted to advise a tyrant," Raymond Aron writes, and "in the shadows exercise influence over the visible actors" like Wormser and Valery Giscard d'Estaing.[19] In the short term, Kojève was content to draw up plans for a "Latin Empire" consisting of France, Italy, and Spain that would protect European independence from both American and Russian hegemony. In recent years evidence has emerged to suggest that Kojève was acting as a Soviet agent while working to secure the formation of the EEC and the signing of the GATT accords.[20]

The concept of recognition was the centerpiece of Kojève's reading of Hegel's *Phenomenology of Mind*. The term itself has a vaguely Kantian provenance and grows out of the intuition that every human being, insofar as we are at least potentially rational agents, should be treated with equal dignity and respect. In Kant's usage the term was both universalist and egalitarian. It meant that each person, regardless of race, gender, or national origin, was entitled to equal respect on the grounds of their humanity alone. In contemporary parlance the concept is used by neo-Kantians such as John Rawls to express the view that political institutions are just only if they afford the equal right of every citizen to the rudimentary conditions of dignity and self-respect.[21]

In his book *Multiculturalism* Charles Taylor shows how the concept of recognition has taken the place of the older aristocratic notion of honor. Honor, in the *ancien régime* sense of the term, was connected to notions of inequality and class hierarchy that fixed one's status in advance. Recognition, by contrast, is an inherently democratic idea that suggests that each individual merits equal dignity and respect regardless of rank. What and who we are cannot be determined from a script written out in advance, but is something to be discovered by the individual in the course of his or her life through a process of social interaction and struggle.

It is in this sense that the term has moved from its Kantian and universalist sense to its more recent sociological meaning. Recognition has come to be seen as a property not of individuals, but of social groups, ethnicities, and cultures vying with one another for equal respect. The idea that groups, not individuals, are the locus of recognition seems to point backward to the premodern idea of ascribed identities, but in fact sanctions the new pluralist or multiculturalist emphasis on the uniqueness of each group and its difference from all others. The "politics of recognition," as it is called, is associated with the rise of multiculturalism and the debates over ethnic and minority rights and whether these are adequately recognized by the contemporary liberal state.[22]

These current debates have all taken place against the backdrop of Kojève's reading of Hegel, although it is surprising how rarely this is acknowledged. To be sure, the concept of the struggle for recognition first came to light in Hegel's famous account of the dialectic of mastery and slavery. Yet in truth, the idea of recognition plays a fairly limited role in Hegel's own thinking. It was not until Kojève that the concept was given a kind of world-historical significance as the all-consuming motor of history.[23]

What distinguishes Kojève's from most contemporary usages of the term is his attempt to give the concept of recognition a grounding in a somewhat old-fashioned philosophical anthropology. His reading of Hegel begins with the question "what am I?" and concludes with the answer that we are the beings who desire recognition. Since the desire to be recognized is the quintessentially human desire, it is necessary to inquire as to exactly what kind of desire it is. Desire is in the first instance an act of negation; it is the expression of a lack or a need on the part of the actor. The simplest form of desire is the desire to satisfy some bodily need or other—hunger, for example. But if we acted only to satisfy our basic biological urges, we would never rise above the level of the animals. The satisfaction of our bodily needs is only a necessary but not a sufficient condition for the fulfillment or "satisfaction" of our specifically human needs.

It is because we have the capacity to desire not only natural objects, but "non-natural" or intellectual ones as well, that we are able to rise above the level of our purely natural history and create a distinctively human world of culture and values. There comes a moment when we are no longer satisfied to appropriate external things around us in Locke's primordial sense of picking apples from a tree, but feel that we must gain the recognition of others. To use a different language, we are beings constituted not only by "first-order desires" to have something, but by "second-order desires" to be something. We have desires to have desires and this is what makes us human. I not only want to have this or that; I want to be this or that and I can only be so if some sign of recognition is conferred by others around me.[24]

The problem, as Kojève, following Hegel, describes it is that the recognition of equal worth is not immediately forthcoming from others. Each wants to be recognized without in turn having to grant recognition to the other, and this one-sided state of affairs leads to a life-and-death struggle for recognition not unlike Hobbes's famous *bellum omnium contra omnes*. It is from the life-and-death struggle in which our passion for honor and prestige is tested against the fear of violent death that the all-important relationship of master and slave develops. This arises because in the struggle one of the parties is unwilling to go all the way, to risk life for the sake of recognition, and agrees to submit to the other, granting recognition without requiring it in return. In short the vanquished party subordinates his own desire for esteem to the biologically stronger desire for self-preservation. The true origin of society does not grow out of a voluntary act of agreement between free and equal agents, but has its beginnings in the inequality between a master class that is prepared to risk everything for the sake of recognition and a slave class that accepts servitude as the price for self-preservation. Kojève's reading of Hegel points not only backward to Aristotle, but forward to Nietzsche.

The dialectic of struggle between master and slave provides the *leitmotiv* of Kojève's reading of history. The conceptual basis for human history is the need of one self-conscious mind to be recognized by another. But the very inequality of the relation of master and slave makes this recognition impossible. The slave grants recognition to the master by the very fact that he is forced to work in the master's service. The master's enjoyment is predicated upon his freedom from work. However, the recognition the master enjoys is conferred not by an equal, but by a degraded tool who is merely employed to satisfy his lord's material comforts. Rather than achieving a level of autonomy, the master comes to realize his dependence on the slave, and this realization creates the worm of discontent. The master may have thought himself a "being for himself." He is in fact a "being for another."[25]

This change in self-consciousness on the part of the master finds a corresponding change on the part of the slave who, through an ironic twist in the dialectic, becomes the mover of humanity toward a higher level of self-awareness. The slave had initially accepted his position out of fear, but through labor he learns to conquer and discipline his fear and in the process to develop a sense of his own worthiness. Work is to be regarded no longer as the biblical curse of Adam, but as the basis for historical becoming or progress. Through work, the slave transforms nature into something other than it originally was; he creates a human world of culture. But through work, the slave not only "humanizes" external nature, he humanizes himself as well. His labor educates him beyond the fear of death and prepares him for a life of freedom. "Work," Kojève writes, "is *Bildung* in the double sense of the word: on the one hand, it forms, transforms, the World, humanizes it by making it more adapted to Man; on the other, it transforms, forms, educates man, it humanizes him by bringing him into greater conformity with the idea that he had of himself."[26]

By liberating the slave from the fear that once held him in thrall, work now becomes the key to human emancipation. "The future and end of history," Kojève says, "belong not to the warlike Master . . . but to the working Slave."[27] The future of history belongs to the once terrorized slave who has learned to conquer his fear and demands to be recognized as a free and equal human being. Indeed, it was this view of history as being made by the workers and for the workers that Kojève claimed to have discovered first in the *Phenomenology*. The belief that the industrial proletariat, the modern-day "wage slaves," are the inheritors of this centuries-old struggle for recognition clearly helped to make Kojève's reading of Hegel so all-important to those young Marxists in search of the metaphysical under-pinnings of their own faith.[28]

Recognition Reconsidered

Let us return to the debate with Strauss. In his "L'action politique des philosophes"—later retitled "Tyrannie et Sagesse"—Kojève applies the lessons of Hegel to Xenophon. Kojève's fundamental premise is that the categories of classical political philosophy are incapable of explaining modern tyranny. Why? In part because Xenophon accepted the ancient belief that the desire for recognition—honor, prestige, admiration—is characteristic only of the "real man", the *aner anderes*. This is tantamount to the pagan or aristocratic "existential view" he had elaborated in his *Introduction to Hegel*. "The quest for glory," he writes, "is specifically and necessarily characteristic only of *born* masters and it is *irremediably* missing from 'servile' natures which, by that very fact, are not truly human" (140).

Kojève's account of the master-slave dialectic seems to have undergone a modification. In the *Introduction to Hegel* he had treated the master and slave as two more or less permanent human archetypes; he now sees them as expressing two historical shapes of being. The pagan or masterly point of view comes at a price. Either the master can continue an endless and ultimately self-consuming struggle for recognition, or he can accept the admiration of slaves. The master thus finds himself in a "contradiction" in the precise Hegelian sense of the term. The result is "essentially tragic" (142). This contradiction is only resolved with the introduction of the "Judeo-Christian" or "bourgeois" viewpoint of the slave. It is only the bourgeois-Christian world that has turned work into the essential human activity, a source of not only satisfaction, but even "joy":

> I think it would be false to say, with Simonides, that *only* the "desire to be honored" and the "joy which comes from honor" makes one "endure *any* labor and brave *any* danger." The *joy* that comes from labor itself, and the desire to *succeed* in an undertaking, can, by themselves alone,

prompt a man to undertake painful and dangerous labors. . . . A man can work hard risking his life for no other reason than to experience the joy he always derives from *carrying out* his project or, what is the same thing, from transforming his "idea" or even "ideal" into a *reality* shaped by his own *efforts*. . . . Thus, although that is an extreme case, a man can aspire to tyranny in the same way that a "conscientious" and "enthusiastic" workman can aspire to adequate conditions for his labor. (140–41)

To put the matter crudely or politically, the problem with the classical understanding is that it rests on too narrow a conception of the self; the circle of recognition remained restricted to only the few or an elite. This is where Kojève finds it necessary to correct Xenophon with Hegel. Tyrants or statesmen—he uses the terms synonymously—all aspire to a kind of universal recognition, the desire to see their authority affirmed by all or at least by the largest possible number. In order to achieve an ever-widening circle of recognition, tyrants will do whatever it takes to expand their recognition pool, whether this entails emancipating slaves, enfranchising women, lowering the age of majority, or making "culture" available to all (146). The desire for recognition is in essence "limitless" and will only be completely satisfied when it is bestowed by the whole of humanity. Only the tyrant—Kojève alludes to Stalin with his "Stakhanovite" system of emulations—will achieve full satisfaction as the gratefully acknowledged architect of the "universal and homogenous state" (138–39).

Strauss's reply to Kojève is a masterpiece of philosophical rhetoric in its own right. He professes to be shocked—in the manner of Claude Raines from *Casablanca*, one suspects—at the "more than Machiavellian bluntness" with which Kojève takes for granted such "terrible things" as atheism and tyranny. At the same time he holds Kojève up as one of "the very few who know how to think and who love to think." "Kojève is a philosopher and not an intellectual" (185, 186). Although he later remarks that Kojève will no doubt object to "our Victorian or pre-Victorian *niaiseries*," Strauss does not mind appearing to play the naif to Kojève's cynical realism. The whole exchange takes on the character of a Platonic dialogue with Strauss taking the part of Socrates to Kojève's tough-talking Thrasymachus.

Strauss begins by taking issue with Kojève's thesis that the desire for recognition is somehow ontologically fundamental, as it were, the desire of all desires. The idea that man is the being who, above all, desires recognition from others in order to be satisfied remains an unproven hypothesis. In a fascinating letter to Kojève of August 1948 Strauss questions whether the desire for recognition does not already presuppose an essentially historicist conception of philosophy. "The deduction of the desire for recognition is convincing if one presupposes that every philosophy consists in grasping the spirit of its time in thought, that is to say if one presupposes everything that is at issue," he writes. "Why should self-consciousness and the striving for recognition not be understood as derivative from the *zoon logon echon* [the rational animal]?"[29] In short, the assumption that man is a being in need of recognition remains to be demonstrated.

In point of fact, Kojève's analysis stems from a misreading of Xenophon and the ancients. Honor merely "seems" to be the end for which the best men strive. "According to the classics," Strauss writes, "the highest good is a life devoted to wisdom or to virtue, honor being no more than a very pleasant, but secondary and dispensable reward" (190). The love or desire for honor is at best a prephilosophic anticipation of the pleasures deriving from wisdom, a good that can be shared with others without being diminished. At its worst, however, the desire for honor can serve as a cover for tyranny:

> One cannot become a tyrant and remain a tyrant without stooping to do base things; hence a self-respecting man will not aspire to tyrannical power. But, Kojève might object, this still does not prove that the tyrant is not motivated chiefly or exclusively by a desire for honor or prestige. He can be motivated, e.g., by a misguided desire to benefit his fellow men. This defense would hold good if error in such matters were difficult to avoid. But it is easy to know that tyranny is base; we all learn as children that one must not give others bad examples and that one must not do base things for the sake of the good that may come out of them. The potential or actual tyrant does not know what every reasonably well-bred child knows, because he is blinded by passion. By what passion? The most charitable answer is that he is blinded by desire for honor or prestige. (191)

The desire for recognition is in fact the result of a very peculiar historical combination of the pagan master morality with the Christian-bourgeois work ethic of the slaves. In opposition to Kojève's and Hegel's dialectical flights of fancy, Strauss prefers to present both alternatives, classical and biblical morality, each in its original pristine form: "Syntheses effect miracles," he writes. "Kojève's or Hegel's synthesis of classical and Biblical morality effects the miracle of producing an amazingly lax morality out of two moralities both of which made very strict demands on self-restraint" (191). The moral laxity of Hegelian ethics, that is, the ethic of recognition, is revealed by the fact that it willingly accepts actions previously regarded as base or criminal as justified by "history" or excuses tyrants because they further the cause of "progress." Such historicist and progressivist doctrines "construct human society," according to Strauss, "by starting from the untrue assumption that man as man is thinkable as a being that lacks awareness of sacred restraints or as a being that is guided by nothing but a desire for recognition" (192).

Strauss's reference here to "sacred restraints" on action is as close as he gets in *On Tyranny* to offering something like a doctrine of natural right. His reference to what every "well-bred child" knows suggests the existence of certain pretheoretical or prephilosophical moral rules of the sort that one should not give bad examples to others or do base things for the sake of good consequences. But no more than Kojève, it should be said, has Strauss demonstrated that a sense of awe or restraint is more primary than the desire for recognition. He has proven at most that without some sense of restraint—he later refers to the "good conscience"—there are no limits to what might be deemed politically justifiable (204). For Strauss, any alleged right of recognition must be derived from a prior awareness that certain ends are unjust or forbidden, such as the desire to extend one's rule over all men and women for the sake of achieving glory and honor. Rather than the goal or end of history, Kojève's universal and homogenous state comes to look more like a vast moral aberration.

At issue, then, is nothing less than the problem of human nature. Kojève recognizes this fact when he writes to Strauss, "If there is something like 'human nature,' then you are surely right in everything."[30] If there are, as Strauss asserts, certain natural restraints on human beings, then it is never right to treat individuals as means to ends or to castigate opponents as "reactionaries" or "enemies of the people" to be exterminated in the name of history. But if, as Kojève believes, we are historical beings all the way down, then there is no reason why human nature should not be remade by those with the politically correct ideology. In the same letter just cited, Kojève continues:

> The task of philosophy is to resolve the fundamental question regarding "human nature." And in that connection the question arises whether there is not a contradiction between speaking about "ethics" and "ought" on the one hand, and about conforming to a "given" or "innate" human nature on the other. For animals, which unquestionably have such a nature, are not morally "good" or "evil," but at most

healthy or sick, and wild or trained. One might therefore conclude that it is precisely ancient anthropology that would lead to mass-training and eugenics.[31]

Philosophical Politics

Central to *On Tyranny* is a question that will run throughout all of Strauss's later writings: namely, what is a philosopher? Is the philosophical life ultimately a form of politics by other means, is the philosopher necessarily an "engaged" intellectual? Or is the philosophical life something radically private, focused on individual, not collective, self-perfection? At issue is the old question of the relation of theory to practice. It is a credit to the exchange with Kojève that there is no beating around the bush. They get straight to the point.

Kojève regards philosophy ultimately as a form of public pedagogy. "One cannot be a philosopher," he asserts, "without wanting to be a philosophical pedagogue" (163). By a philosophical pedagogue he means a teacher or instructor to princes. The philosopher is someone who seeks to "realize" his ideas through the actions of tyrants and statesmen. As examples he refers to Plato's voyage to Sicily and Spinoza's collaboration with De Witt. Philosophy is, in the final instance, judged by its capacity to elicit practitioners who can be educated or convinced to help bring the philosopher's ideas about in history. For this reason, Kojève avers, philosophers have perennially been attracted to tyranny, since gaining the ear of a single individual is more likely to be productive of quick results than the messy and less certain process of attempting to educate an entire society (164).[32]

The criterion of philosophical truth is, following the Hegelian line, a form of success in practice (163). We know a doctrine is true, or at least has a greater share of relative truth, to the degree that it is taken up, espoused, and adopted by society—to the extent, that is, that philosophy becomes public philosophy. The chief defect of ancient philosophy, at least in its "Epicurean" form, was its tendency to isolate itself from public life. In this context Kojève takes Simonides to task for acting not like a philosopher, but like a "typical Intellectual" who erects his ideal utopia and then takes cover behind it as if in some inner citadel (137). Such isolationism not only cuts off philosophy from the lifeblood of history, but essentially renders it without criteria of truth. How can one validate the proof of a philosophy when it is locked away in its Epicurean garden? And what is true of Epicureanism is true for all later attempts to render philosophy accountable to some kind of elite, from Pierre Bayle's Republic of Letters to various

other academies, think tanks, or cloisters. All such efforts to shut philosophy off from history can only lead to a kind of solipsistic narcissism
(153–55).

Beginning from Kojève's premise that all men desire recognition and the
wider the better, it follows that only a philosophy that ultimately achieves
recognition by humanity as a whole can be considered the final or true philosophy. In fact it would cease to be philosophy at all in the sense of a quest
for wisdom, and would become completed wisdom, in Hegelian terms
Wissenschaft. If philosophy is governed by a desire to rule, then it must
seek to establish either directly a rule of the philosopher or, more likely, the
rule of the philosopher's pupil. This idea presupposes a specific vision of the
philosopher's relation to Being that Kojève calls one of "radical Hegelian
atheism":

> If Being creates itself ("becomes") in the course of History, then it is not
> by isolating oneself from History that one can reveal Being (transform it
> by *Discourse* into the *Truth* man "possesses" in the form of *Wisdom*). In
> order to reveal Being, the philosopher must, on the contrary, "partici-
> pate" in history, and it is not clear why he should then not participate
> in it *actively*, for example, by advising the tyrant, since as a philosopher,
> he is better able to govern than any "uninitiate." (152)

Kojève clearly knows these are fighting words, and Strauss responds
accordingly. It is not clear that philosophers desire the same kind of recognition sought by statesmen. For philosophers, it is not approval as such that
they seek, but approval from their peers, that is to say, from the competent
minority. This dependence on the approval of the few need not lead to the
kind of radical subjectivism Kojève fears. "The classics were fully aware of
the essential weakness of the mind of the individual," Strauss writes, and
they took pains to correct it (194). For this reason the philosopher must
seek out others of his kind on whom to test his ideas. The cultivation of
friendship becomes, then, one of the highest offices of philosophy.

To be sure, Strauss agrees with Kojève regarding the dangers of self-
referentiality that come from "the cultivation and perpetuation of common
prejudices by a closely knit group of kindred spirits" (195). He appears to be
fully cognizant of all the dangers later associated with "Straussianism."[33]
But if one danger to philosophy comes from "the snobbish silence and whis-
pering of the sect," an even greater danger derives from the attempt to turn
philosophy into a mass ideology. What good does it do, Strauss taunts, "if
the tenets of the sect are repeated by millions of parrots instead of a few

dozens of human beings?" (195). Does recognition or consensus confer truth? "*If* we must choose between the sect and the party," he writes, "we must choose the sect" (195; emphasis added).

The dangers to philosophy become apparent once it is adapted to the conditions of mass rule. The temptation to turn philosophy into propaganda might seem irresistible especially to a Machiavellian politician. In his essay "Why We Remain Jews" Strauss recalls a lesson from the interwar socialism of his youth:

> It was an axiom: "Anti-Semitism is the socialism of fools" and therefore it is incompatible with intelligent socialism. But again, one can state the lesson that Hitler gave Stalin in very simple words, as follows. The fact that anti-Semitism is the socialism of fools is an argument not against, but for, anti-Semitism given the fact that there is such an abundance of fools, why should one not steal that very profitable thunder.[34]

Stalin's pogroms and other anti-Semitic policies were not only a way of securing his rule; they also served to gain the support and recognition of the large non-Jewish majority of his citizens. In principle, it would seem that Kojève should have no argument with this.

The verification of philosophy is not dependent on either the "subjective certainty" of the philosopher or the sect or the recognition of the mass political party. Philosophy, as Strauss understands it, is a matter of knowledge, but knowledge of one's ignorance. Such philosophy is "zetetic" or, as he adds parenthetically, "skeptic in the original sense of the term":

> Philosophy as such is nothing but genuine awareness of the problems, i.e., of the fundamental and comprehensive problems. It is impossible to think about these problems without becoming inclined toward a solution, toward one or the other of the very few typical solutions. Yet as long as there is no wisdom, but only quest for wisdom, the evidence of all solutions is necessarily smaller than the evidence of the problems. Therefore the philosopher ceases to be a philosopher at the moment at which the "subjective certainty" of a solution becomes stronger than his awareness of the problematic character of that solution. At that moment the sectarian is born. (196)

Strauss's zeteticism—the belief that there are no permanent solutions, only permanent problems—begs a number of important questions. What is a permanent problem? How do we know when a problem is permanent?

How do we know that such problems cannot be solved? Moreover, despite his affirmation of skepticism, Strauss sometimes claims to know more than he allows. His statements cited earlier regarding "awareness of sacred restraints" or the "good conscience" seem to imply much more than the Socratic awareness of ignorance.

Strauss's zetetic conception of philosophy points to a fundamental difference with Kojève's understanding of the theory-practice problem. For Kojève, the aim of philosophy is to make us feel "at home" in the world; its goal is to "reconcile" us to reality. This is the Hegelian dream of a world where philosophy is realized in the institutions and practices of everyday life and where these institutions in turn express every facet of a fully developed human intelligence. Only when all traces of the "unhappy consciousness" have been dissipated will philosophy have come to paint its gray on gray. It is a conception of philosophy as absolute worldliness.

By contrast Strauss regards the aim of philosophy as securing a certain "detachment" from the world (199). Philosophy must continually struggle to resist "the most potent natural charm," which is the "unqualified attachment to human things as such" (203). Philosophy is neither more nor less than "the quest for the eternal order, or for the eternal causes or causes of all things . . . within which history takes place, and which remains entirely unaffected by history" (212). This alienation of the philosopher from the city is not a "tragedy" to be overcome, but the necessary condition for the existence of philosophy. A philosopher at home in the world cannot be a true philosopher. "The conflict between philosophy and city," Strauss writes in a deliberately provocative sentence, "is as little tragic as the death of Socrates" (206).

The quest for the eternal order of causes does not render the philosopher misanthropic. To the contrary, we have no direct access to the eternal order of nature except insofar as it is an expression or reflection of the human soul. The soul remains the microcosm of nature. While resisting the "collective egoisms" bred of politics and attachments to one's own city, the philosopher is necessarily attracted to people of a certain sort, namely, those in possession of a well-ordered soul. It is only through the well-ordered soul that the philosopher is allowed a "glimpse" of the eternal order of nature (201).

But what, one wants to know, is a well-ordered soul? Strauss's answer to this question seems to be "we know one when we see it." He speaks of "the immediate pleasure" we feel when exposed to signs of human nobility (202). Later he refers to the feeling of "self-admiration" or "self-satisfaction" that arises not from external recognition from others, but from the possession of a "good conscience" (204). The defense of philosophy is, then, based on a form of hedonism—a higher hedonism, to be sure, but one that can only be confirmed by the pleasure felt by the philosopher alone. In a letter to Strauss Kojève refers to the appeal to the moral conscience as a criterion for truth. He asks whether Torquemada or Drezhinski suffered from "bad consciences."[35] One has to wonder whether the appeal to self-admiration does not ultimately confirm Kojève's reservations about the narcissism and "subjective certainty" of the philosopher.

The political action of philosophy—to the extent that philosophy admits a public side—consists in various fishing expeditions for new or potential philosophers. This can only be done by entering the marketplace and coming into contact with different kinds of human souls. For the rest, it is sufficient to satisfy the city that philosophers are not atheists, that they revere the gods the city worships, and that they are good citizens (205–6). The temper of philosophical politics necessarily will be moderate. Rather than seeking to realize the best regime where philosophers rule, philosophy knows not to expect redemption from politics. The philosophical politician "will not engage in revolutionary or subversive activity," but "will try to help his fellow man by mitigating, as far as in him lies, the evils that are inseparable from the human condition" (200).

Strauss's phrase, "the evils that are inseparable from the human condition," sets the limits of his philosophical politics. Although he nowhere defines precisely what he means by "evil," it seems to be connected to the transgression of certain natural or sacred boundaries that set limits to humanity (192). It is in this context that he refers to doctrines of unlimited progress and the conquest of nature as "destructive of humanity" (178). It is precisely because evil is ineradicable, Strauss warns, that our expectations of politics must be modest. This idea is connected further to his zetetic conception of philosophy. "Zetetic politics," in the words of Victor Gourevitch, "is a scaling down of what we may hope to achieve, and hence of what we ought to attend."[36]

The End of History

The best-known aspect of the Strauss-Kojève exchange is their debate over the end of history and the possibility of a post-historical future. It is this aspect of their debate that has been picked up recently by Francis Fukuyama in his best-selling *The End of History and the Last Man*.[37] But while Fukuyama saw the end of history as the triumph of the post–cold war capitalist democracies of the West, Kojève saw the future as resting with the great Eastern tyrannies, Soviet Russia and Communist China, exercising power in the name of a universal, homogenous empire.

The doctrine of the end of history is inseparable from the Enlightenment's idea of progress and the kind of optimism that regards history as a rational process leading to both materially and morally higher stages of being. To derive ends or purposes from the evidence of history has been notoriously difficult, if not fatally flawed. In Kant's relatively gentle form of this doctrine, history is regarded as a progressive movement culminating in a confederation of republics overseen by a league of nations to ensure perpetual peace.[38] Although the doctrine is most frequently associated with Hegel, he himself never uses the term *das Ende der Geschichte*. Nevertheless, there is a strong teleological component underlying his philosophy of history that regards the historical process as culminating in the modern state. This state is not to be confused with the Prussian monarchy, but is more like the constitutional *Rechtstaat* based on the separation of public and private spheres and the rule of law. Such a state on Hegel's own terms was neither universal nor homogeneous, but retained significant degrees of social inequality and hierarchy; nor would the realization of such a state put an end to all future wars and revolutions. Hegel remained deeply opposed to the Kantian idea of perpetual peace as representing the triumph of bourgeois civil society and anticipating an age of demoralization and decline.[39]

Kojève's end of history thesis is far more indebted to Marx's eschatological reading of history as a leap from necessity to freedom. In a footnote to the *Introduction to Hegel* Kojève reminds us that this "Hegelian theme, among many others, was taken up by Marx" at the end of the third volume of *Kapital*. Hence Marx made a distinction between "the realm of necessity (*Reich der Notwendigkeit*) and the realm of freedom (*Reich der Freiheit*)." The former consists of "History properly so-called, in which men ('classes') fight among themselves for recognition and fight against Nature by work," while the latter refers to that "beyond [*jenseits*] in which men (mutually recognizing one another without reservation) no longer fight, and work as little as possible (Nature having been definitively mastered—that is, Harmonized with Man)."[40]

The end of history will mean not only the achievement of social harmony, but the pacification of historical negating action of any kind such as wars and revolutions. The transition to the universal and homogeneous state will culminate in "the disappearance of Man"—not, to be sure, the biological phenomenon *homo sapiens*, but "Man properly so-called—that is, Action negating the given . . . or, in general, the Subject opposed to the

Object." The disappearance of man at the end of history will also mean the end of philosophy, because when "Man himself no longer changes essentially, there is no longer any reason to change the (true) principles which are the basis of his understanding of the World and himself."[41]

The meaning of Kojève's end of history thesis comes to light as a synthesis of the pagan morality of the masters and the bourgeois-Christian morality of the slaves. This idea received its first rudimentary incarnation in the attempts of Alcibiades and later Alexander to break out of the confining straitjacket of the ancient city and to create a universal empire. Yet the fact that Alcibiades was a student of Socrates and Alexander a disciple of Aristotle meant that their ideas of empire were still predicated upon a rigid class hierarchy of masters and slaves, conquerors and conquered (170). The idea of a universal empire based on universal human equality only came into being with the Edict of Carcalla, but more specifically with Saint Paul and the rise of Christianity as the universal church. But this was still an equality based on the Judeo-Christian idea of belief in a single God. It was not yet equality in the political sense of the term (172–73).

It is only in "our day," Kojève believes, that "the universal and *homogenous* State has become a *political* good as well" (172). This is the state that Napoleon—Hegel's hero on horseback—helped to inaugurate, but which has only come to fruition in the modern tyranny of Soviet Russia (Salazar's Portugal is also mentioned—139). Modern tyrants like Stalin and Mao will help to bring to fruition what Napoleon could only imagine, that is, a state that is both universal because it allows no room for expansion and homogenous because it unites all previously disparate classes, races, and nations into a single humanity.[42] Only in the universal and classless society can the conditions for universal recognition be fully satisfied. All that remains is for the Hegelian philosopher to describe this happy race in the plenitude of its existence.

In opposition to Kojève's celebration of modern tyranny, Strauss wondered whether this condition of a homogenous mankind could possibly prove satisfying even in its own terms. There are, he argued, "degrees of satisfaction." The satisfaction of the ordinary citizen who enjoys an equality of opportunity and is recognized for his humble achievements is scarcely comparable to the satisfaction felt by the "Chief of State" who alone is "really satisfied" (207–8). Will this not result in the restitution of new hierarchies of rank?

Strauss raises against Kojève the same charge that Nietzsche brought against Hegel, namely, that the end of history—the transition from the realm of necessity to the realm of freedom—would result not in universal satisfaction, but in a kind of generalized aimlessness and loss of meaning. In Marx's utopian vision of a society where men "hunt in the morning, fish in the afternoon, rear cattle in the evening, and criticize after dinner," Nietzsche saw nothing so much as the world of the "last man," the one great herd without a shepherd. The complete satisfaction of desire, even if possible, would prove to be not a blessing but a curse. It would certainly be the end of philosophy:

> The state through which man is said to become reasonably satisfied is, then, the state in which the basis of man's humanity withers away, or in which man loses his humanity. It is the state of Nietzsche's "last man." Kojève in fact confirms the classical view that unlimited technological progress and its accompaniment, which are indispensable conditions of the universal and homogenous state, are destructive of humanity. It is perhaps possible to say that the universal and homogenous state is fated to come. But it is certainly impossible to say that man can reasonably be satisfied with it. If the universal and homogenous state is the goal of History, History is absolutely "tragic." (208)

It is clear from their exchange that Kojève believes that the rational tyranny described by Xenophon has become "an almost commonplace reality" today (138). He refers to Simonides's advice that the tyrant distribute honors and prizes as rewards for good works as being fully implemented in Stalin's system. Strauss cannot accept that the Stalinist system is the good or ideal tyranny proposed by Xenophon. In the first place, he notes that a good tyranny would most likely see a decline of the role of the secret police and the labor camps, a point on which Kojève is ominously silent. He also asks whether, if Stalin really is a good tyrant, he regards all his fellow citizens as comrades, and he can travel freely within or outside the Soviet Union without anything to fear. The inference Strauss draws is that the good tyranny is as much an impossibility today as it was in the time of Xenophon (188–89).

The issue between them is ultimately less whether the Soviet Union and the "Final Tyrant" represent the end stage of history than whether such an idea is coherent even in principle. Here Strauss plays the Left-Hegelian opening up the possibility of the endless play of the dialectic to Kojève's Right-Hegelian emphasis on the final closure of reason and history. There is no thesis that will not generate its own antithesis. "There is no reason for despair as long as human nature has not been conquered completely," Strauss counsels, "as long as sun and man still generate man" (209). What is brought into being will ultimately pass away and even the universal state will generate a "nihilistic negation" unilluminated by any positive goal except a desire to reassert the possibility of human freedom. Strauss claimed to find this abstract nihilistic negation preferable to "the indefinite continuation of the inhuman end" (209).

Kojève himself had occasion to reconsider the meaning of the end of history. The universal and homogenous state is "good," he admitted in a letter to Strauss, not because it satisfies any higher moral criteria, but simply because it comes last. It will put an end to all forms of historical negation. In a deeply disturbing but highly prescient passage that sounds like something out of *A Clockwork Orange,* Kojève speculates on what form post-historical life will assume:

> In the final state there naturally are no more "human beings" in our sense of an historical human being. The "healthy" automata are "satisfied" (sports, art, eroticism, etc.) and the "sick" ones get locked up. As for those who are not satisfied with their "purposeless activity" (art, etc.), they are the philosophers (who can attain wisdom if they "contemplate" enough). By doing so they become "gods." The tyrant becomes an administrator, a cog in the "machine" fashioned by automata for automata.[43]

Kojève developed these thoughts further in the second edition of his *Introduction to Hegel,* where he came to wonder whether the end of history would not also signify the end of humanity. In a lengthy footnote he questioned whether the complete satisfaction of human desire promised at the end would mean not the fulfillment but the "re-animalization" of humanity. If labor, struggle, and work have brought us to our present height, there might be reason to think that the abolition of necessity would result in the abolition of humanity. "Hence it would have to be admitted," Kojève wrote in a remarkable statement, "that after the end of History, men would construct their edifices and works of art as birds build their nests and spiders spin their webs, would perform musical concerts after the fashion of frogs and cicadas, would play like young animals, and would indulge in love like adult beasts. But one cannot then say that 'this makes Man happy.'"[44]

In the same note Kojève left no doubt that the completion of world history announced by Hegel in 1806 had now been accomplished in the effectively "classless" societies of both the contemporary United States and Soviet Russia. If, he said, "the Americans give the appearance of rich Sino-

Soviets," this is only because "the Russians and Chinese are still poor but proceeding to get richer." In either case, Kojève thought he saw in the triumph of the "American way of life" the actual completion of "post-history" and the return of mankind to the "eternal present."[45]

Kojève greeted the possibility of an end of history with the kind of stoic acceptance one would expect from a Hegelian wise man. Even if he later realized that the universal homogenous state will not make us happy, there would be no point in fighting history. "The history of the world is the world's court of judgment," Hegel wrote.[46] The point of philosophy at the end of history is not to change the world, but to interpret it. It is impossible to tell just how seriously Kojève took his own assessment. Those who knew him have commented on his irony and sense of playfulness. Raymond Aron recalled a saying of Kojève's: "Human life is a comedy, we have to play it seriously."[47]

Strauss, who refused to regard philosophy as the product of its time, saw in resistance to history a source of human nobility. "Warriors and workers of all countries, unite," he wrote, playing on Marx, "while there is still time to prevent the coming of 'the realm of freedom.' Defend with might and main, if it needs be defended, 'the realm of necessity' " (209).[48] Thinking perhaps of the Spartans at Thermopylae or the Jews at Masada, Strauss held that there is virtue in going down with the ship, with "guns blazing and flags flying" even if this means the embrace of a lost cause. Such doomed efforts may still "contribute greatly toward keeping awake the recollection of the immense loss sustained by mankind" and therefore "strengthen the desire and hope for its recovery."[49] Only by resistance can we hope to keep alive "the elementary and unobtrusive conditions of human freedom" (27).

CHAPTER SEVEN

Strauss's America

Let us beware of the danger of pursuing a Socratic goal with the means, and the temper, of Thrasymachus. Certainly, the seriousness of the need of natural right does not prove that the need can be satisfied. A wish is not a fact. Even by proving that a certain view is indispensable for living well, one proves merely that the view in question is a salutary myth: one does not prove it to be true. — Leo Strauss, Natural Right and History

Introduction

Over the past decade the work of Leo Strauss has increased in importance to the point that today he has emerged as one of the most distinctive and influential voices of the last century. Once considered a brilliant, if idiosyncratic, interpreter of works in the tradition of political philosophy, he has come to be considered more and more as a philosopher in his own right. Strauss philosophized largely through the medium of the commentary, while at the same time bringing the genre of the commentary to new philosophical heights. Although he typically referred to himself by the more humble epithet of "scholar," one can say without exaggeration that Strauss helped to reopen certain fundamental problems of political philosophy. Although he bequeathed no formal system or doctrine, he did leave a very characteristic way of posing problems.[1]

At the same time, the influence of Strauss cannot be separated from the growth of "Straussianism" as a school of political thought—or a "cult," as its detractors would say. On the face of it, the emergence of Straussianism is no different from the development of any other philosophical school that grows up around powerful and influential teachers. There are Rawlsians,

Habermasians, Arendtians, and so on. No one seems to care. To be sure, all of these thinkers have their friends and detractors, but their names do not call forth an intense, almost visceral response from critics. You can take them or leave them. This is not the case with Strauss. To know him is to either love him or hate him. There is no middle ground. What makes Straussianism so different? One thought is that to a greater degree than other competing schools, Straussians have sought to influence policy, to put their ideas into practice, either directly through work in the government or indirectly through think tanks and other shapers of public opinion. In fact Strauss is widely regarded both by some of his friends and by virtually all of his enemies as responsible for shaping the direction of the conservative movement in America.[2]

Certainly Strauss's work has never lacked for detractors. Although it was once fashionable to mock his sometimes overwrought language about the "decline of the West" and his attempt to view the great political thinkers of the past as addressing transcendent issues beyond their age, it has now become virtually *de rigueur* to denounce his influence from beyond the grave, as it were, on a host of contemporary policies. According to a signed *New York Times* editorial in November 1994, Strauss was the *eminence grise* behind the Gingrich Revolution and the Republican takeover of the House of Representatives. A decade later the *Times* (and virtually every other national and even international newspaper) would see the hand of Strauss behind the Bush administration's war in Iraq and its policy of preemption.[3]

Leaving aside the conspiratorial nature of most of these charges, which often presuppose long and complex genealogies and lines of influence for which there is little direct evidence, there are a number of questions worth considering. What were Strauss's politics? Was he a conservative (neo- or otherwise) or a kind of liberal? What was his vision of America and its role in the world?

The Philosophical Significance of Politics

The expression "political philosophy" has two distinct meanings. It can mean the philosophical examination of politics or it can mean the political treatment of philosophy. In the first case it denotes an object of inquiry, in the second a distinctive manner of writing or rhetoric.[4]

In the first and more common usage of the term, political philosophy denotes a branch of philosophy in general. The term "political" represents a distinct subject matter distinguishable from other philosophical topics like ethics, logic, or the philosophy of mind. The central questions of political philosophy, therefore, concern such things as the proper distribution of power, the place of justice, and the role of tradition or authority. In its most comprehensive sense political philosophy represents "the attempt to replace opinions about the whole by knowledge of the whole."[5] It is "the attempt truly to know both the nature of political things and the right, or the good, political order."[6]

But Strauss is not content to regard political philosophy as one branch of knowledge among others. Politics is not for him one sphere of society or culture equal in rank to the ethical, the aesthetic, or the religious. Political philosophy represents for him a kind of first philosophy. That is to say, it represents the foundation or ultimate presupposition of all other branches of philosophy. There is, in other words, a priority attributed to the political that does not hold for other realms of being. To be sure, it is not at all obvious why political philosophy should have this importance. Why should study of the political take precedence over the contemplation of the unchanging structure of first principles? Or why should politics not be seen as subordinate to the ever-changing ebb and flow of History? What is the source of this belief about the priority of the political?[7]

The priority of political philosophy grows out of the basic structure of human experience. Our fundamental orientation in the world is practical, not theoretical. All action is undertaken for a purpose that is either preservation or change. We seek either to preserve things the way they are or to change them for the better. All action, therefore, presupposes some notion of the good for which all things are done. Insofar as our actions do not take place in a vacuum but are always *inter homines*, we are necessarily forced to think in political terms. We must think not only what is good for me, but what is good for us. Some notion of intersubjectivity or the common good is already implicit in the basic structure of experience.

The basic principles of action—the "what" of human experience—are revealed through the differing opinions we have concerning the good. As Strauss likes to say, "opinion is the element of society."[8] By opinion, however, Strauss does not mean the kind of information elicited through questionnaires or polling data studied by contemporary political scientists. Rather, he is referring to certain special kinds of human experience—the experience of right and wrong, of justice, of how a society should be governed—that the philosophical tradition has referred to by the term "natural right."[9] As such, opinion is not just an isolated preference or set of preferences, but presupposes a structured way of life. It achieves its highest or authoritative expression in law or codes of law as enacted by legislators and statesmen. Law gives shape to our fundamental experiences of right and wrong, of who should rule and be ruled. Ultimately what Strauss means by the fundamental experience of natural right concerns the oldest of political questions: not "who governs?" but "who should govern?"

Strauss, surprisingly, seems to admit an element of subjectivity into his investigation of the natural. The natural is revealed through opinion about nature. In what respect, though, are some forms of opinion or experience, and not others, thought to be coterminous with natural right? In particular Strauss regards contemporary historicism or what he calls "the experience of history" as distorting or concealing the possibility of natural right. Like Heidegger and the phenomenological school, Strauss appeals to a certain kind of original or originary experience uncontaminated by the presence of later theoretical or scientific constructions. "The 'experience of history,'" he writes, "and the less ambiguous experience of the complexity of human affairs may blur, but they cannot extinguish, the evidence of those simple experiences regarding right and wrong which are at the bottom of the philosophic contention that there is a natural right."[10] In other words, although modern-day forms of relativism may conceal certain fundamental forms of experience, they cannot ultimately abolish the intuition that there are permanent problems that are coeval with humanity. "The fundamental problems," he continues, "such as the problem of justice, persist or retain their identity in all historical change, however much they may be obscured by the temporary denial of their relevance and however variable or provisional all human solutions to these problems may be."[11]

Although Strauss's recovery of the political is directed against contemporary efforts to deny the existence of natural right, there is an oddly historical, if not historicist, component to his own thought. Strauss believes that ancient political philosophy has a privileged starting point for the investigation of natural right. But why should antiquity as such occupy this position? Why should the basic or fundamental experience of natural right be less available to us now than at any time in the past? Why should the Greek account of political life be regarded as more authentic to experience and not itself determined by previous civic, theological, and mythological traditions?[12] If certain forms of experience are indeed fundamental or natural, then presumably they should be recoverable by anyone at any time and at any place. The two biblical passages that are used as epigraphs for *Natural Right and History* are a case in point (II Samuel 12; I Kings 21). It is revealing that Strauss cites these passages unadorned. Presumably, one does not need to know their source, original language, or context to grasp immediately their meaning. In what language or in what culture is it ever right for a rich man to steal from a poor one? Although the term "natural right" is of Greek origin, it presumably bespeaks experiences available to everyone.

The ancients occupy a privileged place not only because they represent the original or classic form of political philosophy, but because their thought is said to be related *directly* to political experience. "Classical philosophy," Strauss writes, "originally acquired the fundamental concepts of political philosophy by starting from political phenomena as they present themselves to 'the natural consciousness,' which is a pre-philosophic consciousness."[13] Classical political thought is said to derive directly from political life, whereas all later thought has been mediated through the tradition of political philosophy. Tradition serves as a distorting filter through which the concepts and categories of classical political philosophy have been refracted. While such concepts as *polis, politeia, kalon,* and the like can be verified by "direct reference" to political phenomena as they appear, all later concepts emerged from a modification of the tradition. It is said to follow that "a tradition of political philosophy, its fundamental concepts cannot be fully understood until we have understood the earlier political philosophy its fundamental concepts from which, and in opposition to which, they were acquired."[14] All later political thought was "directly or indirectly" determined by the idea of progress, and this more than anything else has prevented a serious engagement with political philosophy in its classic form.

The problem confronting Strauss or any Straussian conception of history is precisely how we living in the present have access to the problem of natural right if in fact the very traditions we inhabit block our access to it. This is made doubly difficult when the world in which we live is now regarded as a product of the very abstractions we have created. "The world in which we live," Strauss writes, "is already a product of science, or at any rate is profoundly affected by the existence of science."[15] As a result it becomes exceedingly difficult to reconstruct those basic experiences out of which political philosophy arose. How can we bootstrap ourselves out of the cave of our current dogmas to recapture the direct experience of political life? Strauss answers as follows:

> To grasp the natural world as a world that is radically prescientific or prephilosophic, one has to go back behind the first emergence of science or philosophy. It is not necessary for this purpose to engage in extensive and necessarily hypothetical anthropological studies. The information that classical philosophy supplies about its origins suffices, especially if that information is supplemented by consideration of the most elemen-

tary premises of the Bible, for reconstructing the essential character of
"the natural world."[16]

The difficulty is compounded in Strauss's eyes by the fact that the modern world—the world created by science and the "experience of history"—
has become deeply alienated from the life-world or the world of
pretheoretic experience, which provides the fertile soil that makes natural
right possible. In a striking formulation of this problem he speaks of the
fact that we inhabit an "artificial cave" even beneath the "ordinary cave"
of political understanding. "People may become so frightened of the ascent
to the light of the sun and so desirous of making that ascent utterly impossible to any of their descendents," he writes, "that they dig a deep pit
beneath the cave in which they were born, and withdraw into that pit."[17] It
remains, ironically, the task today of historical studies ("new and most artificial tools") simply to recreate the architecture of the natural cave of ordinary experience.

Even if we cannot have access to the natural world directly, we can at
least approach it indirectly through the works of ancient political philosophy. "Political philosophy," we have seen, "is that branch of philosophy
which is closest to political life, to non-philosophic life, to human life."[18]
We find ourselves in the ironic or paradoxical situation where the only
way to have access to the natural world, or what Strauss calls the "pre-
scientific" or "pre-philosophic" world, is through historical investigations
of ancient authors.[19] One reason why Strauss's elaborate and paraphrastic
commentaries on Thucydides, Plato, Xenophon, and Aristotle have caused
so much consternation among readers is that they are often simply asking
the wrong questions. Strauss is not reading them so much to discover new
information as to recover the meaning of philosophy in "its original
Socratic sense." By philosophy in its original sense he means an awareness
of the limitations of knowledge, that is, "awareness of the fundamental
problems and, therewith, of the fundamental alternatives regarding their
solution that are coeval with human thought."[20]

The Political Meaning of Philosophy

There is, however, a second definition of political philosophy that regards
it less as a subject matter or a branch of knowledge and more as a manner
of treating philosophy. "The adjective 'political' in the expression 'political
philosophy' designates not so much a subject matter as a manner of treatment," Strauss writes.[21] Political philosophy means the political or politic

treatment of philosophical themes. From this point of view, the term "political philosophy" describes the political situation of philosophy.

Strauss stresses the tension—the necessary and fruitful tension— between philosophy understood as the quest for knowledge of the best regime and the needs and requirements of political life. "Philosophy or science, the highest activity of man, is the attempt to replace opinion about 'all things' by knowledge of 'all things'; but opinion is the element of society; philosophy or science is therefore the attempt to dissolve the element in which society breathes, and thus it endangers society."[22] Philosophy, so understood, requires an intransigent devotion to the idea of truth, an uncompromising reliance on one's own reason alone, whereas political life remains the realm of opinion that necessarily acquires the form of civic dogmas and other articles of faith. This tension between philosophy and the city is a variation of what Strauss refers to as the "theologico-political problem," that is, the tension between reason and faith as alternative sources of authority. Philosophy, it must be remembered, has not always been protected by legal and constitutional decrees. Philosophers have not always been free to speak and to publish freely and have therefore had to adopt various literary guises to protect themselves and their teachings from public harm. This lesson was learned too late by the first political philosopher, who was sentenced to death for the crime of impiety against the gods of the city.

The primacy of political philosophy grows out of an awareness of the precarious situation of philosophy vis-à-vis society. It is somehow taken for granted by modern scholars that philosophy always had social or political status. Strauss regards this as a profound mistake.[23] Throughout large swaths of human history, society has recognized no intrinsic right to philosophize. The trial of Socrates and the excommunication of Spinoza are but the most obvious cases, but there is a range of examples drawn from Athens of the classical period, the Muslim countries of the early Middle Ages, and France, England, Holland, and Germany of the seventeenth and eighteenth centuries. Persecution is not exclusively a feature of tyrannical or totalitarian regimes, but can take place, as the above examples indicate, even during "comparatively liberal periods."[24] It may take the harsh form of the *auto da fé* or the gentler form of social ostracism exercised by democratic societies.[25] Strauss recognizes that democratic societies may even impose their own forms of self-censorship that inhibit, even if they do not absolutely forbid, certain forms of free expression.[26] Consider the way contemporary "political correctness" serves to prevent the expression of certain opinions deemed unspeakable. For this reason Strauss raised the possibility that philosophers had to adopt various strategic ways of writing in order to express dangerous or unpopular truths. The strategy of esoteric writing came to take various forms, but was always undertaken with an eye to the preservation of philosophy.

It is now possible, thanks to the publication of Strauss's correspondence, to date his discovery of esoteric writing back to the late 1930s.[27] Esoteric writing was for him not simply the recovery of a literary genre; it coincided with his discovery of political philosophy in its classic sense. Esoteric writing was the form political philosophy took as a matter of self-defense. Strauss's claim about the tension between philosophy and society rests upon a second premise. The passage quoted above about the disproportion between philosophy and society continues as follows:

> Hence philosophy or science must remain the preserve of a small minority, and philosophers or scientists must respect the opinions on which society rests. To respect opinions is something entirely different from accepting them as true. Philosophers or scientists who hold this view about the relation of philosophy or science to society are driven to employ a peculiar manner of writing which would enable them to reveal what they regard as the truth to the few, without endangering the unqualified commitment of the many to the opinions on which society rests.[28]

Strauss recognizes that his assumption that political philosophers wrote in such a way as to be understood by only a few and misunderstood by the many is bound to be repugnant to every "decent reader."[29] The shocking suggestion is that philosophers themselves are not decent people. This claim has been met with furious indignation by those who believe, or want to believe, not only that philosophers are respectable, but that no respectable person would ever speak or write in a way deliberately to deceive others. Would philosophers ever lie? The liar, according to Harry Frankfurt's definition, is someone who purposefully leads us away from the truth or from a correct apprehension of reality to something he knows to be false. The liar is, ironically, someone who is respectful of the truth precisely to the degree that he desires to lead his audience away from it.[30] Does Strauss claim, then, that philosophers must lie?

The answer is clearly "no." Philosophy does not engage in the kind of systematic deception characteristic of the liar, but the responsibility to speak the truth must always be balanced with other ends such as the desire for self-preservation and the philosopher's sense of responsibility to the society in which he lives. It is not the responsibility of philosophy to puncture cherished illusions, especially if there is no likelihood that these illusions will be replaced by something better. Philosophy exercises its political function in knowing when to speak and when to keep silent. Philosophers may thus write in ways that deliberately conceal or obscure through the use of secrecy and obfuscation, that may not amount to lies but fall somewhere short of full disclosure. Philosophy is certainly under no obligation to deliver total transparency. To say that one has a commitment to the truth does not require one to shout it from the rooftops. The naïve view that philosophers must always speak the truth, the whole truth, and nothing but the truth is based on the nonhistorical assumption that all writers in the past wrote like those in the present or that the situation faced by them was essentially like our own.

Strauss sometimes presents the case for esoteric writing as a purely historical or sociological thesis about the conditions under which political philosophy has been practiced in the past. One cannot downplay the impact that events from the recent historical past, like Nazi Germany and the cold war, had on Strauss's conception of philosophy. In the introduction to *Persecution and the Art of Writing* he even refers to his thesis as an instance of "the sociology of knowledge."[31] Does this mean, then, that the need for esoteric writing may eventually wither away in liberal societies where speech and publishing is protected? Is a reconciliation of philosophy and society, of theory and practice, as it were, ever imaginable? At one place Strauss concedes the point of a critic that one cannot merely assume an essential hostility between philosophy and society any more than one can assume an essential harmony between them.[32] It is in large measure an empirical point the degree to which society is open to philosophy. There were and are societies "in which men can attack in writings accessible to all both the established social or political order and the beliefs on which it is based." As examples Strauss mentions the Third Republic in France and post-Bismarckian Wilhelmine Germany.[33] Oddly, he does not mention the United States, nor does he comment on the wisdom of such unfettered liberalism.

Elsewhere, however, Strauss makes a much stronger case for esoteric writing, presenting the hostility between philosophy and society as virtually axiomatic. There is a "necessary conflict" between them that requires esotericism.[34] So long as there is hostility to philosophy and philosophers, deceptive speech will have to be adopted, if only as a matter of prudence or self-regard. At one point he presents his argument in the form of a "syllogism": "Philosophy is the attempt to replace opinion by knowledge; but opinion is the element of the city, *hence* philosophy is subversive, *hence* the philosopher must write in such a way that he will improve rather than subvert the city."[35] Of course, Strauss recognizes that political leaders have used philosophy from time to time to support their rule as well as to attack their enemies. But this has been at best a marriage of convenience. The tension between political philosophy and society is not an incidental historical or sociological fact; it is rather a "necessary" condition for the existence of philosophy as such. The idea of an eventual harmony between philosophy and society would spell the end of philosophy as a critical activity.[36]

Still, Strauss considers the self-protection of philosophy to be merely "the most obvious and the crudest reason" for esoteric writing.[37] There is also a philanthropic dimension that regards discretion as the highest form of social obligation.[38] Philosophers have a duty not to upset the decent opinion on which society rests. "A political teaching," Strauss writes, "which addressed itself equally to decent and indecent men would have appeared to them [the ancients] from the outset as unpolitical, that is, as politically, or socially, irresponsible."[39] For this reason, he continues, "the political community cannot tolerate a political science which is morally 'neutral' and which therefore tends to loosen the hold of moral principles on the minds of those who are exposed to it."[40] Philosophers have a duty to satisfy society that they are not atheists, that they do not desecrate the things that society holds dear, and that they revere the laws.[41] Strauss begs the question of just who the "decent men" are and on what principle we can distinguish between the decent and the indecent. The term is intended as a conversation-stopper. He seems to assume that if you have to ask you probably aren't one, and if you are one, you don't need to ask.[42]

Only when philosophy adopts a mask of public discretion can it begin to fulfill its highest function, namely, the recruitment of potential new philosophers. Esoteric writing is, above all, a pedagogic tool. As any teacher (or poker player) knows, one does not show one's hand all at once. One does so rather little by little, depending on the quality of the player as well as the quality of the hand. This is the true meaning of political philosophy. Its aim is "to lead the qualified citizens, or rather their qualified sons, from the political life to the philosophic life."[43] Such an activity will necessarily be regarded as corrupting the youth. To avoid this charge, it is necessary to adopt the "Odyssean" strategy of beginning with opinions that are widely shared or "first for us" and only dialectically leading to those that culminate in the practice of the philosophic life.[44] In this way, and only in this way, does the philosopher demonstrate his love for "the puppies of his race."[45]

Strauss's study of esoteric writing has naturally given rise to the suspicion that he practices what he preaches. Did Strauss's readings of esoteric writers itself conceal an esoteric teaching? The possibility cannot be easily dismissed. If all writing must face the conflict between philosophy and society, then the same must be held for Strauss. If persecution covers a range of phenomena from "the most cruel type, as exemplified by the Spanish Inquisition, to the mildest, which is social ostracism," then even the most free and liberal society, even the United States, cannot be entirely free of the possibility of persecution.[46] As we have seen, Strauss does not rule out the possibility of an end to all forms of persecution, but he adds that such a goal is unattainable in any but "the most halcyon conditions." He cites the American author Archibald MacLeish to the effect that "the luxury of the complete confession, the uttermost despair, the farthest doubt should be denied themselves by writers living in any but the most orderly and settled times."[47] Needless to say, Strauss did not believe that he was living either in "the most halcyon" age or "the most orderly and settled times."

A clue to Strauss's view is his statement that under some circumstances the precarious position of philosophy vis-à-vis society "was not in every respect a misfortune for philosophy."[48] The fact is that persecution can be functional. The fact of persecution has aided philosophers in developing ever more subtle methods of writing and communication to escape detection by the censors. People living in times of persecution have had to become far more careful writers than those living in freer and more liberal eras. This was certainly true for writers like Alfarabi and Maimonides who gave to esotericism its philosophically richest form. Just as importantly, persecution has guaranteed the private character of philosophy and its freedom from the enchantments and entrapments of political power. It is not merely that philosophy necessarily corrupts society; society, at least the promise of rank and prestige, necessarily corrupts philosophy. To be sure, this is not to say that a repressive political order is justified on the grounds of the modes of resistance it creates. It is to suggest that a liberal society in which thought and speech are legally protected carries with it risks of its own kind that need to be carefully monitored.

The Lockean Roots of the American Republic

Strauss's writings on esotericism quite naturally lead to a consideration of his views on America. What did Strauss think of his adopted country? Paradoxically, Strauss has relatively little to say directly about the American regime, although his writings have helped to generate an important body of literature on the founding period and other critical turning points in American politics.[49] It is also widely known that there is a deep rift between Straussians—the so-called East and West Coast schools—regarding Strauss's legacy for the study of America.[50]

At its most basic level Strauss treated the American polity as a product of modernity and the Enlightenment. The American regime was a product of the new political science initiated by Hobbes, Locke, and Montesquieu, who in turn shaped the thinking of the founders. Yet at the same time Strauss also stressed the classical antecedents of the American political tradition. The Declaration of Independence, with its appeal to natural rights, is not only Lockean in origin, but points back to a long tradition of natural right going back to Aristotle and the Stoics. The *Federalist*'s commitment to institutions like the separation of powers and a system of checks and balances was not merely the creation of Montesquieu, but grew out of the ancient theory of the mixed regime in Aristotle and Polybius. And the framers' view that the Senate would serve as a deliberative body insulated from the popular pressures of direct election seemed to recreate the Ciceronian idea of a liberally educated class of gentlemen who could impart necessary civic qualities of leadership and responsibility to the rest of society. The American regime appears to be an amalgam—an unsteady and perhaps even incoherent amalgam—of ancient and modern principles. How did Strauss evaluate this mix and what are its prospects?

There is little doubt that Strauss was deeply grateful to the country that offered him shelter from Nazi tyranny. This sense of gratitude is apparent from the opening pages of *Natural Right and History*, his first book to address a large audience of American social scientists. In his introductory remarks Strauss expresses alarm that the idea of the universal rights of man has become virtually incomprehensible today due to the rise of the German historical consciousness, with its view that all standards of right and judgment are historically relative. This attack on the very foundations of a theory of natural right has been exacerbated by contemporary "value-neutral" social science:

> Our social science may make us very wise or clever as regards the means for any objectives we might choose. It admits being unable to help us in discriminating between legitimate and illegitimate, between just and unjust, objectives. Such a science is instrumental and nothing but instrumental: it is born to be the handmaid of any powers or any interests that be. What Machiavelli did apparently, our social science would actually do if it did not prefer—only God knows why—generous liberalism to consistency: namely, to give advice with equal competence and equal alacrity to tyrants as well as to free peoples.[51]

Strauss traces the current attack on the doctrine of natural right to the fact-value distinction and its claim that while facts and causal relations between facts are a legitimate form of knowledge, values belong to the realm of arbitrary taste and preference. We can have a perfect science of social facts, but such a science must be silent on issues affecting questions of the human good or what kind of regime is best. This disposition is the root cause of modern nihilism that Strauss defines as "the view that every preference, however evil, base or insane, has to be judged before the tribunal of reason to be as legitimate as any other preference."[52] A social science that can no longer confidently assert the superiority of freedom over tyranny is today part of the problem of modern society.[53]

Natural Right and History presents itself in the first instance as a patriotic effort to recover the American tradition of natural right from its corruption by German historicism and relativism. But appearances can be misleading. The same rules that Strauss applies to the reading of other books should be applied to his own. One rule of thumb Strauss attributes to careful writers is that they will put their popular or exoteric points at both the beginning and end of their works. These are the places where most readers will turn to discover a summary statement of an author's point of view, and they will often read no further. However, a careful writer—one who does not wish to be understood too quickly—will often bury his true beliefs in obscure or out-of-the-way parts of the text, usually near the center of the work, by which time most readers will have been lulled to sleep, that is, in places "least exposed to the curiosity of superficial readers."[54]

One should always appear pious and patriotic at the beginning and end of one's discourse and put one's true beliefs in the middle not only to avoid giving offense and incurring the consequences, but in order to gain the confidence of one's readers. At least this is the strategy followed by the most careful writers of the past. The strategy Strauss attributes to the most careful writers seems to be a reflection on his own manner of composition: "He would use many technical terms, give many quotations and attach undue importance to insignificant details; he would seem to forget the holy war of mankind in the petty squabbles of pedants. Only when he reached the core of the argument would he write three or four sentences in that terse and lively style which is apt to arrest the attention of young men who love to think."[55]

Now consider the Locke chapter in *Natural Right and History*.[56] Strauss accepted the view, less popular today than it once was, that Lockean ideas formed the theoretical foundation of the new American republic. It is not an exaggeration to say that Strauss's judgment on Locke *is* his judgment on

America. Yet this chapter closely follows Strauss's description of cautious writing set out above. The chapter occurs approximately two thirds of the way through the book, consists of forty-nine densely written pages, contains numerous quotations and detailed footnotes, and engages in scholarly quarrels with other readers. In short, it appears to bore. Only occasionally does Strauss provide those "terse and lively" sentences designed to engage the curiosity of those patient readers who "love to think." More than anywhere else in the book Strauss appears here to be following his own precepts regarding "a forgotten kind of writing."

Strauss takes it for granted that Locke was a prudent writer and as such "he reaped the reward of superior prudence: he was listened to by many people, and he wielded an extraordinarily great influence on men of affairs and on a large body of opinion." The essence of prudence means knowing "when to speak and when to keep silent."[57] Contemporary controversies over Locke's alleged theoretical incoherence often miss the point because these have less to do with Locke's intellectual deficiencies than with his peculiar reticence in expressing his true opinions. In the *Second Treatise* in particular Locke wrote not as a philosopher, but as an Englishman addressing not philosophers but Englishmen.[58] Writing in the same spirit that Macaulay attributed to those statesmen responsible for passing the Toleration Act of 1689, Locke preferred to bury all of his controversial premises behind a veil of secrecy, as it were. His preferred mode of self-presentation was that of a "cautious man of affairs" seeking "to enlist all respectable prejudices in the service of the good cause."[59]

Strauss's interpretation of Locke's prudence rests on a number of highly controversial decisions. In the first place he believes that Locke was careful not to reveal the truly radical character of his doctrine of natural right, preferring to invoke the eminently respectable name of Richard Hooker ("the judicious Hooker"), the great representative of the Thomistic tradition in the England of his time. Precisely by invoking Hooker and the Thomistic doctrine of natural law, Locke obscures his real intellectual debt to Hobbes's materialistic and non-teleological teaching about nature. Although Locke pays due regard to the great tradition of natural law stretching back beyond Thomas to the early church fathers and the Stoics, a careful reading of his teaching cannot conceal that he "deviated considerably from the traditional natural law teaching and followed the lead given by Hobbes."[60] This lead was to put the doctrine of natural law on an utterly materialist and hedonist foundation substituting for an ethic of duty and obligation the absolute right of individual self-preservation. Each person in the state of nature has the absolute right of judge, jury, and executioner over what constitutes a possible threat to his or her self-preservation. In place of a transcendent moral law, Locke proposes the right of free individual subjectivity. Accordingly, "Locke could not have recognized any law of nature in the proper sense of the term."[61]

Strauss interprets Locke as sugar-coating the harsh, even unpalatable teachings of Hobbes. Locke goes out of his way to distinguish himself from Hobbes and Spinoza, whose "justly decried names" he pretends not even to know and which Strauss gleefully exposes.[62] It was Locke's genius to have provided a kind of placebo effect that disguised an otherwise bitter pill. At issue between them is whether the natural law can be reduced to a doctrine of prudent self-regard as Hobbes maintains, or whether it requires a correlative doctrine of moral duties as Locke seems to insist. At least on the surface Hobbes regards the state of nature as a condition of absolute liberty governed by an absolute right to do whatever it is in our power to do, while for Locke the state of nature was always a moral condition in which our obligation to respect the rights, including the property, of others followed from the fact that they have corresponding duties to respect us. It is precisely because of Locke's apparent equivocation over the status of natural law, balancing unsteadily between a naturalistic and a moral foundation, that Strauss awarded to Hobbes the title of the true founder of liberalism. It is due to the primacy of rights over duties and the identification of the state with a protector of rights that Strauss can maintain that "the founder of liberalism was Hobbes."[63] The irony could not escape Strauss's attentive readers: Hobbes, not Locke, was the true founder of America.

Strauss's interpretation of Hobbes forms a fitting propaedeutic to his reading of Locke's political theory proper. He is, of course, well aware that this reading of Locke stands in "shocking contrast" to what is generally thought: that Hobbes and Locke stand as polar opposites.[64] Unlike many readers, Strauss pays scant attention to Locke's views on such matters as limited government, his theory of representation, competitive elections, or the separation of powers, even his defense of rights as a hedge against arbitrary government. Instead he focuses almost exclusively on Locke's theory of property, which he calls "almost literally the central part" and "certainly [the] most characteristic part" of his political teaching.[65] The Lockean emphasis on property merely amplifies the Hobbesian primacy of self-preservation and the means necessary to achieve it. In particular, Locke's theory of private property begins the deflection of political philosophy in the direction of political economy that would be "perfectly expressed" in Madison's statement from *Federalist,* 10 that "the first object of government" is the protection of "different and unequal faculties of *acquiring* property."[66] The assimilation of Locke to the American founding could not be more "perfectly expressed."

Strauss accepts the view that Locke's theory of property is at the root of the modern "spirit of capitalism" in virtually the same sense analyzed by Weber.[67] But unlike Weber, who traced the spirit of capitalism back to Puritan asceticism, Strauss regards capitalism as the outcome of Locke's revolutionary break with the previous natural law tradition. In the lengthiest footnote in *Natural Right and History* Strauss criticizes Weber for regarding capitalism as the outcome of changes taking place in the sphere of theology rather than as "a break that took place on the plane of purely philosophic or rational or secular thought." Buried deep in this note is Strauss's contention that the capitalist spirit is the outcome of a prior revolution in philosophy and its *"conscious break"* with the philosophical teaching of natural law. This break, he continues, preceded the advent of Puritanism by at least a century and has its true source in the thought of Machiavelli. Puritan theology turned out to be only the "carrier" of secular philosophical ideas that made their way into England by way of Bacon, Hobbes, and Locke.[68]

To return to Locke: while the ancient and medieval doctrine of natural law had sought limits on the amount of capital accumulation deemed morally permissible, Locke used natural law for precisely the opposite purpose, that is, to emancipate the right of acquisition from all prior restraints. Strauss notes that Locke's later followers were often confused by his use of the highly traditional language of natural law to defend the right of property. This is because "they took for granted what Locke did not," namely that "the unlimited acquisition of wealth is not unjust or morally wrong."[69] He is in agreement with the Marxist historian C. B. MacPherson that Locke was in effect the creator of modern bourgeois society.[70] Locke defended the right of unlimited accumulation not by appealing to "a nonexistent absolute right of property," but on the prudential and utilitarian grounds of its contribution to the public welfare. One can see from this statement why there are no Straussian libertarians. Even an alleged right of private property must first justify itself before the bar of "public happiness or the temporal prosperity of society."[71] Only on political grounds can it be determined that selfishness is more advantageous to the common good than altruism. The true benefactors of humanity are not those who help others, but those who help themselves. "Unlimited appropriation without concern for the need of others is true charity" is Strauss's summary statement of Lockean ethics.[72]

The result of Locke's emancipation of the right of property accumulation was to produce an even more "radical change" in the natural law than that of Hobbes. The centrality of labor shifted the center of the moral universe away from nature toward individual creativity as the source of all value. "Not resigned gratitude and consciously obeying or imitating nature, but hopeful self-reliance and creativity become henceforth the marks of human nobility," Strauss writes of the revolution wrought by Locke.[73] For Strauss, Locke was an all-out "hedonist" for whom man is effectively "emancipated" from all the bonds set by nature as well as all social and political arrangements that are not the outcome of our free agreement or consent. Again, unlike many readers who might find Locke's emancipation of the individual a cause for celebration, Strauss tends to see it as the cause of so many contemporary dissatisfactions.[74] The result of the emancipation of labor from all teleological conceptions of the good life has been to render life "aimless." We seek pleasure, but no longer know what to find pleasure in. The only goal is the avoidance of pain and anxiety, but the desire to avoid anxiety becomes, ironically, a cause of anxiety. In the final analysis Strauss agrees with Weber in his rather dark view of the modern "disenchanted world." "Life is the joyless quest for joy" is Strauss's dyspeptic judgment of life under the Lockean dispensation.[75]

Strauss's writing on Locke has produced a large and largely inconclusive literature on whether he got Locke right.[76] The issue typically ignored is not whether Strauss's Locke is the true Locke, but what function Locke plays in Strauss's writing. Locke is presented not simply as one philosopher among others, but as America's philosopher-king. Strauss agrees with Louis Hartz and other historians of the era that America is the Lockean nation par excellence, although he disagrees on just what that means. Hartz emphasized the dominance of Locke in America to explain not only the absence of socialism, but also the absence of all other alternatives to the overriding consensus regarding liberal beliefs and practices. Although Hartz is often taken to be celebrating the liberal consensus that has governed American political life, he was in fact highly critical of the "irrational" character of this Lockean consensus that in effect prohibited debate over first principles.[77]

Strauss, too, regarded America as something of a Lockean remnant in a world increasingly governed by more radical forms of modernity. He frequently contrasted the ancient aristocratic republics concerned with a high order of moral virtue to the "low but solid" ground of modern constitutional democracies based on self-interest and the desire for comfortable preservation.[78] While acknowledging the theoretical radicalism of Lockean principles—their profound rupture with both the classical and the biblical traditions represented by the twin poles of Athens and Jerusalem—Locke's

own prudence to some degree successfully disguised the nature of this radicalism by emphasizing his links with the past. America thus remained
something of a theoretical anomaly protected by its Lockean origins from
the gusts of later modernity. The question is what to do about it.

Strauss is silent about the development of Lockeanism in American politics, but at least two implications seem to be present. His overt teaching
based on the introduction to *Natural Right and History* is a recovery of the
possibility of natural right from both German historicism and its peculiar
American variant, Deweyan progressivism.[79] The book as a whole can be
read as an attempt to redirect American public philosophy away from the
kind of progressivism that may have served it well during the early part of
the twentieth century, but which has gradually become exhausted and may
prove unequal to the coming struggle with the Soviet Union.[80] The book
sets out a kind of irredentist strategy for reappropriating an earlier phase of
modernity as a prophylactic against the corrosive effects of Rousseau,
Marx, and Nietzsche. Indeed, *Natural Right and History* is nothing if not
an invitation to American readers to take seriously their political founding
and the philosophic ideas that gave rise to it. The American founding represented the first wave of modernity in the fullness of its theoretical vigor
and self-confidence. It is necessary to recover some of that confidence today
through the critique of historicism.[81]

Strauss's deeper teaching, however, is that such efforts at reappropria-
tion either are doomed to failure or result in fateful concessions to modernity regarding the role of rights, commerce, and technology.[82] At times he
appears to adopt a form of historicism himself in regarding late modernity
as working out the premises and consequences that were only implicit in
early modernity. On this account, the true nature of the revolution wrought
by Locke was not seen by his contemporaries, but could only have been
brought to light by later thinkers like Rousseau who were able to observe
more fully its effects. Rousseau attacked Locke's bourgeois man in the
name of Roman virtue and citizenship. His was a movement of return.
Rousseau's protest against modernity, however, led not to a return to pre-
modernity, but rather to even more radical forms of modernity.[83]

Strauss sometimes writes as if America has been uniquely resistant to
both the great heights and the great depths of European modernism.
Ironically, Strauss was himself the product of a high European modernism
whose influence he frequently deplores.[84] He is entirely silent on how such
figures as Thoreau, Emerson, Whitman, James, and others helped to shape
a distinctively American modernist literary and intellectual culture. No
more than any other country could America hope to escape the influence of

the second and third waves of modernity initiated by Rousseau and
Nietzsche respectively. The idea of a return to a pristine vision of America
before the advent of romanticism, progressivism, and today multiculturalism is to invoke a kind of nostalgia for a golden age that never properly
existed in the first place. Instead America is the site where the many facets
of modernity have been working themselves out. America, in the words of
Joseph Cropsey, is a moment in the comprehensive "self-dissatisfaction"
that is modernity.[85] A return to Lockeanism is not the cure to the pathologies of modern politics. The pathologies of modernity are already the
pathologies of Locke.

A Machiavellian Moment

Strauss would have found laughable the attempt to bathe the American
founding in the warm glow of antiquity. The American founding, in Carey
McWilliams's phrase, was "a decisively modern event."[86] The true founder
of modernity, as Strauss barely alludes to above, was neither Hobbes
nor Locke, but Machiavelli. "It was Machiavelli," he wrote, "that greater
Columbus, who had discovered the continent on which Hobbes could erect
his structure."[87] Machiavelli was Professor Moriarty to Hobbes's Sherlock
Holmes, his evil *Doppelganger*. Machiavelli said what no Englishman, not
even Hobbes and certainly not Locke, could afford to say openly, namely,
that in politics we have to operate entirely on our own without recourse
to either natural or supernatural guidance. Even as plain-spoken an
Englishman as Hobbes had to sanitize ("mitigate") his teachings by
employing traditional-sounding terms like natural law if they were to prove
acceptable to an Anglo-Saxon audience. Machiavelli's amoral love of glory
and his celebration of warriors like Hannibal and Scipio were turned by
Hobbes into the pedestrian desire for self-preservation and by Locke into
the right to property. This emancipation of acquisitiveness, while apparently a minor modification of Hobbes, was to have revolutionary consequences. Locke showed how it was possible to achieve peacefully and for
the benefit of all what Machiavelli had believed was only attainable
through war. Economics was simply warfare fought through other means.
"Economism," Strauss wrote in one of those terse and lively sentences, "is
Machiavellianism come of age."[88]

Machiavelli was deliberately relegated to only a bit part in *Natural
Right and History* in order to downplay his influence on the modern natu-
ral rights tradition.[89] But the role of Machiavelli in the rise of modern
Roman-style republicanism should not be underestimated. Machiavelli's

admiration for ancient Rome is said to be but the flip side of his rejection of ancient political philosophy. His revolt against the ancient philosophers led him to substitute patriotism or "merely political virtue" for moral virtue and the contemplative ideal. Taking his bearings from "the effectual truth of things," he sought the means for creating a republic that could be actualized through human doings rather than dependence on fortune or providence. The American founding was but the first successful attempt to translate Machiavellian republicanism into practice.[90]

The role of Machiavelli and "civic republican" thought on the American founding has become a subject of sustained controversy in recent years.[91] Machiavelli's appeal to patriotic feeling and a politics of the common good is said to offer an alternative to the purely rights-based juridical liberalism of Lockean natural rights. But unlike many current defenders of Machiavellian republicanism, Strauss did not attempt to gild the lily. Machiavellian virtue meant devotion to the public good, but the public good was merely a form of "collective selfishness." Since the good of one public may well clash with the good of another, war and the preparation for war were never far from Machiavelli's main concerns. It was his admiration for "the lupine politics of republican Rome" that led Machiavelli to emphasize the extreme situations in political life, the most extreme of which necessitates the founding and re-founding of regimes. Foundings are inherently problematic, and Machiavelli delighted in bringing out their morally ambiguous character. They always entail violence or, in the Roman case, fratricide. It is not the recognition of this fact alone that constitutes the "Machiavellian" character of Machiavelli's writings, but his claim that all future legitimacy grows out of murder.[92]

Strauss explicitly addresses the relation between Machiavelli and the American founding in the introduction to his *Thoughts on Machiavelli*. Here he indicates that there are "good reasons" for presenting a book on Machiavelli to an American audience in particular. "The United States of America may be said to be the only country in the world which was founded in explicit opposition to Machiavellian principles," Strauss writes.[93] He continues this thought:

According to Machiavelli, the founder of the most renowned commonwealth of the world was a fratricide: the foundation of political greatness is necessarily laid in crime. If we can believe Thomas Paine, all governments of the Old World have an origin of this description; their origin was conquest and tyranny. But "the Independence of America [was] accompanied by a Revolution in the principles and practice of

Governments": the foundation of the United Sates was laid in freedom
and justice. "Government founded on a moral theory, on a system of
universal peace, on the indefeasible hereditary Rights of Man, is now
revolving from west to east by a stronger impulse than the Government
of the sword revolved from east to west." This judgment is far from
being obsolete. While freedom is no longer a preserve of the United
States, the United States is now the bulwark of freedom. And contemporary tyranny has its roots in Machiavelli's thought, in the
Machiavellian principle that the good end justifies every means. At least
to the extent that the American reality is inseparable from the
American aspiration, one cannot understand Americanism without
understanding Machiavellianism which is its opposite.[94]

Here Strauss puts forward his own version of American exceptionalism
("The United States of America may be said to be the only country in the
world which was founded on explicit opposition to Machiavellian principles"). This passage deliberately begs a number of important questions. Of
all the countries of the world, how did America manage miraculously to
escape contamination by Machiavelli? And if America was developed in
"explicit opposition" to Machiavellian principles, what are the sources of
its resistance? One answer would be to follow Tocqueville in regarding the
sources of American liberty as lying in the nation's Puritan background, or
to see in the Declaration of Independence a unique combination of
Lockean, biblical, and Ciceronian ideals. But note that this is precisely
what Strauss does not say. Instead he cites Tom Paine, the most pro-
Enlightenment, proto-Jacobin figure of eighteenth-century America, to the
effect that America is founded on a new moral system of "universal peace"
and on the "indefeasible hereditary Rights of Man" that he goes on to say
have acquired a kind of world-historical significance "revolving from west
to east." The cited passage sounds more like Kant's theory of a cosmopolitan history and perpetual peace—a key moment in Strauss's "second wave"
of modernity—than anything one might find in either the classical or the
biblical tradition.

Nor is this all. Strauss acknowledges that contemporary tyranny has its
source in the Machiavellian dictum that the ends justify the means. What
he does not acknowledge (at least not here) is that Machiavelli is also the
unique source for the revival of modern republicanism and a kind of civic-
minded idealism. He includes *The Federalist Papers* as among the works
influenced by the revival of Machiavellian republicanism that became "one
of the most powerful trends of modern political thought."[95] There is a

universalism to Machiavelli's thought—that is, he offers advice equally to principalities and republics—but in the passage cited above Strauss deliberately suppresses Machiavelli's role in the renaissance of Roman-style republicanism. Why? One is reminded of the following passage: "If a master of the art of writing commits such blunders as would shame an intelligent high school boy, it is reasonable to assume that they are intentional, especially if the author discusses, however incidentally, the possibility of intentional blunders in writing."[96] Strauss may be guilty of overstating the case for contemporary high school education, but he provides an unambiguous insight into his own manner of writing.

Strauss goes on to reveal his deeper understanding in a passage where he shifts from the active to the passive voice:

> But we cannot conceal from ourselves the fact that the problem is more complex than it appears in the presentation by Paine and his followers. Machiavelli would argue that America owes her greatness not only to her habitual adherence to the principles of freedom and justice, but also to her occasional deviation from them. He would not hesitate to suggest a mischievous interpretation of the Louisiana Purchase and of the fate of the Red Indians. He would conclude that facts like these are an additional proof for his contention that there cannot be a great and glorious society without the equivalent of the murder of Remus by his brother Romulus.[97]

Strauss offers this correction to his earlier formulation by offering a Machiavellian or "mischievous interpretation" of American policy. Given that Strauss himself evidently enjoyed offering his own mischievous interpretations of such received figures as Locke, one cannot avoid the conclusion that he regards the mischievous interpretation as the true interpretation. His use of the word "occasional" in the phrase "occasional deviation" above is a clear and unambiguous imitation of the term *occasione*, which Machiavelli uses to indicate the contingent, erratic, and unpredictable nature of politics that can only be provisionally controlled through the actions of creative statesmen, whether in the mold of Cesare Borgia or of Thomas Jefferson. He offers this interpretation, again, not in his own voice, but by citing Henry Adams's *History of the United States during the Administrations of Thomas Jefferson* to highlight the Machiavellian character of the acquisition of the Louisiana Territory.

Adams never mentions Machiavelli or Machiavellianism by name, although there can be no doubt that his treatment of Jefferson in particular is intended to bring out the contradiction between his democratic ideals and the actual practice of his statecraft. Consider the following passage from the *History* where Adams presents his summary judgment on Jefferson's machinations in the purchase of Louisiana:

> Even in 1804 the political consequences of the act were already too striking to be overlooked. Within three years of his inauguration Jefferson bought a foreign colony without its consent and against its will, annexed it to the United States by an act which he said made blank paper of the Constitution; and then he who had found his predecessors too monarchical and the Constitution too liberal in power . . . made himself monarch of the new territory and wielded over it, against its protests, the power of its old kings.[98]

Throughout the *History* Adams takes special delight in exposing just how far Jefferson was willing to depart from his high democratic ideals in order to achieve his political ambitions. The fact that Strauss elsewhere refers to Adams as "the best American historian I know" suggests how seriously he takes this view.[99] Jefferson's acquisition of Louisiana may not have been the equivalent of Romulus's murder of Remus, but it suggests that, as Strauss puts it above, the problem of America is "more complex" than any theory of American immaculate conception would imply.

Burning Down the House

The debate over the origins of the American republic is not a piece of "self-forgetting and pain-loving antiquarianism."[100] Origins determine outcomes. The founding of nations, as Tocqueville reminds us, affects the entire course of their history.[101] The issue is whether by highlighting the "low but solid"—perhaps not even quite so solid—origins of American republicanism, Strauss is not denigrating the case for America. By appealing to the Lockean and even Machiavellian foundations of America, does Strauss deny to the regime those higher qualities of virtue, nobility, and the possibility of statesmanship? Can a regime dedicated to the pursuit of happiness ever satisfy the deepest longings of the human soul? The answer is "obviously not," but then Strauss never for a moment imagined the purpose of politics was to satisfy our deepest longings.

Strauss was not a legislator. He did not propose any wholesale vision for the reform of American politics or endorse any particular set of public policies. He certainly did not write to produce an ideology, that is, a body of doctrine intended to serve as a blueprint for political action. He was, so far as I am aware, a member of no political party.[102] Although he has come to be associated with conservatism, it is probably more accurate to say that he saw politics neither from the Right nor from the Left but from above.[103] "It is safer," Strauss wrote, "to try to understand the low in the light of the high than the high in the light of the low."[104] If by "the high" he meant the philosophical life and all that attends to it, then one can only conclude that one should never judge philosophy by the standards of politics, but should rather judge politics by the standards of philosophy. The question is not whether Strauss provides an ennobling picture of American democracy, but whether American democracy provides a safe haven for philosophy. This remains, as Strauss likes to say, an open question.

Strauss was neither a conservative nor a liberal in any of the standard uses of those terms. He preferred instead to tweak some of the differences between them. Liberals, he wrote in the 1960s, oppose the war in Vietnam while favoring the war on poverty, while conservatives would have it the other way round. Conservatives abhor violent change, yet one of the most conservative, if not reactionary, organizations in America was called the Daughters of the American Revolution. Conservatives typically prefer diversity to unity and the particular to the universal, but is this not to abandon the idea of the unity of truth that has been the core of the philosophical tradition?[105] If anything, Strauss defined his philosophical position as skeptical, recognizing that there were no permanent answers, only permanent problems in philosophical life. At the moment one's belief in the certainty of the solutions comes to outweigh awareness of the problematic character of all solutions, "the sectarian is born."[106]

Strauss may not have been a legislator, but he was an educator whose proposals took the form of a reform of his own chosen discipline. He had the fortune—or maybe the misfortune—to write at a time when the rise of the behavioral study of politics and its confidence about the capacities of modern science were at their height.[107] Strauss did not call for a new political science, but for a restoration of certain classical approaches to the study of politics. Rather than propose a "city in speech" (Plato) or "new modes and orders" (Machiavelli), he chose the more modest task of offering advice to his fellow political scientists about how they might improve their craft. This does not mean that Strauss longed to recreate the conditions of the ancient *polis*. But he did try to revive certain features of ancient political science precisely for the insight they shed on the conditions of modern democracy.

Strauss was a teacher of political science in its classic sense. This does not mean resurrecting certain ancient philosophical dogmas as an answer to contemporary problems. His teaching sought instead to focus on the relation of philosophy to society as the ancients understood this. Modern political science suffers from two contrary failings. In its aspiration to become scientific, it repeats the failure of Socrates as depicted in the *Clouds* of Aristophanes. The Aristophanic Socrates is depicted as a natural scientist and cosmologist investigating the first causes of things at the expense of human knowledge, knowledge of laws and morality. Modern political science, often speaking the abstract language of mathematical economics, is like the Aristophanic Socrates, that is, characterized by its remoteness and alienation from the concerns of the city. Such a science is not so much dangerous as laughable because of its very ignorance of those things that every well-brought-up citizen already knows. The fact that Aristophanes's comedy ends with Socrates's think tank being burned to the ground by a disgruntled disciple should give political scientists pause for thought.[108]

At the same time modern political science is beset by a desire to be useful. This means that political science takes its bearings not from how things ought to be, but from what is. It must cease to be concerned with questions about the best regime and must concentrate on the control of what is within our power to achieve. Political science proves its utility by focusing on the Is and not the Ought. But by focusing narrowly on the behavioral foundation of politics, political science tends to lose sight of the distinction between well-ordered and faulty regimes. Judgment and evaluation are as much a part of the language of political science as are description and explanation. A political science that cannot use terms like tyranny or freedom (except perhaps in quotation marks) is not a science of politics at all. A political science that cannot address the differences between good and bad, better and worse, is at best a parody of a science.[109]

At the center of Strauss's political science stands the concept of the regime or the way in which institutions are structured in any community.[110] Every community, even the diverse polyglot societies of advanced modernity, constitutes an ordered whole in which the arrangement of powers and offices structures human behavior. Instead of explaining politics by the behavior of interest groups or ethnicities, Strauss showed how the behavior of these groups is fundamentally dependent upon the regime, its governing principles and standards. Each regime represents not only an organization of powers and institutions, but a collective judgment on the relative justice of those institutional arrangements. Every regime contains in its laws and policies a collective judgment on what is just and unjust, and it is this judgment, however imperfectly expressed, that bestows a fundamental legitimacy on the nature of the regime. Strauss was an institutionalist before the term was invented.

The centrality of regime politics is connected to Strauss's conception of the primacy of the political. Political science remains for Strauss not simply one social science among others, but the architectonic discipline that guides the rest. Behavioralism and its successor approaches have all attempted to reduce political life to certain subpolitical economic, psychological, or sociological variables. Accordingly, they either distort what is properly political or confuse the political with the nonpolitical. While the behavioralist orientation was interested only in what could be studied *en masse* and reduced to a set of statistical regularities, today's rational choice approach regards politics as a marketplace where individual preferences are formed and utilities are maximized. What is specifically political is either bleached out or explained away. By reducing all politics to choice and all choices to preferences, the new political science fails to grasp how the constitution and its fundamental laws shape the character of its citizen body.

Strauss's emphasis on the primacy of the regime is at odds not only with behavioral and rational choice approaches to the study of politics, but with much of contemporary "normative" theory as well. Although Strauss did not live to comment on the "new normativism," as it has been called, his response to it would not be difficult to discern.[111] Typical of such approaches are works like John Rawls's *A Theory of Justice* and Jürgen Habermas's *A Theory of Communicative Rationality*. Each of these works advances theories of justice or democracy (called by Habermas "an ideal speech situation") that are presented as standards against which to criticize current policies. These theories are in turn derived from certain norms of public rationality that are said to constrain what can and cannot be used in justifying public policy. Such approaches are curiously antipolitical, as they assume the primacy of certain normative or ethical standards from which politics are then deduced rather than starting with the centrality of the regime and asking what kinds of public policies help to preserve or change a given order. For Strauss, by contrast, it is only by staying close to the surface of things that it becomes possible to penetrate to the heart of things.[112]

It is the very abstractness of so much political science, its increasing remoteness from the substantive issues of political life, that Strauss warns against. "Political science," he reminds us, "stands or falls by the truth of the pre-scientific awareness of things."[113] Political science must begin from the opinions and perspectives of the ordinary citizen. This is not to say the aim of political science is simply to reproduce citizen opinion in all of its complexity, but a science that has become radically detached from that opinion is in danger of losing sight of the very phenomena it seeks to explain. The purpose of political science is not to stand above or outside the political community as an entomologist observing the behavior of ants, but to serve as a civic-minded arbitrator of disputes in order to restore peace and stability to conflict-ridden situations. Political science is not simply a value-neutral science, but a practical engagement with political life. We are today in danger of losing touch with the questions and insights that are the original motivation for understanding political life. In place of these basic questions has arisen a narrow-minded focus on "methodology" and the philosophy of explanation that often overshadow the life-and-death issues that make up the substance of politics.[114]

For Strauss political science remained first and foremost a practical discipline. Its main function was the education of citizens and future leaders. But as that great pre-Straussian philosopher Karl Marx once asked, "who will educate the educators?" Strauss's concern was clearly with educating the next generation of teachers of political science. Accordingly, he focused on those texts that put issues of political education front and center—works like Plato's *Laws*, Machiavelli's *Discourses*, and Montesquieu's *Spirit of the Laws*, to name but the most prominent. Despite the obvious differences between ancients and moderns, these works subordinated their strictly "theoretical" teachings to such practical considerations as the different kinds of regimes and laws appropriate to them, the character of the citizen body, and the ways of achieving preservation and change. Furthermore, these works were written in the language of their time, were relatively free of jargon, and presented the case for the moral seriousness of politics in the strongest possible terms.[115]

As an institutionalist, Strauss taught his readers to take the constitution seriously, above all its structure of rights and responsibilities. He worried about the tendency of contemporary political science to neglect constitutional formalities by focusing on mass behavior or, as it is called today, collective action problems. Strauss witnessed at first hand the destruction of the Weimar constitution due to the rise of a populist movement that cared little for constitutional forms and catered to the basest instincts of the population. "The Weimar Republic was weak" was Strauss's judgment on its inability to defend itself from its enemies.[116] The same kind of attack on constitutionalism was evidenced in the 1960s when radicals disparaged representative government and "procedural justice" in the name of direct participatory democracy. Recent proposals for more deliberative democracy and calls for publicly funded days of national deliberation are merely watered-down versions of the populist assault on the Constitution.[117]

Strauss wrote to strengthen those aspects of American public life that would prevent constitutional democracy from devolving into mass democracy. "We are not permitted to be flatterers of democracy," he wrote, "precisely because we are friends and allies of democracy."[118] But the friend and ally of democracy is not the same thing as a democrat. Strauss was not a partisan of any regime precisely because he was a political philosopher. Philosophy demands a zone of independence for the mind that effectively transcends political obligations and loyalties. This did not prevent him from recognizing, however, that "liberal or constitutional democracy comes closer to what the classics demanded than any alternative that is viable in our age."[119] Strauss's qualifier ("comes closer") suggests that while liberal democracy may be the best available regime, there is still considerable latitude in what form a liberal or constitutional government may take. The task of political science today is to teach neither a scientific detachment from one's country and its traditions nor a fanatical partisanship that regards the distinction between friend and enemy as the primordial political experience, but rather an "unhesitating loyalty to a decent constitution and even to the cause of constitutionalism."[120]

CHAPTER EIGHT

WWLSD; or, What Would Leo Strauss Do?

Tyranny is a danger coeval with political life. — *Leo Strauss*, On Tyranny

Introduction

A virtual truism among journalists and various media pundits is that Leo Strauss has exercised a profound and demonic influence on the foreign policy of the George W. Bush administration. It is taken for granted that the war in Iraq was the brainchild of figures like Paul Wolfowitz, Richard Perle, and William Kristol, all labeled as "neo-conservatives" and all of whose thinking is said to derive from a common source in the philosophy of Strauss.

The association of Strauss with the foreign policy of the Bush administration began just at the time the United States entered the war with Iraq. The chief intellectual architect of the war was thought to be Paul Wolfowitz, a former ambassador to Indonesia and a Ph.D. in Political Science who had studied with Allan Bloom as an undergraduate and had taken graduate courses with Strauss and Albert Wohlstetter at the University of Chicago. Long before the current fascination began, Wolfowitz figured in a minor role in Saul Bellow's novel *Ravelstein*, his fictionalized account of his late friend and colleague Allan Bloom.

On the basis of this connection journalists constructed elaborate intellectual genealogies to show the influence of Strauss or "Straussians" (like Bloom and Harvey Mansfield) on a range of opinion makers and policy analysts. Respectable journalists like Seymour Hersh writing for *The New Yorker* and Pulitzer Prize–winning biographer Sam Tannenhaus writing for *Vanity Fair* fell into the trap of assuming guilt by the most fanciful association. On their own admission very few, if any, of these journalists had ever read the work of Strauss; instead they relied on the work of other journalists already making the same claim. There emerged a self-reinforcing circle of prejudice and innuendo.

Added to this, especially in the European press, has been a thinly veiled strain of anti-Semitism. Strauss was himself a Jewish refugee from Hitler's Germany, and many of his students were Jewish. This provided evidence, for those prepared to believe it, of a Jewish cabal whose real purpose was alleged to be the defense of Israel. The ugly innuendo was that this group of "neo-cons"—as *New York Times* columnist David Brooks put it, "con" being short for conservative, "neo" for Jewish—was using its influence in foreign policy as a tool to advance Israeli interests. I will not even mention some of the kookier theories of a Jewish conspiracy, although a quick look at the Web would be sufficient to show how widespread this virus has become.

As if all this were not enough, the name of Strauss has even appeared in a recent Broadway play written by Academy Award–winning actor (and antiwar activist) Tim Robbins. In this play, titled *Embedded*, Robbins depicts the war in Iraq as manipulated by a sinister cabal who periodically throughout the play shout "hail to Leo Strauss." In the play's program, the audience is told that Strauss believed that democracy was "best defended by an ignorant public pumped up on nationalism and religion." This would be laughable if it were not evidence for a kind of McCarthyism of the Left. How has this come about?

When Leo Strauss died, just over thirty years ago, his influence was confined to a small group of students of political philosophy who were for the most part intrigued by his recovery of the great quarrel between the ancients and the moderns. A few others were similarly influenced by Strauss's rediscovery of the tradition of esoteric writing, according to which great thinkers of the past often hid their most provocative thoughts under complex layers of dissimulation and contradiction. Perhaps following some of his great predecessors, Strauss preferred to remain silent on political matters, rarely if ever venturing into the territory of contemporary commentary. One searches his writings almost in vain for references to current affairs, much less policy prescriptions. He once described himself as "one of those who refuse to go through open doors when one can enter just as well through a keyhole."[1] How, then, did this most reticent and secretive of modern thinkers become a virtual poster child for the current administration's war in Iraq?

The Crisis of the West

The opening gambit of Strauss's political philosophy is his diagnosis of what he calls the "crisis of the West." In the introduction to *Natural Right and History*, still his most influential book, Strauss describes this crisis as precipitated by the rise of the German historical consciousness or the historical sense. Writing in the years immediately after World War II, he traces the decline of the Lockean doctrine of natural rights as embodied in the American Declaration of Independence and the rise of a form of historical relativism that regards all standards of right and justice as relative to their own time and place. "It would not be the first time," Strauss avers, "that a nation defeated on the battlefield . . . has deprived its conquerors of the most sublime fruit of victory by imposing on them the yoke of its own thought."[2]

Strauss returned to this theme again in the introduction to his book *The City and Man*. Here he indicates that the crisis of the West consists in a loss of confidence, "in the West's having become uncertain of its purpose."[3] The purpose of the West he identifies with certain public documents issued between the two World Wars. These documents—one thinks of Woodrow Wilson's famous Fourteen Points—stated that the goals of a just society were to be a "universal league of free and equal nations, each nation consisting of free and equal men and women."[4] This loss of confidence, he avers, is today more than a "strong but vague feeling"; it has acquired the character of "scientific exactitude" among social scientists who are no longer able to regard the principles of the universal and prosperous society as anything more than an ideology superior in neither truth nor justice to innumerable other ideologies.[5]

This loss of confidence derives from two sources, both of which are indigenous to the West. The first is what Strauss elsewhere calls the "experience of history," that is, the belief that there are many different cultures each of which must be regarded as the legitimate equal of every other. The West is thus to be understood as just one culture among many whose ends or ways of life cannot be ranked according to any hierarchy or follow any overall pattern of development. Cultures are unique and irreducible to one another. Western or liberal views of humanity and justice must be seen as "culture-bound," reflecting or expressing the dominant values of one particular society. The attempt to impose one culture or way of life on another is thus seen as a violation of the most fundamental principle of the modern science of culture, namely, universal toleration or the principle of respect for all cultures. Today what Strauss called the experience of history goes under the name of multiculturalism.[6]

The second source of dissatisfaction with the West derives from a very different kind of experience, the experience of communism. For communism originally presented itself as merely carrying out more fully or completely what Western liberalism had originally promised. Drawing on the teachings of Kant, Marx came to believe that democracy could not be possible in a single state, but ultimately would have to extend to the entire globe; hence the universal state or classless society. But Marx ignored Kant's warning that a world state could only produce a "soulless despotism." It was only over time that Marxism came to reveal itself not as the fulfillment of the West but its antithesis. The ends of communism could not be separated from the means necessary to establish it. To be sure, one could argue that the brutality of the means as well as key departures from Marxian universalism such as Stalin's policy of "socialism in one country" fly in the face of the principles of communism. But Strauss retorts that it is opposed to the principles of communism to separate the ends from the historical process by which they are established. Communism would remain for the "foreseeable future" the opponent of Western liberalism. "We see that the victory of Communism," Strauss writes, "would mean indeed the victory of originally Western natural science but surely at the same time the victory of the most extreme form of Eastern despotism."[7]

Contrary to the views of many critics who regard him as an enemy of liberalism or democracy, Strauss makes clear that the danger to the West comes not from liberalism but from our loss of confidence in it. This loss of confidence was precipitated by certain currents in modern philosophy that made notions of right or justice, previously regarded as rooted in certain permanencies of human nature, appear to be nothing more than myths or ideologies. A society that regards its highest ideals as no more than an arbitrary collection of value judgments can certainly not feel confident in its sense of purpose. The question Strauss asks his readers to consider is whether liberal democracy has within itself the resources to regain its sense of direction. To what might one turn?

The Turn to Classical Political Philosophy

Strauss's search for an answer to the crisis of the West led him on a long and circuitous journey into the history of political philosophy both ancient and modern. The crisis of the West has not been precipitated by the contradictions of capitalism, as the Marxists believed, or by the secularization of society, as the Weberians maintained. In order to understand this crisis and what to do about it one must return to its deepest roots in the philosophy of classical antiquity.

The core of classical political philosophy—the central idea from which all the spokes radiate—is the concept of the regime. "Regime" is our translation of the Greek word *politeia*, which signifies both the way power is shared in a community and something like the fundamental law of the land, the constitutional principles that order a society. The regime refers to more than the form of government in the relatively narrow legal sense; it refers to the entire way of life of a society, its habits, customs, and moral beliefs, as when we speak of the *ancien régime* in France.[8]

The regime has (as we might say today) both a factual and a normative component. It is descriptive of the actual distribution of powers and offices within a political community; and it maintains an ideal of human character and conduct to which citizens ought to aspire. Classical political philosophy meant essentially regime analysis. It focused not only on the distinctive features that constitute a particular society, but also on the small number of different regime types that have appeared and will continue to recur throughout human experience. Although regimes will vary as to how they distribute honors and offices—whether to the one, the few, or the many—there are certain features that all regimes have in common.

In the first place, every regime represents an organization of human needs and dispositions. Although the first cause of human society may be the need for preservation, every community exists to foster certain distinctively human traits and characteristics such as love, affection, friendship, and a concern for others. Each regime, therefore, is entrusted with shaping a certain sense of right and wrong, just and unjust ways of behavior that distinguish it from other regime types.

Second, the ancients understood a regime to be possible only in a relatively small or "closed" society. The conditions of mutual trust and common affection that hold society together are only possible within a small *polis*-like community. Moral behavior, the ancients believed, arises from the sense that we have obligations to others. These obligations are felt most strongly to those with whom we have direct attachments—family, friends, compatriots—and radiate out from there. Such particular loyalties and attachments are not the morally arbitrary products of a genetic lottery, as so many contemporary philosophers believe, but are the building blocks of society without which morality withers and dies.

The ancients regarded the regime to be something irremediably particular. This is not to say that Strauss attributed to the ancients a conception of political life as an ongoing struggle between "friend and enemy" in Carl

Schmitt's sense of the term. He did, however, regard the different regimes as organized around sets of constitutionally irreducible organizing principles. In this context, the idea of a cosmopolitan or universal society—an issue to which we will turn later—was for Strauss synonymous with global despotism. The various pathologies of modern mass society are very much a consequence of the effort to create a potentially unlimited open society. In one of Strauss's most provocative assertions, he writes: "An open or all-comprehensive society will exist on a lower level of humanity than a closed society, which, through generations, has made a supreme effort toward human perfection."[9]

Finally, the ancients reserved the highest role of political life for the work of the statesman or legislator. Statesmanship represented for them the highest form of non-philosophic life. The true statesmen—the "fathers of the Constitution," as we might say—establish the permanent framework within which later politicians may handle changing and contingent situations. Freedom and empire are the two outstanding goals sought by those most serious about human excellence. It is the statesman, not the ordinary citizen or good man, who is distinguished above all by the love of fame and honor.[10]

The question Strauss leaves us with is this: what can we today learn from the ancients? In what sense can ancient prescriptions serve as modern remedies? Strauss is deeply aware that his investigations were no more than "tentative or experimental," that one cannot expect classical political philosophy to supply "recipes" for today's use. "Only we living today," he cautions, "can possibly find a solution to the problems of today."[11] Still, he has frequently been accused of attempting to propose the small, tight-knit social patterns of the ancient *polis* as a solution to the problems of a modern, complex, socially differentiated civil society. Nothing in fact could be farther from the truth.

Modern Solutions to Ancient Dilemmas

Strauss is famous for his recovery of the quarrel between the ancients and the moderns and his own stated "preference" for the theory of classical natural right.[12] This did not blind him to the many ways in which early modern political thinkers were indebted to the ancients. In particular, the modern doctrine of the separation of powers celebrated in the works of Locke, Montesquieu, and the *Federalist* authors is a direct descendant of the ancient theory of the mixed regime found in Aristotle and Polybius. How did this transition occur?

According to the ancients, the best practical regime—which, incidentally, also went by the term *politeia*—featured a power-sharing arrangement between the various classes and social groups that made up the
community. Although the best regime might still have been considered one
governed by philosopher-kings, a healthy dose of realism dictated a preference for a mixed constitution where the aristocracy shares power with the
people. Ancient republicanism was still dominated by an aristocratic class
called gentlemen (*kaloikagathoi*)—not philosophers in the strict sense, but
men of inherited wealth and property who are open to liberal education.
The ancients regarded the gentleman as "the political reflection, or imitation, of the wise man." Accordingly, gentlemen are said to have this in
common with the philosopher, "that they 'look down' on many things
which are highly esteemed by the vulgar or that they are experienced in
things noble and beautiful." The gentlemanly class will be drawn from the
urban patriciate who are best suited to obey the laws by knowing how to
rule and be ruled in turn.[13]

Far from disparaging the model of aristocratic republicanism, early
modern political philosophers eagerly sought means of reproducing it even
in changed political conditions. How to produce a new ruling aristocracy,
not of wealth and birth, but of talent and intellect? To this end, modern
political writers like Locke set about composing educational treatises that
would shape the character and habits of mind of the new ruling class.
Similarly, the *Federalist* authors tried to create a complex system of checks
and balances that would favor representatives of broad and enlightened disposition. Even the archetypal American democrat, Thomas Jefferson, wrote
to John Adams expressing the view that the best government is one that
provides "the most effectually for a pure selection of the natural *aristoi* into
offices of the government."[14]

Of course, the differences between ancient and modern republicanism
must always be kept in mind. While the Roman republic was based on certain permanent and hereditary distinctions between patrician and plebeian,
modern American republicanism was carried out on a broad base of equality. But even within this broadly egalitarian body, certain institutional
measures were adopted to promote persons of quality. The principle of election, it must be recalled, was considered by the framers to be an aristocratic
institution designed to select individuals of virtue and ability. "Under the
most favorable circumstances," Strauss writes, "the men who will hold the
balance of power will then be the men of the learned professions. In the best
case, Hamilton's republic will be ruled by the men of the learned professions."[15] By the learned professions, he means principally the law. But this,

as Strauss recognizes, is "the best case." He also recognizes that there is no guarantee that men of the legal profession will be liberally educated, at least in the classical sense.

Strauss realized that the case for liberal democracy stands or falls with the case for liberal education. To state the matter bluntly: liberal education is elitist. It presupposes a hierarchy of talent and intellect. But unlike ancient republicanism, modern republicanism is devoted to the principle of equality, that "all men are created equal." There seems to be a fatal disproportion between the claims of education and the claims of democracy. The question is how to make democracy open to liberal education.

To his credit Strauss offers no easy answer to this question. Democracy in the original sense of the term meant a universal aristocracy, a regime where everyone was entitled to the fruits of a liberal education.[16] This proved unworkable. But today modern democracy has become mass democracy, and mass democracy is ruled by mass culture. To be sure, mass culture is compatible with, even presupposes, a high degree of scientific and technical expertise. What one finds is a highly developed scientific specialization and division of labor coexisting with a mass culture that panders to our lowest tastes and desires.

Under these circumstances what we call education is often not liberal education at all, but at most a form of democratic indoctrination:

> There exists a very dangerous tendency to identify the good man with the good sport, the cooperative fellow, the "regular guy," i.e., an overemphasis on a certain part of social virtue and a corresponding neglect of those virtues which mature, if they do not flourish, in privacy, not to say solitude: by educating people to cooperate with each other in a friendly spirit, one does not yet educate non-conformists, people who are prepared to stand alone, to fight alone "rugged individualists." Democracy has not yet found a defense against the creeping conformism and the ever-increasing invasion of privacy which it fosters.[17]

Although Strauss proposes liberal education as "the counterpoison to mass culture," he also recognizes other, equally powerful dangers to the future of liberal democratic regimes.[18]

The Threat of Universalism to the Autonomy of Politics

A central tenet of Strauss's political teaching is that the defense of liberal democracy is today the highest act of statesmanship. This meant understanding and confronting the differences between liberal democracy and its chief competitors, which in Strauss's time meant principally Marxian communism. Liberalism and Marxism are both children of modern philosophy and as such appear to be limbs of the same tree. Yet they derive from very different phases or "waves" of modernity. Liberalism is a product of modernity's first wave, with its belief in natural rights and civil and political liberties; Marxism belongs to modernity's second wave, with its historical and later historicist critique of rights as a form of "bourgeois" freedom. The best regime was understood by Marxism to be the universal classless society brought into being not through prudence or intelligent statecraft, but through the historical process.

Strauss's critique of Marxian universalism was carried out in his exchange with the great Hegelian philosopher Alexandre Kojève. For Kojève, the dialectic of world history ("the struggle for recognition") would only be brought to completion in what he called the "universal and homogenous state." Only in a universal classless society could the conditions for complete human emancipation be satisfied. A softer version of this conviction has been held by Wilsonian idealists as well as contemporary European social democrats who have relaxed the demand for a world state and would be content with a global federation of all existing and emergent states under the auspices of a fortified UN and international courts of justice.

Strauss was deeply resistant to this kind of cosmopolitanism or global citizenship, whose ultimate end is the withering away of the sovereign state. This is in part due to his belief that statecraft only comes to light in something particular. The universal homogenous state has as its end the replacement of politics with administration and the reduction of prudent judgment to the technical rules of expertise. Following the analysis of Max Weber, Strauss envisaged a nightmare world composed of "specialists without spirit, sensualists without heart." Unlimited technological progress and the increase in economies of scale that go with it are "destructive of humanity." The world state would resemble nothing so much as the world of Nietzsche's "last man."[19]

The real danger to humanity posed by universalism in either its hard or soft variety is to the future of liberty. One cannot help noting the irony that Marxism, which grows out of a legitimate demand to recognize the freedom and dignity of every individual, leads to a system of brutality and tyranny that denies its very premises. For Strauss, we find ourselves in a situation unprecedented in human history:

We are now brought face to face with a tyranny which holds out the threat of becoming, thanks to "the conquest of nature" and in particular human nature, what no earlier tyranny ever became: perpetual and universal. Confronted by the appalling alternative that man, or human thought, must be collectivized either by one stroke and without mercy or else by slow and gentle processes, we are forced to wonder how we could escape from this dilemma. We reconsider therefore the elementary and unobtrusive conditions of human freedom.[20]

The end of communism and the waning of the cold war after 1989 have done nothing to abate the force of Strauss's warning. The dangers to liberal democracy today lie less in the Marxian theory of class struggle and the classless society than in a revivified form of religious fundamentalism with its furious denunciation of liberal democracy. Unlike most social scientists, who had consigned issues of religion and ethno-nationalism to the dustbin of history, Strauss kept alive what he called the permanence of the "theologico-political problem."[21]

The theologico-political problem remains at the core of every society because every society is constituted by opinion, and underlying these opinions are often conceptions of God or the gods. It is only necessary to remind ourselves that Socrates, the first political philosopher, was put to death by the city of Athens for his challenge to the ancestral deities. Ever since Socrates, political philosophers have had to manage a way to do justice both to the city's beliefs and opinions and to the calling of philosophy, which could not but throw these opinions into doubt. This becomes especially problematic in societies with revealed religious traditions, like Judaism, Christianity, and Islam, where the religion in question also claims to be the unique source of truth. The famous tension between reason and revelation—what Strauss called metaphorically by the names of Athens and Jerusalem—was in effect a debate over whether society should be governed by reference to human reason or by divine law.[22]

Every society is, then, constituted in part by its answer to the theologico-political problem. In modern Western societies this has meant that religion has agreed to occupy an autonomous inner sphere of conscience and moral belief separate from the public sphere of law and statecraft. This separation of public and private spheres of life has gradually, haltingly, and incompletely become the norm for modern democratic constitutions over the past three hundred years. Even in the United States, which is officially committed to a secular political culture, the line between religion and politics remains forever shifting and dependent upon swings in public opinion. Although Strauss endorsed the liberal separation of society into separate public and private spheres as the solution to the theologico-political problem most conducive to the freedom of philosophy, he was keenly aware of the moral force of religion and the power of the passions from which it arose. The danger to society from politically reawakened forms of religious fundamentalism always remained for him a living possibility.

The Case for Israel

The theologico-political problem was most clearly delineated by the situation of Judaism in modern society. This was for Strauss not just an abstract, theoretical problem, but a living, existential one. From an early age, Strauss was a committed Zionist. His reasons for this grew out of the real-life experience of the Jews in interwar Germany. Germany was during this period a republic dedicated to a balance between the principles of 1789 and the highest traditions of German philosophy. But the problem with the German Weimar Republic was its failure to protect the Jews. The failure of a constitutional government to protect its Jewish citizens served as a lifelong reminder of the vulnerability of a people who lack sovereign power over their destiny.[23]

Strauss's defense of the Jewish state was not the result of religious or ethnic nationalism. Rather, it grew out of a clear-eyed awareness of the failure of liberal democracy. Liberalism had promised the Jews acceptance and toleration, but at the cost of assimilation and loss of collective identity. The condition of the modern Jew is one of "external freedom and inner servitude," in the words of Ahad Ha'am. At the same time that it was professing toleration of all religions, the liberal state proved incapable of protecting Jews from recurrent outbreaks of anti-Semitism. It is perhaps no coincidence that systematic doctrines of anti-Semitism rose to prominence during the period of greatest political liberalization. Liberalism presupposes the distinction between the state and civil society, the public and the private spheres of life. While the state proper may be officially secular and hence neutral to religion, this could not prevent, indeed may have encouraged, the rise of anti-Semitic ideologies in the sphere of civil society. Hence the "Jewish Question," as it became known, was not solved by liberalism, but rather shifted from the public to the private sphere. Liberalism had failed the Jews and unwittingly revealed its own limitations.

Most importantly, Strauss's Zionism grew out of a need to preserve the moral core of Judaism during a period of assimilation and the "progressive" leveling of tradition. A Jewish state was necessary not merely to ensure

Jewish survival, but for the sake of Jewish self-respect. The concept of self-respect (*Selbstachtuung* in German) is a term Strauss uses frequently when mentioning the Zionist enterprise. "The moral spine of Judaism was in danger of being broken by the so-called emancipation, which in many cases had alienated them from their heritage, and yet not given them anything more than merely formal equality," Strauss wrote in a rare public utterance. "Political Zionism was the attempt to restore that inner freedom, that simple dignity, of which only people who remember their heritage and are loyal to their fate are capable."[24]

Strauss praised Leon Pinsker, Theodor Herzl, and especially Vladimir Jabotinsky for their efforts to restore a sense of Jewish pride and dignity through the creation of a state under hopelessly difficult conditions: a small, endangered republic surrounded by a numerically superior and hostile Arab population. Strauss no doubt saw in the tiny, embattled Jewish state the same quality of spiritedness or "heart" that inspired the ancient Greek city-states to stand together and fight against their wealthier and better-armed Persian enemy. The establishment of a Jewish state was, for Strauss, one of the bright spots on the contemporary political landscape. He described the spirit of Israel as one of "heroic austerity supported by the nearness of biblical antiquity."[25]

To be sure, Strauss was not unaware of and made clear the limits of Zionism. Zionism presented a purely social or political solution to the Jewish problem. In the deepest sense, it was less an answer to than an expression of this problem. Zionism could only offer the Jews a state like other peoples. It could not in any theological sense bring an end to the exile (Galut). "The establishment of the state of Israel," Strauss wrote, "is the most profound modification of the Galut that has occurred, but is not the end of the Galut."[26] If we consider the Jewish problem as emblematic of the social problem of discrimination—a term which, by the way, Strauss always used in quotation marks—then the establishment of the state of Israel, far from solving this problem, may even have exacerbated it. From this point of view the Jewish problem most clearly represents "the most manifest symbol of the human problem insofar as it is a social or political problem."[27]

The Necessity for Statecraft

Strauss's awareness of the crisis of the West speaks largely to a failure of nerve or confidence about the fundamental aspiration of Western liberal democracies. Drawing on his own experience, he argued that the failure of

Weimar grew out of the inability of responsible elites to defend the cause of constitutional government from radical challenges from both the Right and the Left. Today the threat to liberal democracy comes not from communism or fascism, but from an energized Islamic fundamentalism that regards itself, whether we choose to acknowledge it or not, as being locked in a life-or-death struggle with the West. One would have thought that this would awaken Western liberalism from the slumber in which it had languished throughout the 1990s. Yet the very cultural relativism—now called multiculturalism—Strauss diagnosed continues very much in evidence. A symptom of this was the expression of self-doubt, if not self-contempt, voiced by many American intellectuals after the attacks of September 11, 2001.

Strauss hardly accepted a Schmittean view of the political universe as divided into mutually hostile camps of friend and enemy. He did maintain a deep awareness of the underlying diversity shaping different regimes. For this reason he was skeptical of Kantian notions of a cosmopolitan society and "perpetual peace." Although convinced of the essential decency of the West, he could never have accepted even Francis Fukuyama's idea of a liberalized version of an "end of history." Strauss supported the idea of a united free Europe, but conceived this along the lines of a *Europe des patries*, not as some kind of supranational state. The nation-state still remained the form of political organization best suited to the exercise of human agency and creative statesmanship. The highest task of the statesman is to resist the illusory belief in some cosmopolitan social order based on universal human recognition and to recover the self-respect deriving from loyalty to particular and competing political traditions.

Strauss had an admiration for the virtue of the statesman as the highest form of non-philosophic life. Among modern statesmen, it was Winston Churchill who elicited his uncompromising admiration. In a letter from 1946 to his fellow émigré, Karl Löwith, Strauss wrote that "A man like Churchill proves that the possibility of *megalopsychia* [greatness of soul] exists today *exactly* as it did in the fifth century B.C."[28] Perhaps the most important function of statecraft is to remind us, the students of politics, of the possibility of greatness.

Strauss returned to this theme almost twenty years later on the occasion of Churchill's death. " 'The death of Churchill," he told his audience, "is a healthy reminder to academic students of political science of their limitations." Churchill's actions on behalf of human freedom were carried out not only through his deeds, but through his speeches and writings, above all his *Life of Marlborough*, which Strauss calls "the greatest historical work written in our century, an inexhaustible mine of political wisdom and understanding which should be required reading for every student of political science." "We are supposed to train ourselves and others in seeing things as they are, and this means above all in seeing their greatness and their misery, their excellence and their vileness, their nobility and their triumphs, and therewith never to mistake mediocrity, however brilliant, for true greatness." [29]

Great statesmen like Churchill—and one could add the names of Lincoln and Weizmann—illustrate the fact that politics is ultimately a matter of prudence or moral judgment. Strauss's point was not to advocate some kind of great man theory of history or to engage in hero worship. Rather, his interest in the problem of statesmanship was always connected to the question of what kind of knowledge is political knowledge. Is politics ultimately a form of theory, susceptible to scientific or statistical generalization, or does it remain firmly grounded in the world of practice and experience? Throughout his writings Strauss remained deeply skeptical of whether political theory had any substantive advice or direction to offer statesmen.

Consider the following example. In an as yet unpublished essay delivered at the New School in the summer of 1942 titled "What Can We Learn from Political Theory?" Strauss explicitly claims that philosophic knowledge is unnecessary for sound policy and the guidance of practical conduct. What is needed by the statesman is akin not to theoretical insight, but to common sense or a shrewd assessment of the situation. He confirms this by a story told about Churchill at the outbreak of World War II:

> I may refer to the story told in England of H. G. Wells meeting Winston Churchill and asking about the progress of the war. "We're getting along with our idea," said Churchill. "You have an idea?" asked Wells. "Yes," said Churchill, "along the lines of our general policy." "You have a general policy," Wells persisted. "Yes," answered Churchill, "the K.M.T. policy." "And what is the K.M.T. policy?" asked Wells. "It is this," replied Churchill: "Keep Muddling Through."[30]

Strauss goes on to remark that while K.M.T. is not a guarantee of success—he refers to the disasters in Singapore and Libya—it is entirely conceivable that one might construct an intelligent postwar international policy with no reference to political philosophy at all. The key to success after the war, he affirms, is an "Anglo-Saxon" preponderance—even an Anglo-Saxon–Russian entente—that remains vigilant about its own liberties and active in the defense of civil liberties worldwide. "To know these

broad essentials of the situation," he avers, "one does not need a single lesson in political philosophy. In fact, people adhering to fundamentally different political philosophies have reached these same conclusions."[31]

Strauss's conception of the autonomy of statecraft, at least its independence from theoretical philosophy, became a theme in *Natural Right
and History* in his treatment of the Aristotelian conception of natural
right.[32] On this understanding, natural right is not so much a transcendent
natural law from which a doctrine of duties and obligations can be derived;
it is rather closer to the actual decisions made by statesmen in concrete situations. Justice (and therefore natural right) resides not in general rules
applicable to any and every circumstance, but in the mutable situations in
which policy makers and politicians find themselves. It is to guarantee the
flexibility or "latitude" of statecraft to respond to new and unforeseen situations that Strauss emphasizes the variability of Aristotelian natural
right. It is, interestingly, this same sense of flexibility that is given expression in a modern book like Montesquieu's *Spirit of the Laws*, a work
Strauss claims that is closer in spirit to the classics than to the more rigid
formulations of the medieval tradition of natural law.[33]

Strauss makes this point in a curiously neglected passage from the very
center of *Natural Right and History*. In a discussion of Aristotle's theory of
natural right he acknowledges the way political decisions grow out of concrete situations and cannot be deduced from a priori rules:

> Let us call an extreme situation a situation in which the very existence
> or independence of a society is at stake. In extreme situations there may
> be conflicts between what the self-preservation of society requires and
> the requirements of commutative or distributive justice. In such situa-
> tions, *and only in such situations*, it can justly be said that the public
> safety is the highest law. A decent society will not go to war except for
> a just cause. But what it will do during a war will depend to a certain
> extent on what the enemy—possibly an absolutely unscrupulous and
> savage enemy—forces it to do. There are no limits which can be defined
> in advance, there are no assignable limits to what might become just
> reprisals.[34]

Strauss's statement here that there are "no assignable limits" to how a
just society may respond to provocation is neither an invitation to all-out
warfare nor a call for global domination. To the contrary, it is a call for
restraint. Only in situations where the life of a society is directly threatened, "and only in such situations," can the rules of ordinary justice be

suspended. Strauss continues as follows: "But war casts its shadow on peace. The most just society cannot survive without 'intelligence,' i.e., without espionage. Espionage is impossible without a suspension of certain rules of natural right. But societies are not only threatened from without. Considerations which apply to foreign enemies may well apply to subversive elements within society."[35]

The above passages seem to be setting out a conception of statecraft somewhere between the idealistic view that there are certain universal moral duties that must always and everywhere be followed and the cynical ("Machiavellian") view that the ends justify the means. The Aristotelian conception of natural right, by contrast, suggests that there is no rule that does not allow exceptions. "Natural right," Strauss writes, "must be mutable to be able to cope with the inventiveness of wickedness."[36] That is to say, the statesman must be allowed to respond to evil by using means that would ordinarily be considered unjust while not forgetting the distinction between extreme and ordinary situations. To be able to distinguish between extreme actions that were justifiable reactions to extreme situations and extreme actions that were simply unjust becomes, then, "one of the noblest duties of the historian."[37] Needless to say, this is a very fine line.

A Touch of Evil

So what are the lessons, if any, for the conduct of American foreign policy?

Strauss would have been deeply skeptical of President Bush's remarks about an "axis of evil" in his State of the Union address after 9/11. To be sure, the use of clear and forceful moral language rather than equivocating talk about moral equivalence is a mark of statesmanship. Yet the administration's rhetoric has been used to turn a war against one particular form of evil into a mission against evil in general. "To rid the world of evil" was already the president's formula for foreign policy as early as September 14, 2001. "This is not a contingent and political, it is an absolute and metaphysical statement," David Bromwich writes, "a promise of salvation such as only religions, until now, have dared to make and only the gods of religions have been supposed to keep." [38]

This turn in the Bush administration's foreign policy rhetoric is echoed by Richard Perle and former White House speechwriter David Frum in their new book, *An End of Evil: How to Win the War on Terror.*[39] By evil the authors mean Islamic terrorism. But evil, as conservative columnist Patrick Buchanan has noted, has been around since Cain slew his brother Abel. If

God accepts the existence of evil in the world, how is it that Perle and Frum propose to end it?[40] The idea that political or military action can be used to eradicate evil from the human landscape is closer to the utopian and idealistic visions of Marxism and the radical Enlightenment than anything found in the writings of Strauss.

Evil is a theme Strauss mentions several times throughout his writings, always in the context of a warning against radical expectations in politics. "It is against nature," he wrote (citing Plato's *Theaetetus*), "that there should ever be a 'cessation of evils.'"[41] Evil is a permanent disposition of the human heart. The task of the statesman is not to try to eradicate the causes of evil, something that would require a permanent war against human nature, but to mitigate its worst effects. Aware of "the limits set to all human action and all human planning," the philosopher-statesman will be modest in his expectations from politics. "He will try to help his fellow man by mitigating, as far as in him lies, the evils that are *inseparable from the human condition*."[42] And in a beautiful passage where he describes the characteristics of the true statesman ("free from the narrowness of the lawyer, the brutality of the technician, the vagaries of the visionary, and the baseness of the opportunist"), Strauss remarks that the spirit of statesmanship is "free from all fanaticism because it knows that evil cannot be eradicated and that one's expectations from politics must be moderate."[43]

Nothing more clearly distinguishes Strauss from the foreign policy of neo-conservatism than his reflections on the intractability of the problem of evil in political life. "Tyranny is a problem coeval with politics," he avers; it is "as old as political science itself."[44] His analysis of tyranny as a disposition of the soul rooted in certain permanencies of human nature should be contrasted to the transformative vision of politics embraced in George W. Bush's Second Inaugural Address. "So it is the policy of the United States," the president avowed, "to seek and support the growth of democratic movements and institutions in every nation and culture with the ultimate goal of ending tyranny in our world."[45] There is a utopianism about this rhetoric that is deeply at odds with Strauss's own sense of cautious reflection on human nature. The rhetoric of "ending tyranny" is in part religious and messianic, but also a part of the Enlightenment's faith that human nature is ultimately perfectible and that evil can be eradicated through an act of political will.[46]

Strauss brought a sharply different sensibility to the understanding of politics, a sensibility shaped by the European experiences of war and totalitarianism and the dangers of political utopianism. This kind of sensibility has gone out of fashion today in part because it does not correlate with any of our current political ideologies. The essence of politics for Strauss is moderation. Echoing Tacitus, Strauss regards moderation as the highest lesson of wisdom.[47] Not the city in perpetual motion (Athens), but the city at rest (Sparta), is closer to his ideal. The dangers of arrogance and imperial overreach exhibited by Periclean Athens should be a sobering counterexample to neo-conservatism's assertion of national greatness.[48]

Far from justifying war, Strauss's writings may plausibly provide a stinging critique of current policy. A central theme of his reading of the *Republic* is the need to tame the fierce and warlike ardor of Adeimantus and Glaucon. Like "noble dogs" they must be taught to distinguish friend from enemy and to moderate their ambition and love of honor (*Republic* 375e-76b). Similarly Strauss warns against the dangers of popular leaders like Alcibiades, who in his bid to conquer Sicily charmed the Athenians into believing that "we shall augment our power at home by this adventure abroad" by "letting them see how little we care for the peace that we are now enjoying." After hearing his speech, Thucydides tells us, the Athenians "all alike fell in love with the enterprise," especially those in the bloom of life who "felt a longing for foreign sights and spectacles" (Thucydides, VI, 18, 24).

"I am not a Marxist," Karl Marx is supposed once to have said. Whether Leo Strauss would have said the same thing about today's Straussians is anybody's guess. Strauss was a skeptic who cautioned against the twin dangers of "visionary expectations" and "unmanly contempt" for politics.[49] His work as a whole must be considered a reflection on the "essential limits" of politics; his ambition was to provide "the broadest and deepest analysis of political idealism ever made."[50]

NOTES

INTRODUCTION

1. Other works to appear in this series included Eric Voeglin, *The New Science of Politics* (Chicago: University of Chicago Press, 1952); Hannah Arendt, *The Human Condition* (Chicago: University of Chicago Press, 1958).

2. For a rearguard defense of Dewey, see Richard Rorty, "Marxists, Straussians, and Pragmatists," *Raritan* (fall 1998): 128–36.

3. Myles Burnyeat, "Sphinx without a Secret," *New York Review of Books* May 30, 1985, 31.

4. See Arthur Schlesinger Jr., "The Making of a Mess," *New York Review of Books*, September 23, 2004, 40; most of what this author claims to know of Strauss draws extensively on Anne Norton, *Leo Strauss and the Politics of American Empire* (New Haven, Conn.: Yale University Press, 2004).

5. James Atlas, "Leo-Cons: A Classicist's Legacy," *New York Times*, May 4, 2003; Atlas's article and the intellectual genealogy on which it draws is based on the previous work by Alain Frachon and Daniel Vernet, "Le Stratège et le Philosophe," *Le Monde*, April 16, 2003; this article was subsequently developed at greater length in their *L'Amérique Messianique: Les guerres des néo-conservateurs* (Paris: Éditions du Seuil, 2004), 59–82; for a counter to many of the purely negative characterizations, see Bret Stephens, "Hands Up, Straussians!" *The Jerusalem Post*, June 4, 2003.

6. Walter Lippmann, *The Public Philosophy* (New York: Little Brown, 1955).

7. Morton J. Frisch and Richard G. Stevens, eds., *American Political Thought: The Philosophic Dimension of American Statesmanship* (New York: Charles Scribner's Sons, 1971).

8. William A. Galston, "A Student of Strauss in the Clinton Administration," in *Leo Strauss, the Straussians, and the American Regime,* ed. Kenneth L. Deutsch and John A. Murley (Lanham Md.: Rowman & Littlefield, 1999), 429–37.

9. See Isaiah Berlin, "Does Political Theory Still Exist?" in *Concepts and Categories,* ed. Henry Hardy (New York: Viking Press, 1979), 143–72.

10. Herbert J. Storing, ed., *What Country Have I? Political Writings by Black Americans* (New York: Saint Martin's, 1970).

11. Leo Strauss, *Socrates and Aristophanes* (New York: Basic Books, 1966).

12. See Descartes, *Discourse on Method*, Part VI; for the background of coercion and intimidation, see Leo Strauss, *Persecution and the Art of Writing* (Glencoe, Ill.: Free Press, 1952), 17, 22, 33; for Locke as an esoteric writer, see "Strauss's America," chapter 7 below.

13. Strauss, *Persecution and the Art of Writing*, 30.

14. Myles Burnyeat, "Utopia and Fantasy: The Practicability of Plato's Ideally Just City," in *Plato 2: Ethics, Politics, Religion, and the Soul*, ed. Gail Fine (Oxford: Oxford University Press, 1999), 300.

15. For some works more sensitive to the rhetorical and dialogical aspects of the *Republic*, see Seth Benardete, *Socrates's Second Sailing: On Plato's "Republic"* (Chicago: University of Chicago Press, 1989); Jacob Howland, *The Republic: The Odyssey of Philosophy* (New York: Twayne, 1993); G.R.F. Ferrari, *City and Soul in Plato's "Republic"* (Chicago: University of Chicago Press, 2005); for a fuller discussion of some of the issues involved, see the essay "Leo Strauss's Platonic Liberalism," chapter 4 below.

16. Strauss, *Persecution and the Art of Writing*, 30.

17. Gérald Sfez, "Leo Strauss: Un criticisme de la preuve," *Revue Philosophique* 130 (2005): 7.

18. Strauss, *Persecution and the Art of Writing*, 73.

19. Leo Strauss to Karl Löwith, "Correspondence of Karl Löwith and Leo Strauss," trans. George Elliott Tucker, *Independent Journal of Philosophy* 5/6 (1988): 183.

20. For an excellent treatment of Strauss's connection to various strands of contemporary literary theory, see Paul Cantor, "Leo Strauss and Contemporary Hermeneutics," in *Leo Strauss's Thought: Toward a Critical Engagement*, ed. Alan Udoff (Boulder, Colo.: Lynne Rienner, 1991), 267–314.

21. Leo Strauss, "Preface to 'Hobbes Politische Wissenschaft,' " in *Jewish Philosophy and the Crisis of Modernity*, ed. Kenneth Hart Green (Albany: SUNY Press, 1997), 453.

22. The expression "What has Athens to do with Jerusalem?" goes back to the early Patristic Tertullian, *De Praescriptione haereticorum*, 7; the issue was addressed prominently in the nineteenth century under the rubric of "Hellenism and Hebraism." See Matthew Arnold, *Culture and Anarchy*, ed. J. Dover Wilson (Cambridge: Cambridge University Press, 1986), 129–44; it was used again in the last century by Lev Shestov, *Athens and Jerusalem*, trans. Bernard Martin (Athens: Ohio University Press, 1966); for a recent treatment, see Jaroslav Pelikan, *What Has Athens to do with Jerusalem? Timaeus and Genesis in Counterpoint* (Ann Arbor: University of Michigan Press, 1997).

23. Leo Strauss, "Progress or Return," in *The Rebirth of Classical Political Rationalism*, ed. Thomas Pangle (Chicago: University of Chicago Press, 1989), 270.

24. Leo Strauss, "Preface to Spinoza's Critique of Religion," in *Liberalism Ancient and Modern* (New York: Basic Books, 1968), 229.

25. Leo Strauss, "Why We Remain Jews," in *Jewish Philosophy and the Crisis of Modernity*, 327.

26. Leo Strauss, *The City and Man* (Chicago: University of Chicago Press, 1964), 241.

27. Leo Strauss, "On the Interpretation of 'Genesis,'" *L'Homme* 21 (1981):5–36.

28. Strauss, "Preface to Spinoza's Critique of Religion," 256.

29. Leo Strauss, *Persecution and the Art of Writing*, 7.

30. Harry V. Jaffa, "The Crisis of the Strauss Divided: The Legacy Reconsidered," *Social Research* 54 (1987): 579–603; for another retelling of this story, see Charles Kesler, "All against All," *National Review*, August 18, 1989, 39–43.

31. Leo Strauss, *On Tyranny Including the Strauss-Kojève Correspondence*, ed. Victor Gourevitch and Michael Roth (Chicago: University of Chicago Press, 2000), 196.

32. Leo Strauss, "Liberal Education and Responsibility," in *Liberalism Ancient and Modern*, 14.

33. Leo Strauss, "A Giving of Accounts," in *Jewish Philosophy and the Crisis of Modernity*, 464–65; emphasis added.

34. Strauss, "What Is Liberal Education?" in *Liberalism Ancient and Modern*, 4.

35. Ibid., 5.

36. Ibid., 24.

37. Strauss, "Preface to Spinoza's Critique of Religion," 239.

38. Strauss, "An Introduction to Heideggerian Existentialism," in *The Rebirth of Classical Political Rationalism*, 29; Leo Strauss, "What Is Political Philosophy," in *What Is Political Philosophy? and Other Studies* (New York: Free Press, 1959), 55.

CHAPTER ONE

1. Harold Bloom, "Foreword" to Yosef H. Yerushalmi, *Zakhor: Jewish History and Jewish Memory* (New York: Schocken Books, 1989), xiii.

2. Leo Strauss, *Die Religionskritik Spinozas als Grundlage seiner Bibelwissenschaft* in *Gesammelte Schriften*, ed. Heinrich Meier (Stuttgart: Metzler, 1996), vol. 1; published in English as *Spinoza's Critique of Religion*, trans. E. M. Sinclair (New York: Schocken Books, 1965).

3. Leo Strauss, *Philosophie und Gesetz: Beiträge zum Verständnis Maimunis und seiner Vorläufer* in *Gesammelte Schriften*, ed. Heinrich Meier (Stuttgart: Metzler, 1997), vol. 2; published in English as *Philosophy and Law: Essays Toward an Understanding of Maimonides and His Predecessors*, trans. Fred Baumann (Philadelphia: Jewish Publication Society of America, 1987).

4. Leo Strauss, "Jerusalem and Athens: Some Introductory Reflections," in *Studies in Platonic Political Philosophy*, ed. Thomas Pangle (Chicago: University of Chicago Press, 1983), 147–73; see also "The Mutual Influence of Theology and Philosophy," *Independent Journal of Philosophy* 3 (1979): 111–18; "Progress or Return?" in *The Rebirth of Classical Political Rationalism*, ed. Thomas Pangle (Chicago: University of Chicago Press, 1989), 227–70; "On the Interpretation of Genesis," *L'Homme* 21 (1981): 5–20.

5. Leo Strauss, "Preface to Spinoza's Critique of Religion," in *Liberalism: Ancient and Modern* (New York: Basic Books, 1968), 224–59. In a letter to Gershom Scholem written in English and dated December 2, 1962, Strauss explained his decision to publish this autobiography as follows: "When studying Hobbes, I observed that what he said and did not say was a function of the heresy laws obtaining at the time of publication of his various works. But then I saw that

in one of his works published at a time of considerable restriction he was more outspoken than ever before. I was baffled until I noted that this book was published when he was already very old, with one foot in the grave and I learned that this condition is conducive to courage. As for me I have had my first two heart attacks, Ergo." Leo Strauss, *Gesammelte Schriften*, vol. 3, ed. Heinrich Meier (Stuttgart: Metzler, 2001), 748.

6. Leo Strauss, *Persecution and the Art of Writing* (Glencoe Ill.: Free Press, 1952), 7.

7. George Steiner, "Inscrutable and Tragic: Leo Strauss's Vision of the Jewish Destiny," *Times Literary Supplement*, November 11, 1997, 4.

8. Strauss, "Preface to Spinoza's Critique of Religion," 224.

9. Leo Strauss, *The City and Man* (Chicago: University of Chicago Press, 1964), 2–4.

10. Strauss, "Preface to Spinoza's Critique of Religion," 230.

11. Leo Strauss, "Preface to *Hobbes politische Wissenschaft*," in *Jewish Philosophy and the Crisis of Modernity*, ed. Kenneth Hart Green (Albany: SUNY Press, 1997), 453.

12. Strauss, *Spinoza's Critique of Religion*, 194; *City and Man*, 241.

13. Strauss, "Mutual Influence of Theology and Philosophy," 113; "Progress or Return?" 270.

14. Leo Strauss, "What Is Political Philosophy?" in *What Is Political Philosophy and Other Studies* (New York: Free Press, 1959), 11.

15. Strauss, "Progress or Return?" 246.

16. Ibid., 251.

17. Leo Strauss, *Natural Right and History* (Chicago: University of Chicago Press, 1953), 81–82; "Progress or Return?" 253–54; see also *History of Political Philosophy*, ed. Leo Strauss and Joseph Cropsey (Chicago: Rand McNally, 1972), 2–3.

18. Strauss, "Progress or Return?" 246–47.

19. Strauss, *Natural Right and History*, 130; see also Leo Strauss, *On Tyranny Including the Strauss-Kojève Correspondence*, ed. Victor Gourevitch and Michael Roth (Chicago: University of Chicago Press, 2000), 191–92.

20. Strauss, "Progress or Return?" 247–48.

21. Strauss, *City and Man*, 1–12; *Liberalism: Ancient and Modern*, v–ix; "The Crisis of Our Time," in *The Predicament of Modern Politics*, ed. Harold Spaeth (Detroit, Mich.: University of Detroit Press, 1964), 41–54.

22. Strauss, *On Tyranny*, 178.

23. Strauss, "What Is Political Philosophy?" 28.

24. Strauss, *Natural Right and History*, 15.

25. Strauss, *Philosophy and the Law*, 11–12; "What Is Political Philosophy?" 45; see also Leo Strauss, *Thoughts on Machiavelli* (Glencoe, Ill.: The Free Press, 1958), 297–98.

26. Strauss, *Philosophy and the Law*, 3–20.

27. "Boldness formerly was not the character of atheists as such. They were even of a character nearly the reverse; they were formerly like the old Epicureans, rather an unenterprising race. But of late they are grown active, designing, turbulent, and seditious." Edmund Burke, cited in *Natural Right and History*, 169.

28. Strauss, *Natural Right and History*, 81–83; *City and Man*, 241.

29. Strauss, *Natural Right and History*, 169; emphasis mine.

30. Strauss, *Spinoza's Critique of Religion*, 172–82.

31. René Descartes, *Discourse on Method*, in *Philosophical Writings of Descartes*, trans. John Cottingham, Robert Stroothoff, and Dugald Murdoch (Cambridge: Cambridge University Press, 1985), vol. 1.

32. Strauss, "Preface to Spinoza's Critique of Religion," 256.

33. Strauss, *Philosophy and the Law*, 18.

34. Alan Bloom, "Leo Strauss," *Political Theory* 4 (1974): 383, speaks of "three phases" in Strauss's development, while Seth Benardete, in "Leo Strauss' 'The City and Man,' " *American Political Science Reviewer* 8 (1978): 1, speaks of a "fundamental change" taking place in his thought.

35. Leo Strauss, "The Zionism of Nordau," trans. Michael Zanc, in *Leo Strauss: The Early Writings, 1921–1932* (Albany: SUNY Press, 2002), 83–88; reprinted in *Gesammelte Schriften*, vol. 2, 315–21.

36. Strauss, "Zionism of Nordau," 85.

37. Ibid., 86.

38. Ibid., 87.

39. Ibid., 84.

40. Ibid., 87.

41. Hermann Cohen, "Spinoza über Staat und Religion, Judentum und Christentum," in *Jüdische Schriften*, ed. B. Strauss (Berlin: Schwetschke, 1924), vol. 3: 290–372.

42. Ibid., 298, 360.

43. Ibid., 37–72.

44. Ibid., 361.

45. Leo Strauss, "Cohen's Analysis of Spinoza's Bible Science," in *Early Writings*, 140–72; reprinted in *Gesammelte Schriften*, vol. 1: 363–86.

46. Strauss, "Cohen's Analysis of Spinoza's Bible Science," 143.

47. Ibid., 144.

48. Ibid., 152.

49. Ibid., 155–56, 161.

50. Immanuel Kant, *Religion within the Limits of Reason Alone*, trans. T. M. Greene and H. H. Hudson (New York: Harper and Row, 1960), 116.

51. Immanuel Kant, *The Conflict of the Faculties*, trans. Mary J. Gregor (New York: Arabis, 1979), 115.

52. Moses Mendelssohn, *Jerusalem or on Religious Power and Judaism*, trans. Allan Arkush (Hanover, N.H.: University Press of New England, 1983), 94.

53. Baruch Spinoza, *Theologico-Political Treatise*, trans. Samuel Shirley (Indianapolis, Ind.: Hackett, 1998), 21.

54. Ibid., 31.

55. Ibid., 38.

56. Cohen, *Jüdische Schriften*, 1:105–24; partial English translation by Eve Jospe, *Reason and Hope: Selections from the Jewish Writings of Hermann Cohen* (New York: W. W. Norton, 1971), 122–27.

57. Cohen, *Jüdische Schriften*, 2:319–27, 328–40; *Reason and Hope*, 164–71.

58. Cohen, *Jüdische Schriften*, 2:73.

59. Ibid., 2:310–11.

60. Strauss, "An Introduction to Heideggerian Existentialism," in *Rebirth of Classical Political Rationalism*, 28; for a sustained examination of Rosenzweig's relation to Heideggerian existentialism see Karl Löwith, "M. Heidegger and F. Rosenzweig or Temporary and Eternity," *Philosophy and Phenomenological Research* (1942): 53–77. See also Peter Eli Gordon, *Rosenzweig and Heidegger: Between Judaism and German Philosophy* (Berkeley: University of California Press, 2003).

61. Franz Rosenzweig, *The Star of Redemption*, trans. William Hallo (New York: Holt, Rinehart, and Winston, 1970), 176–77.

62. Rosenzweig, *The Star of Redemption*, 213.

63. Ibid.: "The [Kantian] moral law is necessarily purely formal and therefore not only ambiguous but open to an unlimited number of interpretations. By contrast the commandment to love one's neighbor is clear and unambiguous in content." The classic of this critique of Kant is still Hegel's *Philosophy of Right*, trans. T. M. Knox (Oxford: Clarendon Press, 1967), para. 135, 89–90.

64. Rosenzweig, *The Star of Redemption*, 217.

65. See Nahum Glatzer, ed., *Franz Rosenzweig: His Life and Thought* (New York: Shocken Books, 1961), 190-208.

66. Strauss, "Preface to Spinoza's Critique of Religion," 237.

67. Cohen, *Jüdische Schriften*, 1:306–30; *Reason and Hope*, 76.

68. Strauss, "Jerusalem and Athens," 168.

69. Leo Strauss, "How to Begin to Study 'The Guide of the Perplexed,' " in Maimonides, *The Guide of the Perplexed*, trans. Shlomo Pines (Chicago: University of Chicago Press, 1963), xi; for some of Strauss's other writings see "Quelques remarques sur la science politique de Maimonide et de Farabi," *Revue des Etudes Juives* 100 (1936): 1–37; "Maimonides' Statement on Political Science," in *What Is Political Philosophy*, 155–69; "The Literary Character of the 'Guide of the Perplexed,' " in *Persecution and the Art of Writing*, 38–94.

70. Strauss, *Philosophy and the Law*, 82–83.

71. See Strauss, *Persecution and the Art of Writing*, 22–37.

72. See Shadia Drury, *The Political Ideas of Leo Strauss* (New York: Saint Martin's, 1988).

73. Nathan Tarcov, "Philosophy and History: Tradition and Interpretation in the Work of Leo Strauss," *Polity* 16 (1983): 19.

74. Maimonides, *Guide of the Perplexed*, 6.

75. Maimonides, *Guide of the Perplexed*. 6–7.

76. Strauss, "How to Begin to Study the 'Guide,' " xiii, xiv.

77. See Elaine Pagels, *Adam, Eve, and the Serpent* (New York: Random House, 1988), 57–72.

78. Gershom Scholem, *Major Trends in Jewish Mysticism* (New York: Schocken Books, 1961), 40–79.

79. Hans Jonas, *The Gnostic Religion* (Boston: Beacon Press, 1963).

80. Gershom Scholem, *The Messianic Idea in Judaism and Other Essays in Jewish Spirituality* (New York: Schocken Books, 1971), 78–141.

81. See Rémi Brague, "Leo Strauss and Maimonides," in *Leo Strauss's Thought: Toward a Critical Engagement*, ed. Alan Udoff (Boulder, Colo.: Lynne Rienner, 1991), 93–114; Kenneth Hart Green, *Jew and Philosopher: The Return to Maimonides in the Jewish Thought of Leo Strauss* (Albany: SUNY Press, 1993).

82. Strauss, *Persecution and the Art of Writing*, 55; emphasis mine.

83. Strauss, "What Is Political Philosophy?" 17.

84. Strauss, *Persecution and the Art of Writing*, 56.

85. Leo Strauss, "On Collingwood's Philosophy of History," *Review of Metaphysics* 5 (1952): 585.

86. Strauss, *Persecution and the Art of Writing*, 37.

87. Strauss, *Natural Right and History*, 74–76; *Philosophy and Law*, 13–14.

88. Strauss, "What Is Political Philosophy?" 50.

89. Strauss, "Preface to Spinoza's Critique of Religion," 225.

90. Strauss, "Progress or Return?" 232.

91. Ibid., 233.

CHAPTER TWO

1. The writings of men like Hermann Cohen, Franz Rosenzweig, and Martin Buber—to say nothing of such "non-Jewish Jews" as Freud and Arendt—would no doubt also have to be considered. An important step in this direction has already been taken by Paul Mendes-Flohr, *Divided Passions: Jewish Intellectuals and the Experience of Modernity* (Detroit, Mich.: Wayne State University Press, 1991).

2. Gershom Scholem, *The Correspondence of Walter Benjamin and Gershom Scholem, 1932–1940*, trans. Gary Smith and Andre Lefevre (New York: Schocken Books, 1989).

3. Leo Strauss, "A Giving of Accounts," in *Jewish Philosophy and the Crisis of Modernity*, ed. Kenneth Hart Green (Albany: SUNY Press, 1997), 459–60.

4. Leo Strauss, *On Tyranny Including the Strauss-Kojève Correspondence*, ed. Victor Gourevitch and Michael Roth (Chicago: University of Chicago Press, 2000). See "Tyranny Ancient and Modern," chapter 6 below.

5. Scholem, *Correspondence*, 24, 156–57, 160, 179, 181; Gershom Scholem, *Walter Benjamin: The Story of a Friendship*, trans. Harry Zohn (Philadelphia: The Jewish Publication Society of America, 1981), 98, 201; Gershom Scholem, *From Berlin to Jerusalem*, trans. Harry Zohn (New York: Schocken Books, 1980), 149. Strauss's most important statement is the autobiographical preface to the English language edition of his *Spinoza's Critique of Religion*, trans. E. M. Sinclair (New York: Schocken Books, 1965); reprinted in *Liberalism: Ancient and Modern* (New York: Basic Books, 1968), 224–59. Strauss contributed an essay, "Notes on Maimonides's Book of Knowledge," to a *festschrift* for Scholem titled *Studies in Mysticism and Religion*, ed. E. E. Urbach, C. Wirszubski, and R.J.Z. Werblowsky (Jerusalem: J. Magnes Press, 1967); reprinted in *Studies in Platonic Political Philosophy*, ed. T. Pangle (Chicago: University of Chicago Press, 1983), 192–204.

6. Michael Meyer, *The Origins of the Modern Jew: Jewish Identity and European Culture in Germany, 1749–1824* (Detroit, Mich.: Wayne State University Press, 1967), 173.

7. See Steven B. Smith, "Hegel and the Jewish Question: In Between Modernity and Tradition," *History of Political Thought* 12 (1991): 87–106.

8. See David Biale, *Gershom Scholem: Kabbalah and Counter-History* (Cambridge: Harvard University Press, 1982), 6–8, 36–38, 152–53.

9. Gershom Scholem, *The Messianic Idea in Judaism and Other Essays in Jewish Spirituality* (New York: Schocken Books, 1971), 304–13.

10. Strauss's views on Weber are most fully stated in *Natural Right and History* (Chicago: University of Chicago Press, 1953), 35–80, esp. 58–62; see also his "The Weber Thesis Re-examined," *Church History* 30 (1961): 100–102.

11. Strauss, *Natural Right and History*, 52.

12. Strauss, *Natural Right and History*, 31–34; Strauss, *On Tyranny*, 25–28.

13. Strauss's writings on Maimonides are a constant across his career. The most important of these include *Philosophie und Gesetz: Beiträge zum Verständnis Maimunis und seiner Vorläufer*, in *Gesammelte Schriften*, ed Heinrich Meier (Stuttgart: Metzler, 1997), vol. 2; "Quelques remarques sur la science politique de Maimonide et de Farabi," *Revue des Etudes Juives* 100 (1936): 1–37; "The Literary Character of the 'Guide of the Perplexed,' " in *Persecution and the Art of Writing* (Glencoe, Ill.: The Free Press, 1952), 38–94; "How to Begin to Study the 'Guide of the Perplexed,' " in *Maimonides' Guide of the Perplexed*, trans. Shlomo Pines (Chicago: University of Chicago Press, 1963), xi–lvi.

14. See Eliezer Schweid, *Judaism and Mysticism According to Gershom Scholem*, trans. David Weiner (Atlanta, Ga.: Scholar's Press, 1985); Moshe Idel, "Rabbinism versus Kabbalism: On G. Scholem's Phenomenology of Judaism," *Modern Judaism* 11 (1991): 281–96.

15. Gershom Scholem, *Major Trends in Jewish Mysticism* (New York: Schocken Books, 1961), 23.

16. For an appreciation see Jürgen Habermas, "Gershom Scholem: The Torah in Disguise," in *Philosophical-Political Profiles*, trans. Frederick Lawrence (Cambridge: MIT Press, 1983), 199–211.

17. Scholem, *Major Trends*, 21, 25, 49; see also Gershom Scholem, *The Origins of Kabbalah*, trans. Allan Arkush (Princeton, N.J.: Princeton University Press, 1990), 18–24.

18. Scholem, *Messianic Idea*, 6, 10.

19. Scholem, *Major Trends*, 246–47, 274, 284–86.

20. Scholem, *Messianic Ideal*, 61–65; see also his monumental study *Sabbatai Sevi: The Mystical Messiah*, trans. R.J Z. Werblowsky (Princeton, N.J.: Princeton University Press, 1973).

21. Scholem, *Messianic Idea*, 78–141.

22. See also Amos Funkenstein, *Theology and the Scientific Imagination: From the Middle Ages to the Seventeenth Century* (Princeton, N.J.: Princeton University Press, 1986), 48–49.

23. Strauss, "Preface to Spinoza's Critique of Religion," 224.

24. Strauss, *Philosophy and Law*, 3–20.

25. Leo Strauss, "Progress or Return?" *The Rebirth of Classical Political Rationalism*, ed. T. Pangle (Chicago: University of Chicago Press, 1989), 270.

26. Scholem, *Major Trends*, 38.

27. Strauss, *Philosophy and Law*, 38–39, 50–58; see also Strauss, "Quelques remarques sur la science politique de Maimonide et Farabi," 1–2.

28. Strauss, "Preface to Spinoza's Critique of Religion," 237: "Whereas the classic work of what is called Jewish medieval philosophy, [Maimonides's] the *Guide of the Perplexed*, is primarily not a philosophic book, but a Jewish book, Rosenzweig's *Star of Redemption* is primarily not a Jewish book, but 'a system of philosophy.'" For Strauss's disagreements with Cohen and Rosenzweig, see "How Jewish Was Leo Strauss?" (chapter 1 above).

29. Scholem, *Major Trends*, 28, 29.

30. Leo Strauss, "How to Begin to Study Medieval Philosophy," in *The Rebirth of Classical Political Rationalism*, 213–16.

31. Letters to Klein, January 20, 1938 and February 16, 1938, in *Gesammelte Schriften*, ed. Heinrich Meier (Stuttgart: Metzler, 2001), vol. 3: 545, 549. Strauss's discovery of esotericism in the work of Maimonides has recently been treated by Laurence Lampert, "Nietzsche's Challenge to Philosophy in the Thought of Leo Strauss," *Review of Metaphysics* 58 (2005): 600–601.

32. Strauss, *Persecution and the Art of Writing*, 22–37; Strauss, "On a Forgotten Kind of Writing," in *What Is Political Philosophy and Other Studies* (New York: The Free Press, 1959), 221–32.

33. For a useful overview see Rémi Brague, "Leo Strauss and Maimonides," in *Leo Strauss's Thought: Toward a Critical Engagement*, ed. Alan Udoff (Boulder, Colo.: Lynne Rienner, 1991), 93–114; Joseph Buijs, "The Philosophical Character of Maimonides's 'Guide'—A Critique of Strauss's Interpretation," *Judaism* 27 (1978): 448–57; Shlomo Pines, "The Philosophic Purport of Maimonides's Halachic Works and the Purport of 'The Guide of the Perplexed,'" in *Maimonides and Philosophy*, ed. Shlomo Pines and Yirmiyahu Yovel (Dordrecht: Martinus Nijhoff, 1986), 1–14; Aviezer Ravitzky, "Samuel Ibn Tibbon and the Esoteric Character of 'The Guide of the Perplexed,'" *AJS Review* 6 (1981): 87–123.

34. See Strauss's "The Literary Character of the 'Guide for the Perplexed,'" in *Persecution and the Art of Writing*, 60–78.

35. Strauss, "What Is Political Philosophy?" in *What Is Political Philosophy*, 40; Strauss, *Natural Right and History*, 178–79.

36. Strauss, "What Is Political Philosophy?" 46–47.

37. Leo Strauss, "Niccolo Machiavelli," in *History of Political Philosophy*, ed. Leo Strauss and Joseph Cropsey (Chicago: Rand McNally, 1972), 274–75.

38. Strauss, "Machiavelli," 286, notes that *The Prince* consists of twenty-six chapters, which is the same numerical value as the letters of the sacred name of God in the Hebrew Tetragrammaton. But Strauss adds, sensibly, that he does not know whether Machiavelli knew this.

39. Strauss, "What Is Political Philosophy?" 44.

40. Ibid., 45; Strauss, "Machiavelli," 288–89.

41. An apparent exception is J.G.A. Pocock, who acknowledges the importance of the date 1666 for the esoteric languages of the sixteenth century but then goes on, inexplicably, to deny that Machiavelli performed the simple mathematics to come up with the number. Pocock, "Prophet and Inquisitor," *Political Theory* 3 (1975): 396–97.

42. Strauss, "What Is Political Philosophy?" 44–45.

43. Ibid., 47–49; Strauss, *Natural Right and History*, 177–202, 248–51.

44. Strauss, "What Is Political Philosophy?" 50–54; Strauss, *Natural Right and History*, 278–79, 315–16, 319–20.

45. Strauss, "What Is Political Philosophy?" 27, 55.

46. Gershom Scholem, *Jews and Judaism in Crisis*, ed. Werner J. Dannhauser (New York: Schocken Books, 1976), 31.

47. Ibid., 32.

48. Ibid., 33.

49. Leo Strauss, "On Collingwood's Philosophy of History," *Review of Metaphysics* 5 (1952): 585.

50. Leo Strauss, *The City and Man* (Chicago: University of Chicago Press, 1964), 4; see also Strauss, *Liberalism: Ancient and Modern*, vi–vii.

51. For the problem of evil, see Leo Strauss, "Jerusalem and Athens: Some Preliminary Reflections," in *Studies in Platonic Political Philosophy*, 168; Strauss, "What Is Political Philosophy?" 28.

52. Strauss, "Relativism," in *The Rebirth of Classical Political Rationalism*, 21; see also Strauss, *On Tyranny*, 208–9.

53. Strauss, *City and Man*, 9.

54. Strauss, "Preface to Spinoza's Critique of Religion," 229 and note.

55. Hannah Arendt, *Eichmann in Jerusalem: A Report on the Banality of Evil* (New York: Viking, 1964).

56. Scholem, *Jews and Judaism in Crisis*, 302; for the issues at stake in this debate, see Raluca M. Eddon, *Israel, "A Light unto the Nations?" Hannah Arendt, Gershom Scholem and the Founding of the Jewish State* (Ph.D. dissertation, Yale University, 2004).

57. For Scholem's role in Brit Shalom, see Biale, *Gershom Scholem*, 97–104; see also Eddon, *Israel, "A Light unto the Nations?"*, chapter 3; for an unusually harsh view of Scholem and the entire Brit Shalom movement, see Yaron Hazony, *The Jewish State: The Struggle for Israel's Soul* (New York: Basic Books, 2000), 196–200.

58. Gershom Scholem, "What Is Judaism?" in *On the Possibility of Jewish Mysticism in Our Time* (Philadelphia: Jewish Publication Society, 1997), 116.

59. Hannah Arendt, "Zionism Reconsidered," in *The Jew as Pariah: Jewish Identity and Politics in the Modern Age*, ed. Ron H. Feldman (New York: Grove Press, 1978), 131–63.

60. Gershom Scholem, *A Life in Letters 1914–1982*, trans. Anthony David Skinner (Cambridge: Harvard University Press, 2002), 330.

61. Scholem, *A Life in Letters*, 331.

62. Scholem, *Jews and Judaism in Crisis*, 305.

63. Ibid., 303.

64. Ibid., 302.

65. Ibid., 71–92.

66. Ibid., 34.

67. Ibid., 292, 294.

68. Ibid., 48.

69. Leo Strauss, "Why We Remain Jews," in *Jewish Philosophy and the Crisis of Modernity*, 319.

70. Carl Schmitt, *The Concept of the Political*, trans. George Schwab (New Brunswick, N.J.: Rutgers University Press, 1976); this edition also contains

Strauss's "Comments on Carl Schmitt's *Der Begriff des Politischen* "; for a discussion that helps elucidate the importance of Schmitt for Strauss's later thought, see Heinrich Meier, *Carl Schmitt and Leo Strauss: The Hidden Dialogue*, trans. J. Harvey Lomax (Chicago: University of Chicago Press, 1995).

71. Schmitt, *The Concept of the Political*, 26.

72. Ibid., 29.

73. Ibid., 55–57.

74. Strauss, "Comments," 98.

75. Ibid., 98.

76. Ibid., 101.

77. Leo Strauss, "The Zionism of Nordau," in *Leo Strauss: The Early Writings (1921–1932)*, trans. and ed. Michael Zanc (Albany: SUNY Press, 2002), 86.

78. Strauss, "Zionism of Nordau," 88.

79. Letter to *National Review*, January 5, 1956, in *Jewish Philosophy and the Crisis of Modernity*, 413–14.

80. Strauss, "Preface to Spinoza's Critique of Religion," 230.

81. Ibid., 256; see also Strauss, *Philosophy and Law*, 18–19.

CHAPTER THREE

1. Leo Strauss, "Das Testament Spinozas," in *Gesammelte Schriften*, ed. Heinrich Meier (Stuttgart: Metzler, 1996), vol. 1: 415–22; trans. by Michael Zanc as "The Testament of Spinoza," in *Leo Strauss: The Early Writings (1921–32)* (Albany: SUNY Press, 2002), 216–33.

2. Strauss, "The Testament of Spinoza," 220. Nietzsche's use of the term "good European" can be found in *Beyond Good and Evil*, trans. Walter Kaufmann (New York: Random House, 1966), 4.

3. Leo Strauss, *Die Religionskritik Spinozas als Grundlage seiner Bibelwissenschaft*, in *Gesammelte Schriften*, vol. 1; for an early appreciation of the work, see Gerhard Kruger, "Review of Leo Strauss's 'Die Religionskritik Spinozas,'" in the *Independent Journal of Philosophy* 5/6 (1988): 173–75. The later reception of Strauss's Spinoza critique has focused almost entirely on Strauss's thesis that Spinoza was an esoteric writer, developed in his essay "How to Study Spinoza's 'Theologico-Political Treatise,'" in *Persecution and the Art of Writing* (Glenco Ill.: Free Press, 1952), 142–201; for a treatment of some of the interpretive issues, see Steven B. Smith, *Spinoza, Liberalism, and the Question of Jewish Identity* (New Haven, Conn.: Yale University Press, 1997), 27–54.

4. For the publication background of the book, see Michael Zanc, "Introduction," in *Leo Strauss: The Early Writings*, 10–11.

5. Leo Strauss, "An Introduction to Heideggerian Existentialism," in *The Rebirth of Classical Political Rationalism*, ed. Thomas Pangle (Chicago: University of Chicago Press, 1989), 28; for Strauss's relation to Rosenzweig, see Leora Batnitzky, "On the Truth of History or the History of Truth: Rethinking Rosenzweig via Strauss," *Jewish Studies Quarterly* 7 (2000): 223–51.

6. Leo Strauss, *Spinoza's Critique of Religion*, trans. E. M. Sinclair (New York: Schocken Books, 1965); the extensive autobiographical preface is reprinted in *Liberalism: Ancient and Modern* (New York: Basic Books, 1968), 241.

7. Leo Strauss, *Das Erkenntnisproblem in der philosophischen Lehre Fr. H. Jacobis,* in *Gesammelte Schriften,* ed. Heinrich Meier (Stuttgart: J. B. Metzler, 1997), vol. 2: 235–92; the Jacobian sources of Strauss's thought have received scant attention, but for some partial exceptions see John Gunnell, "Strauss before Straussianism: Reason, Revelation, and Nature," in *Leo Strauss: Political Philosopher and Jewish Thinker,* ed. Kenneth Deutsch and Walter Nicgorski (Lanham, Md.: Rowman & Littlefield, 1994), 109–10; David Janssens, "The Problem of the Enlightenment: Strauss, Jacobi, and the Pantheism Controversy," *Review of Metaphysics* 56 (2003): 605–32.

8. For Strauss's negative judgment on the dissertation, see "A Giving of Accounts," in *Jewish Philosophy and the Crisis of Modernity,* ed. Kenneth Hart Green (Albany: SUNY Press, 1997), 460.

9. Rémi Brague, "Leo Strauss and Maimonides," in *Leo Strauss's Thought: Towards a Critical Engagement,* ed. Alan Udoff (Boulder, Colo.: Lynne Rienner, 1991), 93–114; Kenneth H. Green, *Jew and Philosopher: The Return to Maimonides in the Jewish Thought of Leo Strauss* (Albany: SUNY Press, 1993).

10. For the context and significance of this debate, see Frederick Beiser, *The Fate of Reason: German Philosophy from Kant to Fichte* (Cambridge: Harvard University Press, 1987), 44–91; David Bell, *Spinoza in Germany from 1670 to the Age of Goethe* (London: Institute of Germanic Studies, 1984), 71–96; see also Paul Franks, "All or Nothing: Systematicity and Nihilism in Jacobi, Reinhold, and Maimon," in *The Cambridge Companion to German Idealism,* ed. Karl Ameriks (Cambridge: Cambridge University Press, 2000), 95–116.

11. For Hume's influence on the German debate, see Beiser, *The Fate of Reason,* 3–4, 11, 54; see also Isaiah Berlin, "Hume and the Sources of German Anti-Rationalism," in *Against the Current* (New York: Penguin, 1977), 181–87.

12. Friedrich Heinrich Jacobi, *The Main Philosophical Writings and the Novel "Atwill,"* trans. George di Giovanni (Montreal: McGill-Queen's University Press, 1994).

13. Ibid., 187.

14. Ibid., 187

15. Ibid., 189.

16. Ibid., 519.

17. Leo Strauss, *Philosophie und Gesetz: Beiträge zum Verständnis Maimunis und seiner Vorläufer,* in *Gessamelte Schriften,* vol. 2; trans. Fred Baumann as *Philosophy and Law: Essays Toward the Understanding of Maimonides and His Predecessors* (Philadelphia: Jewish Publication Society, 1987).

18. Strauss, *Philosophy and Law,* 5.

19. Strauss wrote several of the introductory essays while working with Alexander Altmann on the *Jubilee-Edition* of Mendelssohn's collected works. The longest and most important of these pieces is the introduction to "Morgenstuden und An die Freunde Lessings," in *Gesammelte Schriften,* vol. 2: 528–605; for Strauss's relation to Mendelssohn see Zanc, "Introduction," 10–11; Meier, *Gesammelte Schriften,* vol. 2: xxxi–xxxii; Janssens, "The Problem of Enlightenment," 605–32.

20. Strauss, *Philosophy and Law,* 7.

21. Ibid., 14.

22. Ibid., 18; cf. 113–14 where Strauss indicates the difference between the new probity that he argues has been attained only on the basis of a dogmatic atheism

and the classical doctrine of the love of truth. For the Nietzschean sources of the doctrine of intellectual honesty, see Nietzsche, *Beyond Good and Evil*, sec. 227; see also *The Gay Science*, trans. Walter Kaufmann (New York: Random House, 1974), sec. 335.

23. Strauss, *Philosophy and Law*, 19.

24. For a more complete discussion of Strauss's relation to Weber, see Nasser Behnegar, *Max Weber, Leo Strauss, and the Scientific Study of Politics* (Chicago: University of Chicago Press, 2003).

25. Leo Strauss, *Natural Right and History* (Chicago: University of Chicago Press, 1953), 74.

26. Ibid., 74–75.

27. Strauss, Preface to Spinoza's Critique of Religion, 224.

28. Ibid., 225.

29. Rathenau, an archetypal German Jew, once wrote: "My people are the Germans, no one else. For me the Jews are a German tribe like the Saxons, the Bavarians, or the Wends." Cited in Isaiah Berlin, "Jewish Slavery and Emancipation," in *The Power of Ideas* (Princeton, N.J.: Princeton University Press, 2000), 170.

30. See Smith, *Spinoza, Liberalism, and the Question of Jewish Identity*, 22–26, 162–65.

31. Strauss, "Preface to Spinoza's Critique of Religion," 241.

32. Ibid., 242.

33. Berthold Auerbach, *Spinoza. Ein historischer Roman* (1837), trans. E Nicholson as *Spinoza. A Novel* (London, 1882); see Paul Lawrence Rose, *Revolutionary Antisemitism in Germany from Kant to Wagner* (Princeton, N.J.: Princeton University Press, 1990), 230–31.

34. Strauss, "Preface to Spinoza's Critique of Religion," 239.

35. Ibid., 244.

36. Ibid., 242–43.

37. Ibid., 243.

38. Spinoza, quoted in Strauss, "Preface to Spinoza's Critique of Religion," 229; I have modified the translation somewhat.

39. For his account of his meeting with Jabotinsky, see Leo Strauss, "Why We Remain Jews," in *Jewish Philosophy and the Crisis of Modernity*, 319; see also "Preface to Spinoza's Critique of Religion," 229: "The establishment of the state of Israel . . . procured a blessing for all Jews everywhere regardless of whether they admit it or not."

40. These issues are considered in Steven B. Smith, "Spinoza's Critique of Election," in *The Jewish Political Tradition*, vol. 2, ed. Michael Walzer (New Haven, Conn.: Yale University Press, 2003), 39–44. Spinoza's attitude toward Hebrew is complicated; for useful treatments of the topic, see Geniève Brykman, *La Judéité de Spinoza* (Paris: Vrin, 1972), 117–30; Warren Zev Harvey, "Spinoza's Metaphysical Hebraism," in *Jewish Themes in Spinoza's Philosphy*, ed. Heidi Ravven and Lenn E. Goodman (Albany: SUNY Press, 2002), 107–14.

41. Strauss notes that Pinsker uses for the motto of his work Hillel's famous phrase, "If I am not for myself, who will be for me? And if not now, when?" while silently omitting the central sentence of Hillel's statement "And if I am only for

myself, what am I?" He refers to this as a "profound" modification of traditional Jewish hopes; see Strauss, "Preface to Spinoza's Critique of Religion," 229. The same phrase was used, to similar effect, in Ruth R. Wisse, *If I Am Not for Myself: The Liberal Betrayal of the Jews* (New York: The Free Press, 1992).

42. Strauss, "Preface to Spinoza's Critique of Religion," 246.

43. For this theme, see Paul Mendes-Flohr, *German Jews: A Dual Identity* (New Haven, Conn.: Yale University Press, 1999).

44. Strauss, "Preface to Spinoza's Critique of Religion," 254; emphasis added.

45. Ibid., 256.

46. Ibid., 255; emphasis added.

47. Ibid., 256.

48. Ludwig Wittgenstein, *Tractatus Logico-Philosophicus*, trans. D. F. Pears and B. F. McGuinness (London: Routledge, 1988), 6, 54.

49. Strauss, "Preface to Spinoza's Critique of Religion," 256.

50. Leo Strauss, "The Law of Reason in the 'Kuzari,'" in *Persecution and the Art of Writing*, 141.

51. Ibid., 140.

52. For an inside look at the worlds of contemporary Jewish orthodoxy, see Aviezer Ravitzky, *Messianism, Zionism, and Jewish Religious Radicalism*, trans. Michael Swirsky and Jonathan Chipman (Chicago: University of Chicago Press, 1996); Ehud Luz, *Parallels Meet: Religion and Nationalism in the Early Zionist Movement*, trans. Lenn Schramm (New York: Jewish Publication Society, 1988).

53. Brague, "Leo Strauss and Maimonides," 103.

54. Strauss, "Why We Remain Jews," 328.

55. Letter to Walter Benjamin, March 29, 1935, in *The Correspondence of Gershom Scholem and Walter Benjamin, 1932–1940*, trans. Gary Smith and André Lefevre (New York: Schocken Books, 1989), 157.

CHAPTER FOUR

1. Karl Popper, *The Open Society and Its Enemies*, vol. 1 (Princeton, N.J.: Princeton University Press, 1962). Popper's critique of Plato has been extensively debated and refuted, but its influence remains powerful. A professor at Oxford used to open his lectures with the words "I shall be talking about Plato the Fascist"—cited by Jasper Griffin, "Plato's Grand Design," *New York Review of Books*, May 6, 1999, 41.

2. I owe this term to Charles Griswold, who of course bears no responsibility for the way in which it is used in this paper; see Charles Griswold, "Platonic Liberalism: Self-Perfection as a Foundation of Political Theory," *Contre Platon*, vol. 2, ed. Monique Dixsuat (Paris: J. Vrin, 1995), 155–95.

3. For an early critique of Strauss's esotericism, see George Sabine, "Review of 'Persecution and the Art of Writing,'" *Ethics* 53 (1953): 220–22; Strauss's reply, "On a Forgotten Kind of Writing," is contained in *What Is Political Philosophy and Other Essays* (Glencoe, Ill.: The Free Press, 1959), 221–32; for a reprise of this debate, see the exchange over Machiavelli between Harvey C. Mansfield, "Strauss's Machiavelli," *Political Theory* 3 (1975): 372–84, and J.G.A. Pocock, "Prophet and Inquisitor," *Political Theory* 3 (1975): 384–401; for even further refinement of some issues, see John Gunnell, "The Myth of the Tradition," *American Political Science*

Review 72 (1978): 122–34, and Nathan Tarcov, "Philosophy and History: Tradition and Interpretation in the Work of Leo Strauss," *Polity* 16 (1983): 5–29, esp. 16–18.

4. See the interesting exchange between Dale Hall, "The 'Republic' and the 'Limits of Politics,' " *Political Theory* 5 (1977): 293–313; and Allan Bloom, "Response to Hall," *Political Theory* 5 (1977): 315–30; for a more recent discussion of Strauss's anti-utopianism, see Melissa Lane, "Plato, Popper, Strauss, and Utopianism: Open Secrets?" *History of Philosophy Quarterly* 16 (1999): 119–42.

5. Myles Burnyeat, "Sphinx without a Secret," *New York Review of Books,* May 30, 1985, 31.

6. See Stephen Holmes, "Truths for Philosophers Alone?" *The Times Literary Supplement,* December 1–7, 1989, 1319–23; Charles Larmore, "The Secrets of Philosophy," *The New Republic,* July 3, 1989, 30–35.

7. Brent Staples, "Undemocratic Vistas: The Sinister Vogue of Leo Strauss," *New York Times,* November 28, 1994. In a subsequent clarification of his views, the *Times*'s editorialist admitted to a reporter from the Jewish *Forward* that he had never studied the works of Strauss but based his opinions entirely on the attacks printed in the *New York Review* and the *TLS* cited above; see James Ring Adams, "New 'Cause of the Holocaust' Found," *Forward,* December 2, 1994, 1–2.

8. Charles Kahn, *Plato and the Socratic Dialogue: The Philosophical Use of a Literary Form* (Cambridge: Cambridge University Press, 1996).

9. Alexander Nehamas, *The Art of Living: Socratic Reflections from Plato to Foucault* (Berkeley: University of California Press, 1998); see also Pierre Hadot, *Philosophy as a Way of Life: Spiritual Exercises from Socrates to Foucault,* trans. Michael Chase (New York: Oxford University Press, 1995).

10. For a comprehensive evaluation of the new trend in Platonic studies, see Charles Griswold, "E Pluribus Unum? On the Platonic 'Corpus,' " *Ancient Philosophy* 19 (1999): 361–97.

11. For other contemporaries of Strauss who emphasized the dialogic form, see Jacob Klein, *A Commentary on Plato's Meno* (Chapel Hill: University of North Carolina Press, 1965), 5–31; Hans-Georg Gadamer, *Plato's Dialectical Ethics,* trans. Robert M. Wallace (New Haven, Conn.: Yale University Press, 1991), 51–65.

12. G.R.F. Ferrari, "Strauss's Plato," *Arion* (fall, 1997): 61.

13. In addition to the work by Kahn mentioned above, see Charles Griswold, ed., *Platonic Writings, Platonic Readings* (London: Routledge, 1988).

14. Leo Strauss, *The City and Man* (Chicago: University of Chicago Press, 1964), 52.

15. Ibid., 55.

16. Leo Strauss, "On a New Interpretation of Plato's Political Philosophy," *Social Research* 13 (1946): 351.

17. Ibid., 351 (emphasis added).

18. Ibid., 352.

19. Ibid.

20. Strauss, *City and Man,* 59.

21. Strauss, "On a New Interpretation of Plato's Political Philosophy," 351.

22. Ibid., 351–52.

23. Leo Strauss, "Correspondence Concerning *Warheit und Methode,*" *The Independent Journal of Philosophy* 2 (1978): 5–6.

24. Strauss, *City and Man*, 61–62.

25. For an excellent treatment of this argument, see Jacob Howland, "The Republic's Third Wave and the Paradox of Political Philosophy," *The Review of Metaphysics* 51 (1998): 633–57.

26. Strauss, *City and Man*, 65, 127.

27. For recent efforts to study the influence of Heidegger on Strauss, see Horst Mewes, "Leo Strauss and Martin Heidegger: Greek Antiquity and the Meaning of Modernity," in *Hannah Arendt and Leo Strauss: German Émigrés and American Political Thought after World War II*, ed. Peter Graf Kielmansegg, Horst Mewes, and Elisabeth Glaser-Schmidt (Cambridge: Cambridge University Press, 1995), 105–20; Catherine Zuckert, *Postmodern Platos* (Chicago: University of Chicago Press, 1996); see also "Destruktion or Recovery?" (chapter 5 below).

28. Strauss, "On a Forgotten Kind of Writing," 221.

29. Leo Strauss, *Natural Right and History* (Chicago: University of Chicago Press, 1953), 18–34; see also Strauss, *Persecution and the Art of Writing* (Glencoe, Ill.: Free Press, 1952), 155–57.

30. Leo Strauss, "Besprechung von Julius Ebbinghaus,'" in *Gesammelte Schriften*, ed. Heinrich Meier (Stuttgart: Metzler, 1997), vol. 2: 439.

31. Strauss, *Persecution and the Art of Writing*, 155.

32. The translation used is Allan Bloom, *The Republic of Plato* (New York: Basic Books, 1968).

33. Strauss, *City and Man*, 123.

34. Ibid., 124–25.

35. Ibid., 125.

36. Ibid., 125.

37. Burnyeat, "Sphinx without a Secret," 35.

38. Strauss, *City and Man*, 64.

39. Ibid., 123.

40. Ibid., 123.

41. Strauss, *Persecution and the Art of Writing*, 16–17; Strauss, "Farabi's Plato," in *Louis Ginsberg Jubilee Volume* (New York: American Academy of Jewish Research, 1945), 382–84.

42. Strauss, *City and Man*, 127.

43. Victor Gourevitch, "Philosophy and Politics, II," *Review of Metaphysics* 22 (1968): 292; the internal quote is from Strauss, *On Tyranny*, 200; for the role of evil, see chapter 8 below, "WWLSD; or, What Would Leo Strauss Do?"

44. Strauss, *City and Man*, 127.

45. Ibid., 138.

46. Ibid., 45.

47. Ferrari, "Strauss's Plato," 45.

48. Strauss, *City and Man*, 128 and footnote 49.

49. The quarrel between philosophy and morality was arguably first expressed by Strauss in his interpretation of Judah Halevi's *Kuzari*; see *Persecution and the Art of Writing*, 95–141.

50. Burnyeat, "Sphinx without a Secret," 32.

51. Strauss, *City and Man*, 119.

52. Burnyeat, "Sphinx without a Secret," 32.

53. Richard Kennington, "Strauss's 'Natural Right and History,' " *The Review of Metaphysics* 35 (1981): 67–68.

54. Strauss, *Natural Right and History*, 32.

55. Ibid.

56. Strauss, *On Tyranny*, 196.

57. Ibid.

58. Strauss, *Persecution and the Art of Writing*, 17.

59. Martha Nussbaum, *The Fragility of Goodness: Luck and Ethics in Greek Tragedy and Philosophy* (Cambridge: Cambridge University Press, 1986), 160–64.

60. For an excellent overview of the place of Socratic skepticism in the ancient world, see Julia Annas, "Plato the Skeptic," and Christopher Shields "Socrates among the Skeptics," in *The Socratic Movement*, ed. Paul A. Vander Waerdt (Ithaca, N.Y.: Cornell University Press, 1994), 309–40, 341–66.

61. Strauss, *City and Man*, 137: "It cannot be the duty of a genuinely just man like Socrates to drive weaker men to despair of the possibility of some order and decency in human affairs, and least of all those who, by virtue of their inclinations, their descent, and their abilities, may have some public responsibility."

62. On the obstacles, both natural and artificial, to the recovery of philosophy, see Strauss, *Persecution and the Art of Writing*, 154–56.

63. Strauss, *Natural Right and History*, 124–26.

64. Ian Loadman, "Historical Sickness: Heidegger and the Role of History in Political Thought," unpublished paper, 25–26.

65. Holmes, "Truths for Philosophers Alone?" 1321.

66. Laurence Lampert, *Leo Strauss and Nietzsche* (Chicago: University of Chicago Press, 1996); Shadia Drury, *The Political Thought of Leo Strauss* (New York: St. Martin's Press, 1988).

67. Larmore, "The Secrets of Philosophy"; Staples, "Undemocratic Vistas"; see also Luc Ferry, *Rights—The New Quarrel between the Ancients and the Moderns*, trans. Franklin Philip (Chicago: University of Chicago Press, 1990), 20–22.

68. See Robert Pippin, "The Modern World of Leo Strauss," in *Hannah Arendt and Leo Strauss*, 139–60; Stanley Rosen, *Hermeneutics as Politics* (New York: Oxford University Press, 1987), 107–23 for two especially astute analyses of the modernity problem.

69. Strauss, *Natural Right and History*, vii.

70. See Strauss's view that the second wave of modernity consists "in a return from the world of modernity to pre-modern ways of thinking" and that "romanticism as a whole is primarily a movement of return to the origins," in "What Is Political Philosophy?" 50.

71. Strauss, *City and Man*, 11.

72. Ibid.; emphasis added.

73. Leo Strauss, "Liberal Educational Responsibility," in *Liberalism: Ancient and Modern* (New York: Basic Books, 1968), 24.

74. Leo Strauss, "The Three Waves of Modernity," in *An Introduction to Political Philosophy: Ten Essays by Leo Strauss*, ed. Hilail Gildin (Detroit, Mich.: Wayne State University Press, 1989), 98.

75. John Stuart Mill, *Autobiography* (New York: Columbia University Press, 1960), 16; for an interesting discussion of Mill's "Platonism," see Peter Berkowtiz,

Virtue and the Making of Modern Liberalism (Princeton, N.J.: Princeton University Press, 1999), 139–40.

76. Strauss, *City and Man*, 131.

77. Ibid.; see also Strauss, "What Is Political Philosophy?" 55.

78. Pierre Manent, *Tocqueville and the Nature of Democracy*, trans. John Waggoner (Lanham, Md.: Rowman & Littlefield, 1996), 132.

79. Strauss, "What Is Liberal Education?" in *Liberalism: Ancient and Modern*, 4.

80. Ibid., 5.

81. See Lane, "Plato, Popper, Strauss, and Utopianism," 120–22.

82. For those surprised to see Strauss in this company, see "Liberal Educational Responsibility," 17–18 where Strauss endorses Mill's scheme for proportional representation.

83. Strauss, *On Tyranny*, 27.

CHAPTER FIVE

1. The most important of these was Strauss's "Anmerkungen zu Carl Schmitt, 'Der Bergriff des Politischen,'" *Archiv fur Sozialwissenschaft und Sozialpolitik* 67 (1932): 732–49; an English translation by E. M. Sinclair appeared as an appendix to Leo Strauss, *Spinoza's Critique of Religion* (New York: Schocken Books, 1965), 331–51. The exchange between Strauss and Schmitt has recently been studied by Henrich Meier, *Carl Schmitt and Leo Strauss: The Hidden Dialogue*, trans. Harvey Lomax (Chicago: University of Chicago Press, 1995); for a thoughtful overview of some of the issues involved, see Robert Howse, "From Legitimacy to Dictatorship—and Back Again: Leo Strauss's Critique of the Anti-Liberalism of Carl Schmitt," *The Canadian Journal of Law and Jurisprudence* 10 (1997): 77–103.

2. Recently Laurence Lampert has found in Strauss's "Note on the Plan of Nietzsche's 'Beyond Good and Evil,'" in *Studies in Platonic Political Philosophy*, ed. Thomas Pangle (Chicago: University of Chicago Press, 1983), 174–91 the hidden plan to Strauss's own teachings; see Laurence Lampert, *Leo Strauss and Nietzsche* (Chicago: University of Chicago Press, 1996). The importance of Nietzsche in Strauss's writings has, of course, been noted before; see Rémi Brague, "Leo Strauss and Maimonides," in *Leo Strauss's Thought: Toward a Critical Engagement*, ed. Alan Udoff (Boulder, Colo.: Lynne Reinner, 1991), 93–114, esp. 104–5.

3. Hwa Yol Jung, "The Life-World, Historicity and Truth: Reflections on Leo Strauss's Encounter with Heidegger and Husserl," *Journal for the British Society for Phenomenology* 9 (1978): 11–25; James F. Ward, "Political Philosophy and History: The Links between Strauss and Heidegger," *Polity* 20 (1987): 273–95; Lawrence Berns, "The Prescientific World and Historicism: Some Reflections on Strauss, Heidegger, and Husserl," in *Leo Strauss's Thought*, 169–81; Horst Mewes, "Leo Strauss and Martin Heidegger: Greek Antiquity and the Meaning of Modernity," in *Hannah Arendt and Leo Strauss: German Émigrés and American Political Thought after World War II*, ed. Peter Graf Kielmansess, Horst Mewes, and Elisabeth Glaser-Schmidt (Cambridge: Cambridge University Press, 1995), 105–20.

4. Leo Strauss, "An Introduction to Heideggerian Existentialism," in *The Rebirth of Classical Political Rationalism*, ed. T. Pangle (Chicago: University of Chicago Press, 1989), 28; Strauss, "Kurt Riezler (1882–1955)," in *What Is Political*

Philosophy and Other Studies (Glencoe, Ill.: The Free Press, 1959), 246: "One has to go back to Hegel until one finds another professor of philosophy who affected in a comparable manner the thought of Germany, nay, of Europe. But Hegel had some contemporaries whose power equalled his or at any rate whom one could compare to him without being manifestly foolish. Heidegger surpasses all his contemporaries by far."

5. Strauss, "Heideggerian Existentialism," 28; "Kurt Riezler," 246.

6. Strauss, "Heideggerian Existentialism," 30–31; "What Is Political Philosophy?" in *What Is Political Philosophy*, 55; "Philosophy as Rigorous Science and Political Philosophy," in *Studies in Platonic Political Philosophy*, 30–31.

7. Victor Farias, *Heidegger and Nazism*, trans. Paul Burrell and Gabriel R. Ricci (Philadelphia: Temple University Press, 1989); a critical appraisal of the maelstrom produced by the book is provided by Thomas Sheehan, "Heidegger and the Nazis," *New York Review of Books*, June 16, 1988, 38–47; see also his "A Normal Nazi," *New York Review of Books*, January 14, 1993, 30–35; among the several works devoted to this issue see Gunther Neske and Emil Kettering, eds., *Martin Heidegger and National Socialism: Question and Answers* (New York: Paragon, 1990) and Richard Wolin, ed., *The Heidegger Controversy: A Critical Reader* (Cambridge: MIT Press, 1993).

8. Strauss, "Philosophy as Rigorous Science," 30.

9. Leo Strauss, "An Unspoken Prologue to a Lecture at Saint John's," *Jewish Philosophy and the Crisis of Modernity*, ed. Kenneth Hart Green (Albany: State University of New York Press, 1997), 450.

10. Strauss, "Philosophy as Rigorous Science," 30.

11. Luc Ferry, *Political Philosophy*, vol. 1: *Rights: The New Quarrel between the Ancients and the Moderns*, trans. Franklin Philip (Chicago: University of Chicago Press, 1990).

12. Ibid., 3.

13. Ibid., 4.

14. Ibid., 3.

15. Ibid., 18.

16. Ibid., 20.

17. Ibid.

18. Ibid., 21.

19. Ibid.

20. Ibid., 20.

21. Martin Heidegger, *An Introduction to Metaphysics*, trans. Ralph Manheim (New Haven, Conn.: Yale University Press, 1959), 38.

22. Ibid.

23. Immanuel Kant, "Idea for a Universal History with a Cosmopolitan Purpose," in *Political Writings*, ed. Hans Reiss, trans. H. B. Nisbet (Cambridge: Cambridge University Press, 1970), 49; "We are *cultivated* to a high degree by art and science. We are *civilised* to the point of excess in all kinds of social courtesies and proprieties. But we are still a long way from the point where we could consider ourselves *morally* mature." Friedrich Nietzsche, *Untimely Meditations*, trans. R. J. Hollingdale (Cambridge: Cambridge University Press, 1983), 3–6, where Nietzsche speaks of "an alien 'cultivatedness' (*unnationale Gebildetheit*) which is

nowadays dangerously misunderstood to constitute culture" and goes on to complain that this confusion is especially rife in Germany, "where there no longer exists any clear conception of what culture is." This distinction runs throughout Thomas Mann, *Reflections of a Nonpolitical Man*, trans. Walter D. Morris (New York: Ungar, 1987), 17: "The difference between intellect and politics includes that of culture and civilization, of soul and society, of freedom and voting rights, of art and literature; and German tradition is culture, soul, freedom and art and *not* civilization, society, voting rights, and literature."

24. Heidegger, *Introduction to Metaphysics*, 37.

25. Ibid., 38.

26. Martin Heidegger, "The Self-Assertion of the German University," in *Martin Heidegger and National Socialism*, 5–13.

27. Heidegger, *Introduction to Metaphysics*, 199.

28. Leo Strauss, *Natural Right and History* (Chicago: University of Chicago Press, 1953), 1–2.

29. Leo Strauss, "Relativism," in *The Rebirth of Classical Liberalism*, 17.

30. Contrast Heidegger, "The Self-Assertion of the German University," 10: "To give oneself the law is the highest freedom. The much-lauded 'academic freedom' will be expelled from the German university; for this freedom was not genuine because it was only negative. It primarily meant lack of concern, arbitariness of intentions, lack of restraint in what was done and left undone" to Strauss, "Relativism," 15–16: "It would be shortsighted to deny that Berlin's formula is very helpful for a political purpose—for the purpose of an anticommunist manifesto designed to rally all anticommunists."

31. Strauss, "Relativism," 13.

32. Ibid., 17; Strauss finds particularly problematic Berlin's endorsement of Schumpeter's view that "To realise the relative validity of one's convictions and yet stand for them unflinchingly, is what distinguishes a civilised man from a barbarian," cited in Isaiah Berlin, "Two Concepts of Liberty," in *Four Essays on Liberty* (Oxford: Oxford University Press, 1975), 172.

33. Leo Strauss, *The City and Man* (Chicago: University of Chicago Press, 1964), 3.

34. Ibid., 3–4.

35. Ibid., 3, 6–7; *Natural Right and History*, 5–6.

36. For Heidegger's critique of Plato see Hans-Georg Gadamer, "Plato and Heidegger," in *The Question of Being*, ed. M. Sprung (University Park: Pennsylvania State University Press, 1978), 44–53; William Galston, "Heidegger's Plato: A Critique of 'Plato's Doctrine of Truth,'" *Philosophical Forum* 13 (1982): 371–84.

37. Hans-Georg Gadamer, "Heidegger and the History of Philosophy," *The Monist* 64 (1981): 436.

38. Martin Heidegger, *Being and Time*, trans. John Macquarrie and Edward Robinson (San Francisco: Harper & Row, 1962), 39.

39. Ibid., 41.

40. Ibid., 43.

41. Ibid., 44.

42. Ibid., 44.

43. Martin Heidegger, *Vorträge und Aufsätze* (Pfullingen: Neske, 1954), 71.

44. Strauss, "An Unspoken Prologue," 450.

45. Ibid., 450.

46. Strauss, "Heideggerian Existentialism," 28: "I had heard Heidegger's interpretation of certain sections of Aristotle, and some time later I heard Werner Jaeger in Berlin interpret the same texts. Charity compels me to limit my comparison to the remark that there was no comparison." One wonders what an uncharitable judgment would have produced.

47. Hannah Arendt, "Martin Heidegger at Eighty," in *Heidegger and Modern Philosophy*, ed. Michael Murray (New Haven, Conn.: Yale University Press, 1978), 295.

48. In his contribution to a *festschrift* for Strauss, his friend Jacob Klein, without mentioning Heidegger by name, relates the following story: "Many, many years ago I attended a series of lectures on Aristotle's philosophy. The lecturer began his exposition as follows: 'As regards Aristotle himself, as regards the circumstances and the course of his life, suffice it to say: Aristotle was born, he spent his life in philosophizing, and died.' " Jacob Klein, "Aristotle, An Introduction," in *Ancients and Moderns: Essays on the Tradition of Political Philosophy in Honor of Leo Strauss*, ed. Joseph Cropsey (New York: Basic Books, 1964), 50.

49. Strauss, *City and Man*, 12: "We contend that [the] coherent and comprehensive understanding of political things is available to us in Aristotle's *Politics* precisely because the *Politics* is the original form of political science. . . . Classical political philosophy is the primary form of political science because the common sense understanding of political things is primary."

50. The first use of this image of a "second cave" or a cave below the cave appears in Strauss's review of Julius Ebbinghaus's *Uber die Fortschritte der Metaphysik*, in *Gesammelte Schriften*, ed. Heinrich Meier (Stuttgart: Metzler, 1997), vol. 2: 439.

51. Leo Strauss, *Persecution and the Art of Writing* (Glencoe, Ill.: The Free Press, 1952), 155–56.

52. Seth Benardete, "Leo Strauss' 'The City and Man,' " *Political Science Reviewer* 8 (1978): 1.

53. Leo Strauss, *Thoughts on Machiavelli* (Seattle: University of Washington Press, 1958), 13.

54. Strauss, *Natural Right and History*, 79–80.

55. Ibid., 7-8.

56. Strauss, "What Is Political Philosophy?" 38.

57. Ibid., 39.

58. For a useful discussion of these issues, see Victor Gourevitch, "Philosophy and Politics, I–II," *Review of Metaphysics* 22 (1968): 58–84, 281–328, esp. 281–99; Laurence Lampert, "The Argument of Leo Strauss in 'What Is Political Philosophy,' " *Modern Age* (winter 1978): 38–46.

59. Strauss, *City and Man*, 11.

60. Ibid.

61. Ibid.

62. Ibid., 9.

63. Strauss, *Natural Right and History*, 81.

64. Strauss, "Heideggerian Existentialism," 28; Strauss, "Kurt Riezler," 246: "Heidegger . . . explicitly denies the possibility of ethics because he feels that there is a revolting disproportion between the idea of ethics and those phenomena which ethics pretended to articulate." See also Strauss, "Philosophy as Rigorous Science," 30: "There is no room for political philosophy in Heidegger's work, and this may well be due to the fact that the room in question is occupied by god or the gods."

65. The two passages in question are Nathan's parable about the rich man's theft of a poor man's lamb in II Samuel 12 and the story of Ahab's covetousness of Naboth's vineyard in I Kings 21.

66. Strauss, *Natural Right and History*, 31–32, 105.

67. Ibid., 127–28.

68. Leo Strauss, *On Tyranny Including the Strauss-Kojève Correspondence*, ed. Victor Gourevitch and Michael Roth (Chicago: University of Chicago Press, 2000), 191.

69. Ibid., 191–92.

70. Strauss, *Natural Right and History*, 130; see also *On Tyranny*, 204, where Strauss argues that the philosopher does not require "recognition" from others but is fortified by an inner sense of self-satisfaction or self-admiration as something "akin to 'the good conscience' which as such does not require confirmation from others." In a letter to Strauss dated September 19, 1950, Kojève suggested that Strauss's appeal to moral conscience is as "problematic" as his [Kojève's] appeal to mutual recognition and then asks: "Did Torquemada or Dzerzhinski have 'bad consciences'?" *On Tyranny*, 255. Kojève's reply seems to miss the point, since neither Torquemada nor Dzerzhinski was a philosopher in Strauss's specific sense of the term. See "Tyranny Ancient and Modern," chapter 6 below.

71. Strauss, *City and Man*, 12.

72. Ibid., 138; Ferry, *The New Quarrel*, 21.

73. Strauss, *City and Man*, 131: "Democracy itself is characterized by freedom which includes the right to say and do whatever one wishes. . . . Hence, we must understand, democracy is the only regime other than the best in which the philosopher can lead his peculiar way of life without being disturbed. . . . Plato himself called the Athenian democracy, looking back on it from the rule of the Thirty Tyrants, 'golden.' " In this context it is interesting that Strauss says three times that Plato deliberately "exaggerates" his critiques of democracy.

74. Strauss, *On Tyranny*, 196.

75. Cf. M. F. Burnyeat, "Sphinx without a Secret," *New York Review of Books*, May 30, 1985, 32: "There is much talk in Straussian writings about the nature of 'the philosopher' but no sign of any knowledge, from the inside, of what it is to be actively involved in philosophy." This accusation seems to have been written in ignorance of Strauss's extensive discussion of the "zetetic" nature of philosophy. This is all the more surprising since the accuser is himself an authority on the history and theory of philosophical skepticism; see M. F. Burnyeat, ed. *The Skeptical Tradition* (Berkeley: University of California Press, 1983).

76. Strauss, *City and Man*, 119–20.

77. Strauss, "The Problem of Socrates," in *Rebirth of Classical Political Rationalism*, 162: "To return to the argument of the *Republic*, by realizing the

essential limitations of the political, one is indeed liberated from the charms of what we now would call political idealism."

78. Strauss, "What Is Political Philosophy?" 28.

79. Strauss, *On Tyranny*, 200.

80. Strauss, "Liberal Education and Responsibility," *Liberalism Ancient and Modern* (New York: Basic Books, 1968), 24.

81. Strauss, "Heideggerian Existentialism," 43–44.

82. See Heidegger, "The Self-Assertion of the German University," 8: "if it is true what that passionate seeker after God and last German philosopher, Friedrich Nietzsche, said: 'God is dead'—[then] we must be serious about this forsakenness of modern human beings in the midst of what is. . . ." See also Heidegger's later lecture "The Word of Nietzsche: 'God is Dead,' " in *The Question Concerning Technology and Other Essays*, trans. William Lovitt (New York: Harper & Row, 1977), 53–112.

83. Heidegger, "The Spiegel Interview," in *Heidegger and National Socialism*, 62; see also "Hölderlin and the Essence of Poetry," in *Existence and Being*, ed. Werner Brock (Chicago: Regnery, 1949), 289: "Hölderlin, in the act of establishing the essence of poetry, first determines a new time. It is the time of the gods that had fled *and* the god that is coming."

84. Hölderlin, "Brot und Wein," cited in Heidegger, "Hölderlin and the Essence of Poetry," 290.

85. Martin Heidegger, "What Are Poets For?" in *Poetry, Language, Thought*, ed. Albert Hofstadter (New York: Harper & Row, 1971), 96.

86. Martin Heidegger, "The Question Concerning Technology," in *Basic Writings*, ed. David Krell (San Francisco: Harper & Row, 1977), 316.

87. Martin Heidegger, *Hölderlins Hymnen 'Germanien' und 'Der Rhein' Gesamtausgabe*, vol. 39, ed. Susanne Ziegler (Frankfurt: Klosterman, 1980), 80–82, 87–89, 141.

88. Heidegger, *Hölderlins Hymnen*, 120, 121: "Das 'Vaterland' ist dast Seyn selbst. . . . Das Vaterland ist keine abstrakte, uberzeitliche Idee an sich, sondern das Veterland sieht der Dichter in einem urspunglichen Sinne geschichtlich."

89. Heidegger, *Basic Writings*, 218.

90. Martin Heidegger, "Memorial Address," in *Discourse on Thinking*, trans. John Anderson and E. Hans Freund (New York: Harper & Row, 1966), 43–57.

91. Heidegger, "The Spiegel Interview," 61: "I think that the task of thinking is precisely to help, within its bounds, human beings to attain an adequate relationship to the essence of technology at all. Although National Socialism went in that direction, those people were much too limited in their thinking to gain a really explicit relationship to what is happening today and what has been under way for three centuries."

92. Heidegger, *Introduction to Metaphysics*, 199. The claim that Nazism grew out of an excess of humanism has given rise to justified incredulity; for a recent attempt to defend the claim see Philippe Lacoue-Labarthe, *Heidegger, Art, and Politics*, trans. Chris Turner (Oxford: Basil Blackwell, 1990), 95–96: "Nazism is a humanism in so far as it rests upon a determination of *humanitas* which is, in its view, more powerful—i.e. more effective—than any other. . . . The fact that this subject lacks the universality which apparently defines the *humanitas* of human-

NOTES TO PAGES 124-127

ism in the received sense, still does not make Nazism an anti-humanism. It simply situates it within the logic, of which there are many other examples, of the realization and the becoming-concrete of 'abstractions.' "

93. Heidegger, "The Spiegel Interview," 54.

96. Strauss, City and Man, 241.

97. Leo Strauss, "Preface to 'Hobbes Politische Wissenschaft,' " in Jewish Philosophy and the Crisis of Modernity, 453.

98. Strauss, "What Is Political Philosophy?" 13.

99. For an argument that Strauss's conception of "prophetology" derives neither from Greek ("athénien") nor Jewish ("hiérosolymatain") but Muslim ("mecquois") sources, see Rémi Brague, "Athènes, Jerusalem, La Mecque: L'interprétation 'musulmane' de la philosophie greque chez Leo Strauss," Revue de Metaphysique et de Morale 3 (1989): 309-36 at 316. At issue is Strauss's use of Avicenna as an authoritative interpreter of Plato's Laws; see Leo Strauss, The Argument and Action of Plato's Laws (Chicago: University of Chicago Press, 1975), 1; Ralph Lerner and Mushin Mahdi, eds., Medieval Political Philosophy: A Sourcebook (Glencoe, Ill.: The Free Press, 1963), 97: "Of this science, the treatment of kingship is contained in the book by Plato and that by Aristotle on the regime, and the treatment of prophecy and the Law is contained in their two books on the laws."

100. Strauss, "How to Begin to Study Medieval Philosophy," in Rebirth of Classical Political Rationalism, 223-24.

101. See Strauss, The Argument and Action of Plato's 'Laws,' 1-3.

102. Strauss, Natural Right and History, 74: "No alternative is more fundamental than this: human guidance or divine guidance. The first possibility is characteristic of philosophy or science in the original sense of the term, the second is presented in the Bible. The dilemma cannot be evaded by any harmonization or synthesis." See also "Jerusalem and Athens: Some Introductory Reflections," in Studies in Platonic Political Philosophy, 147-73.

103. Strauss, Natural Right and History, 81-83; City and Man, 241.

104. Strauss, Natural Right and History, 169.

105. Strauss, "Mutual Influence of Theology and Philosophy," The Independent Journal of Philosophy 3 (1979): 116.

106. Leo Strauss, "Preface to Spinoza's Critique of Religion," in Liberalism: Ancient and Modern, 254.

109. Strauss, "What Is Political Philosophy?" 50.

110. Strauss, "Jerusalem and Athens," 149-50; but contrast this to the opening paragraph of Strauss's "Niccolo Machiavelli," in History of Political Philosophy, ed. Leo Strauss and Joseph Cropsey (Chicago: Rand McNally, 1972), 271-72.

111. Strauss, "Mutual Influence of Theology and Philosophy," 111, 113.

112. Leo Strauss, "The Zionism of Nordau,," in Leo Strauss: The Early Writings (1921-1932), trans. Michael Zanc (Albany: SUNY Press, 2002), 86.

113. Strauss, "Heideggerian Existentialism," 31.

114. Strauss, "Preface to Spinoza's Critique of Religion," 230.

115. Ibid., 230.

116. Strauss, "What Is Political Philosophy?" 40.

117. Strauss, "Heideggerian Existentialism," 29; "What Is Political Philosophy?" 55.

118. Strauss, "Heideggerian Existentialism," 29.

119. Ibid.

120. Strauss, "What Is Political Philosophy?" 55; see also Karl Löwith, "M. Heidegger and F. Rosenzweig or Temporality and Eternity," *Philosophy and Phenomenological Research* 3 (1942): 75: "[Heidegger's] political commitment . . . was not—as naïve people thought—a deviation from the main path of his philosophy, but a consequence of his concept of historical existence which only recognizes truths that are relative to the actual and proper."

121. Strauss, "What Is Political Philosophy?" 55.

122. Ibid., 27: "The biggest event of 1933 would rather seem to have proved, if such proof was necessary, that man cannot abandon the question of the good society, and that he cannot free himself from the responsibility for answering it by deferring to History or to any other power different from his own reasons."

123. Emile Fackenheim, *To Mend the World: Foundations of Future Jewish Thought* (New York: Schocken Books, 1982), 169–70.

124. Heidegger's views on Marx are surprisingly sympathetic; see *Basic Writings*, 219 where Marx is praised for recognizing "the homelessness of modern man" as "an essential and significant" element of modern history: "Because Marx by experiencing estrangement attains an essential dimension of history, the Marxist view of history is superior to that of other historical accounts."

125. For some of the recent political appropriations of Heidegger see Michael E. Zimmerman, *Heidegger's Confrontation with Modernity: Technology, Politics, Art* (Bloomington: Indiana University Press, 1990), 248–74.

126. Heidegger's infamous statement that the mechanized production of foodstuffs is "the same thing" as the "production of corpses" in Auschwitz is cited in Lacoue-Labarthe, *Heidegger, Art, and Politics,* 34.

127. Strauss, *On Tyranny,* 212.

CHAPTER SIX

1. Leo Strauss, *On Tyranny: An Interpretation of Xenophon's Hiero.* Foreword by Alvin Johnson (New York: Political Science Classics, 1948).

2. For Johnson's role in establishing the university-in-exile, see Claus-Deiter Krohn, *Intellectuals in Exile: Refugee Scholars and the New School for Social Research,* trans. Rita and Robert Kimber (Amherst: University of Massachusetts Press, 1993), 22–23, 58–59; for Strauss's place in the faculty, see 74–76.

3. Leo Strauss, *De la Tyrannie. Précédé de Hiéron de Xénophon et suivi de Tyrannie et Sagesse par Alexandre Kojève* (Paris: Gallimard, 1954).

4. Leo Strauss, *On Tyranny.* Revised and enlarged edition including Alexandre Kojève, "Tyranny and Wisdom" and Strauss's "Restatement on Xenophon's 'Hiero' " (New York: Free Press, 1963).

5. Leo Strauss, *On Tyranny. Including the Strauss-Kojève Correspondence,* ed. Victor Gourevitch and Michael Roth (Chicago: University of Chicago Press, 2000). Unless otherwise noted, all further citations of *On Tyranny* will be to this edition.

6. Allan Bloom, "Leo Strauss," *Political Theory* 4 (1974): 383.

7. For some of the more useful commentaries, see George Grant, "Tyranny and Wisdom: A Comment on the Controversy between Leo Strauss and Alexandre Kojève," *Social Research* (1964): 45–72; Victor Gourevitch, "Philosophy and Politics I–II," *Review of Metaphysics* 22 (1968): 58–84, 281–328; Nicola Chiaromonte, "On Modern Tyranny: A Critique of Western Intellectuals," *Dissent* 16 (1969): 137–50; Michael Roth, "Natural Right and the End of History: Leo Strauss and Alexandre Kojève," *Revue de Metaphysique et de Morale* 3 (1991): 407–22; Robert Pippin, "Being, Time, and Politics: The Strauss-Kojève Debate," *History and Theory* 2 (1993): 138–61.

8. Strauss, *On Tyranny,* 22. Subsequent citations of this work will be parenthetical in the text, by page number.

9. Strauss to Kojève, undated, in *On Tyranny,* 222.

10. Strauss to Kojève, August 8, 1948, in *On Tyranny,* 239.

11. Strauss to Kojève, September 4, 1949, in *On Tyranny,* 245.

12. Kojève to Strauss, March 29, 1962, in *On Tyranny,* 308.

13. Strauss to Kojève, May 29, 1962, in *On Tyranny,* 309.

14. The most complete biography of Kojève to date is Dominique Auffret, *Alexandre Kojève: La philosophie, L'Etat, et la fin de l'Histoire* (Paris: Bernard Grasset, 1990). The literature on Kojève's influence on subsequent French thought has become quite extensive, but for some of the better studies, see Vincent Descombes, *Modern French Philosophy* (Cambridge: Cambridge University Press, 1983), 9–47; Barry Cooper, *The End of History: An Essay on Modern Hegelianism* (Toronto: University of Toronto Press, 1984); Michael Roth, *Knowing and History: Appropriations of Hegel in Twentieth-Century France* (Ithaca, N.Y.: Cornell University Press, 1988); for a personal account of Kojève as a thinker and personality, see Allan Bloom, "Kojève, le philosophe," *Commentaire* 9 (1980): 116–19; Stanley Rosen, "Kojève's Paris: A Memoir," in *Metaphysics in Ordinary Language* (New Haven, Conn.: Yale University Press, 1999), 258–78; see also Raymond Aron, *Memoirs: Fifty Years of Political Reflection,* trans. George Holoch (New York: Holmes & Meier, 1990), 65–69.

15. As is appropriate for someone who chose to work behind the scenes as an adviser to princes, as it were, Kojève's name is virtually absent from the standard literature on the formation of the EU, but for those influential in French policy making, he was acknowledged as a leading figure; see Olivier Wormser, "Mon ami Alexandre Kojève," *Commentaire* 9 (1980): 121–22; Robert Marjolin, *Architect of European Unity: Memoirs, 1911–1986,* trans. William Hall (London: Weidenfeld & Nicholson, 1989), 52–53; Kojève's role in the world of high French policy is treated extensively in Auffret, *Alexandre Kojève,* 301–56; Aron tells the story that Giscard d'Estaing was an admirer of Kojève and after delivering a speech inspired by him, asked "Well, Kojève, are you happy?" *Memoirs,* 67.

16. See Leo Strauss, *The Political Philosophy of Hobbes: Its Basis and Genesis,* trans. Elsa M. Sinclair (Chicago: University of Chicago Press, 1966), 58.

17. Alexandre Kojève, *Introduction à la lecture de Hegel*, ed. Raymond Queneau (Paris: Gallimard, 1947); an abridged English translation was published under the title *Introduction to the Reading of Hegel*, trans. James H. Nichols, Jr., ed. Allan Bloom (New York: Basic Books, 1968).

18. Alexandre Kojève, *Essai d'une histoire raisonnée de la philosophie paienne* (Paris: Gallimard, 1968, 1973); *Le Concept, le Temps, et le Discours* (Paris: Gallimard, 1990); *Kant* (Paris: Gallimard, 1973).

19. Aron, *Memoirs*, 67.

20. The story was broken in *Le Monde*, September 16, 1999, 14; for a reply see Edmund Ortigues, "Pour l'honneur d'Alexandre Kojève," *Le Monde*, October 3, 1999, 17.

21. For a general account of how the concept of recognition fits into recent debates on communicative ethics and deliberative democracy, see Axel Honneth, *The Struggle for Recognition: The Moral Grammar of Social Conflicts*, trans. Joel Anderson (Cambridge, Mass.: Polity Press, 1995); Patchen Markell, *Bound by Recognition* (Princeton, N.J.: Princeton University Press, 2003).

22. Charles Taylor, *Multiculturalism: Examining the Politics of Recognition* (Princeton, N.J.: Princeton University Press, 1994), 25–73.

23. The remainder of this section draws on Steven B. Smith, "Hegelianism and the Three Crises of Rationality," *Social Research* 4 (1989): 943–73.

24. Kojève, *Introduction to Hegel*, 6–8, 39–41, 192–93.

25. Kojève, *Introduction to Hegel*, 43–48.

26. Kojève, *Introduction to Hegel*, 52.

27. Kojève, *Introduction to Hegel*, 23.

28. See Allan Bloom, "Introduction," in *Introduction to Hegel*, vii: "Kojève is the most learned, the most profound of those Marxists who, dissatisfied with the thinness of Marx's account of the human and metaphysical grounds of his teaching, turned to Hegel as the truly philosophic source of that teaching."

29. Strauss to Kojève, August, 22, 1948, in *On Tyranny*, 237.

30. Kojève to Strauss, October 29, 1953, in *On Tyranny*, 261.

31. Kojève to Strauss, October 29, 1953, in *On Tyranny*, 262.

32. The relation between philosophy and tyranny has been the subject of Mark Lilla, *The Reckless Mind: Intellectuals in Politics* (New York: NYRB, 2001); see also Chiaromonte, "On Modern Tyranny."

33. For some of the dangers, see Nathan Tarcov, "On a Certain Critique of 'Straussianism,' " *Review of Politics* 52 (1991): 3–18.

34. Leo Strauss, "Why We Remain Jews," in *Jewish Philosophy and the Crisis of Modernity*, ed. Kenneth Hart Green (Albany: SUNY Press, 1997), 316–17.

35. Kojève to Strauss, September 19, 1950, in *On Tyranny*, 255.

36. Gourevitch, "Philosophy and Politics II," 307.

37. Francis Fukuyama, *The End of History and the Last Man* (New York: Free Press, 1992). Although the article and the book on which his article was based have been subjected to a mountain of commentary, for one of the better replies, see Howard Williams, David Sullivan, and Gwynn Matthews, *Francis Fukuyama and the End of History* (Cardiff: University of Wales Press, 1997).

38. The best treatments of this theme in Kant remain William A. Galston, *Kant and the Problem of History* (Chicago: University of Chicago Press, 1975);

Yirmiyahu Yovel, *Kant and the Philosophy of History* (Princeton, N.J.: Princeton University Press, 1980).

39. See Steven B. Smith, *Hegel's Critique of Liberalism: Rights in Context* (Chicago: University of Chicago Press, 1989), 140–45, 156–64, 236–37.

40. Kojève, *Introduction to Hegel*, 159.

41. Kojève, *Introduction to Hegel*, 158–59.

42. For Kojève's favorable references to Mao, see Letter of October 29, 1953, in *On Tyranny*, 262: "Your Bible quote about the land of the fathers is already most problematic. From it one can of course deduce a condemnation of collectivization in the USSR and elsewhere. But with it one also justifies permanently preserving a Chinese peasant's animal-like starvation existence (before Mao-Tse Tung)." The reference to a biblical citation is to the epigraph to *Natural Right and History*.

43. Kojève to Strauss, September 19, 1950, in *On Tyranny*, 255.

44. Kojève, *Introduction to Hegel*, 159.

45. Kojève, *Introduction to Hegel*, 160–61.

46. Hegel cited in Kojève, *Introduction to Hegel*, 185.

47. Aron, *Memoirs*, 67.

48. See also Leo Strauss, "Relativism," in *The Rebirth of Classical Political Rationalism*, ed. Thomas Pangle (Chicago: University of Chicago Press, 1989), 21.

49. Leo Strauss, *Natural Right and History* (Chicago: University of Chicago Press, 1953), 318.

CHAPTER SEVEN

1. Leo Strauss, "An Introduction to Heideggerian Existentialism," in *The Rebirth of Classical Political Rationalism*, ed. Thomas Pangle (Chicago: University of Chicago Press, 1989), 29–30.

2. For a recent attempt to view Strauss as a public philosopher, see Kenneth L. Deutsch and John A. Murley, eds., *Leo Strauss, the Straussians, and the American Regime* (Lanham, Md.: Rowman & Littlefield, 1999).

3. The best treatment of this topic is Alain Franchon and Daniel Vernet, *L'Amérique Messianique: Les guerres des néo-conservateurs* (Paris: Éditions du Seuil, 2005).

4. Leo Strauss, "On Classical Political Philosophy," in *What Is Political Philosophy and Other Studies* (New York: Free Press, 1959), 93–94.

5. Leo Strauss, "What Is Political Philosophy?" in *What Is Political Philosophy*, 11.

6. Strauss, "What Is Political Philosophy?" 12.

7. Heinrich Meier, "Why Political Philosophy?" *Review of Metaphysics* 56 (2002): 391.

8. Leo Strauss, "On a Forgotten Kind of Writing," in *What Is Political Philosophy*, 222.

9. Strauss, *Natural Right and History*, 129–30; Leo Strauss, *On Tyranny Including the Strauss-Kojève Correspondence*, ed. Victor Gourevitch and Michael Roth (Chicago: University of Chicago Press, 2000), 191–92.

10. Strauss, *Natural Right and History*, 31–32.

11. Ibid., 32.

12. These questions have been lucidly explored by Robert Pippin, "The Unavailability of the Ordinary: Strauss on the Philosophical Fate of Modernity," *Political Theory* 3 (2003): 335–58; see also Stanley Rosen, "Leo Strauss and the Possibility of Philosophy," *Review of Metaphysics* 53 (2000): 541–64.

13. Leo Strauss, "Political Philosophy and History," in *What Is Political Philosophy*, 75.

14. Ibid., 75.

15. Strauss, *Natural Right and History*, 79.

16. Ibid., 79–80.

17. Leo Strauss, *Persecution and the Art of Writing* (Glencoe, Ill.: Free Press, 1952), 155; see also "Leo Strauss's Platonic Liberalism" (chapter 4 above).

18. Strauss, "What Is Political Philosophy?" 10.

19. The relation between historical analysis and philosophical criticism has been usefully dealt with by Nathan Tarcov, "Philosophy and History: Tradition and Interpretation in the Work of Leo Strauss," *Polity* 16 (1983): 5–29.

20. Strauss, *Natural Right and History*, 32.

21. Strauss, "On Classical Political Philosophy," 93.

22. Strauss, "On a Forgotten Kind of Writing," 221.

23. Strauss, *Persecution and the Art of Writing*, 18.

24. Ibid., 33.

25. See Alexis de Tocqueville, *Democracy in America*, trans. Harvey Mansfield and Delba Winthrop (Chicago: University of Chicago Press, 2000), 244: "Princes had so to speak made violence material; democratic republics in our day have rendered it just as intellectual as the human will that it wants to constrain. Under the absolute government of one alone, despotism struck the body crudely, so as to reach the soul; and the soul, escaping from those blows, rose gloriously above it; but in democratic republics, tyranny does not proceed in this way; it leaves the body and goes straight for the soul."

26. The epigraph by Macaulay that Strauss uses at the head of *On Tyranny* is a case in point; for the full context of Macaulay's remarks, see Thomas Babbington Lord Macaulay, *The History of England from the Accession of James II* (New York: Harper, 1899), vol. 5, 70–72.

27. Strauss reports his discovery of esoteric writing in a series of letters to Jacob Klein in 1938 and 1939; see Leo Strauss, *Gesmmmelte Schriften*, vol. 3, ed. Heinrich Meier (Stuttgart: Metzler, 2001), 548–83; Strauss's discovery of estericism has been recently discussed in Laurence Lampert, "Nietzsche's Challenge to Philosophy in the Thought of Leo Strauss," *Review of Metaphysics* 58 (2005): 585–619.

28. Strauss, "On a Forgotten Kind of Writing," 221–22.

29. Strauss, *Persecution and the Art of Writing*, 35; see Pippin, "The Unavailability of the Ordinary," 348–49.

30. Harry Frankfurt, *On Bullshit* (Princeton, N.J.: Princeton University Press, 2005), 55–57.

31. Strauss, *Persecution and the Art of Writing*, 7.

32. Strauss, "On a Forgotten Kind of Writing," 229–30; for the critic, see Yvon Beleval, "Pour une Sociologie de la Philosophie," *Critique* 9 (1953): 852–66.

33. Strauss, "On a Forgotten Kind of Writing," 224; elsewhere Strauss referred to the Wilhelmine Germany of his youth as "perhaps not in every respect

admirable, but keeping an admirable order everywhere" where "such things as pogroms would have been absolutely impossible." See Leo Strauss, "Why We Remain Jews," in *Jewish Philosophy and the Crisis of Modernity*, ed. Kenneth Hart Green (Albany: SUNY Press, 1997), 313.

34. Strauss, "On a Forgotten Kind of Writing," 227, 229.

35. Leo Strauss, "A Giving of Accounts," in *Jewish Philosophy and the Crisis of Modernity*, 463.

36. Strauss, "On a Forgotten Kind of Writing," 229; Strauss, *On Tyranny*, 206.

37. Strauss, *Persecution and the Art of Writing*, 17.

38. Ibid., 35–36.

39. Strauss, "On Classical Political Philosophy," 89.

40. Ibid., 90.

41. Strauss, *On Tyranny*, 205–6.

42. Strauss, *Natural Right and History*, 128–29; Strauss, *On Tyranny*, 201–2.

43. Strauss, "On Classical Political Philosophy," 93–94.

44. Strauss, *Natural Right and History*, 142.

45. Strauss, *Persecution and the Art of Writing*, 36.

46. Ibid., 32.

47. Ibid., 34.

48. Ibid., 21.

49. Among some of the most significant contributions to the study of American politics are Harry V. Jaffa, *Crisis of the House Divided: An Interpretation of the Issues in the Lincoln-Douglas Debates* (Chicago: University of Chicago Press, 1958), and *The New Birth of Freedom: Abraham Lincoln and the Coming of the Civil War* (Lanham, Md.: Rowman & Littlefield, 2000); Charles Kesler, ed., *Saving the Revolution* (New York: Free Press, 1987); Ralph Lerner, *The Thinking Revolutionary: Principles and Practice in the New Republic* (Ithaca, N.Y.: Cornell University Press, 1987); Harvey C. Mansfield, *America's Constitutional Soul* (Baltimore, Md.: Johns Hopkins University Press, 1991); Herbert J. Storing, ed., *What Country Have I? Political Writings by Black Americans* (New York: St. Martin's, 1970); *The Complete Anti-Federalists* (Chicago: University of Chicago Press, 1981).

50. See Charles Kesler, "All Against All," *National Review*, August 18, 1989, 39–43.

51. Strauss, *Natural Right and History*, 3–4.

52. Ibid., 42.

53. Strauss, *On Tyranny*, 177.

54. Strauss, *Persecution and the Art of Writing*, 185.

55. Ibid., 24.

56. Strauss's chapter on Locke has arguably proved to be the most controversial of his writings; for a range of views indebted to Strauss, see Richard H. Cox, *Locke on War and Peace* (Oxford: Clarendon Press, 1960); Nathan Tarcov, *Locke's Education for Liberty* (Chicago: University of Chicago Press, 1984); Ruth W. Grant, *John Locke's Liberalism* (Chicago: University of Chicago Press, 1987); Thomas Pangle, *The Spirit of Modern Republicanism: The Moral Vision of the American Founders and the Philosophy of Locke* (Chicago: University of Chicago Press, 1989); Michael Zuckert, *Launching Liberalism: On Lockean Political Philosophy* (Lawrence: University of Kansas Press, 2002). The most important of the

anti-Straussian readings of Locke is still John Dunn, *The Political Thought of John Locke: An Historical Account of the Argument of the "Two Treatises of Government"* (Cambridge: Cambridge University Press, 1969).

57. Strauss, *Natural Right and History*, 165.

58. Ibid., 220–21.

59. Ibid., 207; the passage from Macaulay that Strauss cites is worth quoting in full: "For it is a well-known maxim of English law that, when a king is misled by pernicious counsel, his counsellors, and not himself, ought to be held accountable for his errors. It is idle, however, to examine these memorable words as we should examine a chapter of Aristotle or of Hobbes. Such words are to be considered, not as words, but as deeds. If they effect that which they are intended to effect, they are rational, though they be contradictory. If they fail of attaining their end, they are absurd, though they carry demonstration with them. Logic admits of no compromise. The essence of politics is compromise. It is therefore not strange that some of the most important and most useful political instruments in the world should be among the most illogical compositions that were ever penned. The object of Somers, of Maynard, and of the other eminent men who shaped this celebrated motion was, not to leave to posterity a model of definition and partition, but to make the restoration of a tyrant impossible, and to place on the throne a sovereign under whom law and liberty might be secure. This object they attained by using language which, in a philosophical treatise, would justly be reprehended as inexact and confused. They cared little whether their major agreed with their conclusion if the major secured two hundred votes, and the conclusion two hundred more. In fact, the one beauty of the resolution was its inconsistency." Lord Macaulay, *The History of England from the Accession of James II*, vol. 2, 574–75.

60. Strauss, *Natural Right and History*, 221.

61. Ibid., 220.

62. Ibid., 210–11

63. Ibid., 181–82.

64. Ibid., 220.

65. Ibid., 234.

66. Ibid., 245.

67. Ibid., 246.

68. Ibid., 61; emphasis added.

69. Ibid., 246.

70. Ibid., 234, note 106; for Strauss's further views, see his "Review of C. B. Macpherson's 'The Political Theory of Possessive Individualism,' " in *Studies in Platonic Political Philosophy*, ed. Thomas Pangle (Chicago: University of Chicago Press, 1983), 229–31.

71. Strauss, *Natural Right and History*, 242.

72. Ibid., 243.

73. Ibid., 248.

74. Ibid., 323.

75. Ibid., 251.

76. For a recent exchange, see James R. Stoner's critique of Michael Zuckert's *Launching Liberalism*, titled "Was Leo Strauss Wrong about John Locke?" and Zuckert's reply, "Perhaps He Was," *Review of Politics* 4 (2004): 553–63, 565–69.

77. See Louis Hartz, *The Liberal Tradition in America* (New York: Harcourt Brace, 1955); for works critical of Hartz's thesis about a single Lockean tradition in America, see Barry Alan Shain, *The Myth of American Individualism: The Protestant Origins of American Political Thought* (Princeton, N.J.: Princeton University Press, 1994); Rogers Smith, "Beyond Tocqueville, Myrdal, and Hartz: Multiple Traditions in America," *American Political Science Review* 87 (1993): 549–66.

78. The phrase "low but solid" has become deeply controversial when applied to America because of its implied criticism of the founding; the phrase was adapted from Churchill, who used it in the context of absolving his famous ancestor from the allegation that he was involved in a plot to murder James II. The full passage runs as follows: "Whatever may be charged against Churchill's morals, no one has impugned his sagacity, especially where his own interests were concerned. If he had murdered King James, William would have been able to reach the throne after enforcing merciless execution upon the criminals who had slain his beloved father-in-law. The greater the severity with which he treated them, the more becoming the auspices under which he would have succeeded. Indeed, it would be vital to him to avenge by every terror known to the law a crime by which he would himself have profited so highly. This accusation, which even Macaulay does not adopt, may be rebutted on these low but solid grounds and consigned to the rubbish heap of Jacobite mendacity." See Winston S. Churchill, *Marlborough: His Life and Times* (London: George Harrap, 1933), vol. 1, 294–95.

79. Strauss's only explicit treatment of Dewey occurs in his "Review of Dewey's 'German Philosophy and Politics,'" in *What Is Political Philosophy*, 279–81.

80. An early appreciation of this aspect of the book is provided by Walter Lippmann, *The Public Philosophy* (New York: Little Brown, 1955).

81. Strauss, *Natural Right and History*, 6.

82. See Victor Gourevitch, "Introduction," in *On Tyranny*, xxi–xxii; see also "What Is Political Philosophy?" 37: "The difference between the classics and us with regard to democracy *consists exclusively* in a different estimate of the virtues of technology" (emphasis added).

83. Strauss, "What Is Political Philosophy?" 50.

84. Robert Pippin, *Modernism as a Philosophical Problem: On the Dissatisfactions of European High Culture* (Cambridge, Mass.: Blackwell, 1991).

85. Joseph Cropsey, "The United States as Regime and the Sources of the American Way of Life," *Political Philosophy and the Issues of Politics* (Chicago: University of Chicago Press, 1977), 14–15.

86. Wilson Carey McWilliams, "Leo Strauss and the Dignity of American Political Thought," *Review of Politics* 60 (1998): 237.

87. Strauss, *Natural Right and History*, 177.

88. Strauss, "What Is Political Philosophy?" 49.

89. Strauss, *Natural Right and History*, 177–80.

90. Strauss makes no effort to examine Cromwell's England, the first effort by a modern Machiavellian statesman to found a republic; his one recognition of Cromwell occurs in *On Tyranny*, 182 with the following enigmatic observation: "The difference between Cyrus and a Hiero educated by Simonides is comparable to the difference between William III and Oliver Cromwell. A cursory comparison

of the history of England with the history of certain other European nations suffices to show that this difference is not unimportant to the well-being of peoples."

91. The most influential of the neo-Machiavellian readings of Machiavelli is J.G.A. Pocock, *The Machiavellian Moment: Florentine Political Thought and the Atlantic Republican Tradition* (Princeton, N.J.: Princeton University Press, 1975); for a more accurate picture of the role of Machiavelli in Anglo-American thought, see Paul Rahe, ed., *Machiavelli's Liberal Republican Legacy* (Cambridge: Cambridge University Press, 2005).

92. Strauss, *Natural Right and History*, 179; Strauss, "What Is Political Philosophy?" 41–42.

93. Leo Strauss, *Thoughts on Machiavelli* (Glencoe, Ill.: Free Press, 1958), 13.

94. Ibid., 13–14.

95. Strauss, "What Is Political Philosophy?" 47; see also his review of Zera Fink's *The Classical Republicans*, in *What Is Political Philosophy*, 290–92.

96. Strauss, *Persecution and the Art of Writing*, 30.

97. Strauss, *Thoughts on Machiavelli*, 14.

98. Henry Adams, *History of the United States during the Administrations of Thomas Jefferson* (New York: Library of America, 1986), vol. 1: 389.

99. Leo Strauss, "Thucydides: The Meaning of Political History," in *The Rebirth of Classical Political Rationalism*, 76. It is not often recognized because of his critique of historicism that Strauss was a great reader of modern histories. In addition to Macaulay's *History of England* cited in *Natural Right and History* and Adams's *History* mentioned in *Thoughts on Machiavelli*, he was a great admirer of Churchill's *Life of Marlborough* ("the greatest historical work written in our century and an inexhaustible mine of political wisdom") and William Prescott's *Conquest of Mexico* and *Conquest of Peru* ("A story more fabulous than any fairytale"—*On Tyranny*, 249).

100. Leo Strauss, *The City and Man* (Chicago: University of Chicago Press, 1964), 1.

101. Tocqueville, *Democracy in America*, 28.

102. I have heard that he voted twice for Adlai Stevenson during the 1950s.

103. See the contribution by Werner J. Dannhauser to the colloquium on "The Achievement of Leo Strauss," *National Review*, December 7, 1973, 1355–57.

104. Leo Strauss, "Preface to Spinoza's Critique of Religion," in *Liberalism Ancient and Modern* (New York: Basic Books, 1968), 225.

105. Strauss, *Liberalism Ancient and Modern*, v–vii.

106. Strauss, *On Tyranny*, 196.

107. For Strauss's assessment of the political science profession, see "An Epilogue," in *Liberalism Ancient and Modern*, 203–23; for an excellent overview and evaluation, see Eugene F. Miller, "Leo Strauss: Philosophy and American Social Science," in *Leo Strauss, the Straussians, and the American Regime*, 91–102.

108. See Leo Strauss, *Socrates and Aristophanes* (New York: Basic Books, 1966), 311–14.

109. Strauss, "What Is Political Philosophy?" 19–21; Strauss, *Natural Right and History*, 52–53.

110. Strauss, "What Is Political Philosophy?" 34–35; Strauss, *Natural Right and History*, 135–37; Strauss, *City and Man*, 45–49.

111. For an excellent treatment of this topic, see James W. Ceaser, *Liberal Democracy and Political Science* (Baltimore, Md.: Johns Hopkins University Press, 1990), 94–113.

112. Strauss, *Thoughts on Machiavelli*, 13.

113. Strauss, "An Epilogue," 211.

114. Ibid., 223; Strauss, "What Is Political Philosophy?" 24–25.

115. For a recent example of this kind of work, see Carnes Lord, *The Modern Prince: What Leaders Need to Know Now* (New Haven, Conn.: Yale University Press, 2003).

116. Strauss, "Preface to Spinoza's Critique of Religion," 224; Strauss, "What Is Political Philosophy?" 26–27.

117. See Amy Gutmann and Dennis Thompson, *Democracy and Disagreement* (Cambridge: Belknap Press, 1996); Bruce Ackerman and James Fishkin, *Deliberation Day* (New Haven, Conn.: Yale University Press, 2004).

118. Strauss, "Liberal Education and Responsibility," in *Liberalism Ancient and Modern*, 24.

119. Strauss, *On Tyranny*, 194.

120. Strauss, "Liberal Education and Responsibility," 24.

CHAPTER EIGHT

1. Strauss, Letter to Alexandre Kojève, August 22, 1948, in *On Tyranny*, 236.

2. Leo Strauss, *Natural Right and History* (Chicago: University of Chicago Press, 1953), 2.

3. Leo Strauss, *City and Man* (Chicago: University of Chicago Press, 1964), 3.

4. Ibid., 4.

5. Ibid., 6–7.

6. Leo Strauss, "Jerusalem and Athens: Some Preliminary Reflections," in *Studies in Platonic Political Philosophy*, ed. Thomas Pangle (Chicago: University of Chicago Press, 1983), 147–49.

7. Strauss, *City and Man*, 3.

8. Strauss, *Natural Right and History*, 135–38; Leo Strauss, "What Is Political Philosophy?" in *What Is Political Philosophy and Other Studies* (New York: Free Press, 1959), 34.

9. Strauss, *Natural Right and History*, 131–32.

10. Ibid., 133–34; Strauss, "On Classical Political Philosophy," in *What Is Political Philosophy*, 83–84.

11. Strauss, *City and Man*, 11.

12. Strauss, *Natural Right and History*, vii.

13. Ibid., 142–43; Strauss, "On Classical Political Philosophy," 85–86; Strauss, "Liberal Education and Responsibility," in *Liberalism Ancient and Modern* (New York: Basic Books, 1968), 15–16.

14. Jefferson, cited in Strauss, "On Classical Political Philosophy," 86.

15. Strauss, "Liberal Education and Responsibility," 16–17.

16. Strauss, "What Is Liberal Education?" in *Liberalism Ancient and Modern*, 4.

17. Strauss, "What Is Political Philosophy?" 38.

18. Strauss, "What Is Liberal Education?" 5.

19. Strauss, *On Tyranny*, 208; Strauss, "Liberal Education and Responsibility," 23.

20. Strauss, *On Tyranny*, 27.

21. Leo Strauss, "Preface to Hobbes's *Politische Wissenschaft*," in *Jewish Philosophy and the Crisis of Modernity*, ed. Kenneth Hart Green (Albany: SUNY Press, 1997), 453.

22. Strauss, *Natural Right and History*, 74–75.

23. Strauss, "Preface to Spinoza's Critique of Religion," in *Liberalism Ancient and Modern*, 224–26.

24. Strauss, "Letter to the Editor," in *Jewish Philosophy and the Crisis of Modernity*, 414.

25. Ibid., 413.

26. Strauss, "Preface to Spinoza's Critique of Religion," 230.

27. Ibid., 230.

28. Letter to Karl Löwith of August 20, 1946, in *Independent Journal of Philosophy* 5/6 (1988): 111; emphasis in original.

29. Leo Strauss, cited in Hillail Gilden, "A Response to Gourevitch," in *The Crisis of Democracy: A Straussian Perspective*, ed. Kenneth Deutsch and Walter Soffer (Albany: SUNY Press, 1987), 118.

30. Leo Strauss, "What Can We Learn from Political Theory?" Leo Strauss Papers, Box 6. Folder 12 Special Collections, Regenstein Library, University of Chicago.

31. Ibid.

32. Strauss, *Natural Right and History*, 156–63.

33. Ibid., 164.

34. Ibid., 160; emphasis added.

35. Ibid., 160.

36. Ibid., 161.

37. Ibid., 161.

38. David Bromwich, "Acting Alone," *Dissent* (winter 2003): 21.

39. David Frum and Richard Perle, *An End to Evil: How to Win the War on Terror* (New York: Random House, 2004).

40. Patrick Buchanan, "No End to War," *The American Conservative*, March 1, 2004.

41. Strauss, *City and Man*, 127.

42. Strauss, *On Tyranny*, 200; emphasis added.

43. Strauss, "What Is Political Philosophy?" 28.

44. Strauss, *On Tyranny*, 22.

45. George W. Bush, "Second Inaugural," January 20, 2005, www.whitehouse.gov.

46. Alain Franchon and Daniel Vernet, *L'Amériquie Messianique: Les guerres des néo-conservateurs* (Paris: Éditors du Seuil, 2004), 77.

47. Strauss, "Liberal Education and Responsibility," 24.

48. Strauss, *City and Man*, 226–36.

49. Strauss, "Liberal Education and Responsibility," 24.

50. Strauss, *City and Man*, 138, 127.

INDEX

Abel, 27
absolutism, 100
abstraction, 3
"Account of the Chariot, The," 37–38
acquisitiveness, 174
action, 122, 158–59
Action politique des philosophes, L' (Kojève), 131, 142
Adam's fall, 50
Adams, Henry, 177–78
Adams, John, 190
Adeimantus, 98, 201
Adorno, Theodor, 132
African-American political thinkers, 5–6
Agudat Israel, 82
Ahavat Yisrael, 57, 59
Akademie für die Wissenschaft des Judentums, 23, 66
Akedah, 33
Akiba ben Joseph, 24
Alcibiades, 152
Alexander the Great, 152
Alfarabi, 7, 82, 103, 166
allegory, 9, 38, 39, 49, 93
Altmann, Alexander, 214n19
altruism, selfishness vs., 171
"Americanism," 124
American regime, 9, 12, 18–19; classical antecedents of, 167, 189–90; classless society and, 154–55; Constitution and, 3, 127, 182; Declaration of Independence and, 8, 25, 112, 167, 176, 186; exceptionalism and, 176; founding of, 2, 4, 5, 167, 168–78, 189; Jewish identity and, 42; modernity and, 173–74; natural

right and, 167, 168, 173; progressivism and, 173; republicanism and, 190–91; Straussians' policy influence on, 88, 157, 184–87, 199; Strauss's views on, 166–67, 175–78, 179; theologico-political problem and, 193–94
"American way of life," 155
Amos, 28
anarchism, 56, 58
ancients and moderns, quarrel of, 4, 5, 65, 104, 105, 106, 109–11, 113, 132, 134, 175, 185, 189
antinomianism, 16, 38, 45, 50, 51, 56, 63
anti-Semitism, 32, 34, 36, 42; liberalism and, 194; political use of, 148; Strauss as target of, 185. *See also* Holocaust
apocalyptic messianism, 50–51, 54, 64
Apology (Plato), 97
aporia, 102
Arendt, Hannah, 57–59, 116, 132–33, 201n1
Argument and Action of Plato's Laws, The (Strauss), 92
aristocracy, 14, 105, 106, 107, 143; ancient republicanism and, 172, 190; democracy as universal, 191; honor and, 139, 142
Aristophanes, 7, 24, 180
Aristotle, 5, 12, 49, 54, 55, 91, 118, 141, 152, 161; golden mean and, 120; Heidegger on, 17, 115–16; mixed regime theory and, 189; natural right and, 167, 198, 199; Strauss's reading of, 11, 116
Aron, Raymond, 15, 133, 138, 139, 155
Art of Living, The (Nehamas), 89
assimilation, 25–26, 30, 82; critics of, 31, 63–64; of German Jews, 34, 35–36, 43,